THE CRIMINALLY INSANE

THE CRIMINALLY INSANE
A Community Follow-up
of Mentally Ill Offenders

Terence P. Thornberry
Joseph E. Jacoby

THE UNIVERSITY OF CHICAGO PRESS
Chicago and London

TERENCE P. THORNBERRY is assistant director and research associate at the Center for Studies in Criminology and Criminal Law at the University of Pennsylvania. JOSEPH E. JACOBY is assistant professor of criminal justice at the University of South Carolina.

To our parents:
Patrick and Rose Thornberry
James and Martha Jacoby

The University of Chicago Press, Chicago 60637
The University of Chicago Press, Ltd., London

Printed in the United States of America
83 82 81 80 79   5 4 3 2 1

This investigation was supported in part by Public Health Service research grant 3R01-MH-23742-0252, National Institute of Mental Health, Center for Studies of Crime and Delinquency.

Library of Congress Cataloging in Publication Data

Thornberry, Terence P
  The criminally insane.

  (Studies in crime and justice)
  Bibliography: p.
  Includes index.
  1. Insane, Criminal and dangerous—Pennsylvania.
2. Pennsylvania. State Hospital for Criminal Insane,
Farview.   3. Criminal behavior, Prediction of.
4. Recidivists—Pennsylvania.   I. Jacoby, Joseph E.,
joint author.   II. Title.   III. Series.
HV8742.U52T56   365'.46   78-10703
ISBN 0-226-79818-6

CONTENTS

FOREWORD

Dangerousness is not so much a state as a state of mind. It is the belief that a person or thing is more likely to cause serious harm than are others of its kind. When dangerousness is attributed to things—bridges, radioactive materials, skateboards—the attribution is usually based on some sort of knowledge, such as of the way radioactivity works or of statistics that show an unusually frequent association with harm.

Sometimes we do the same with people. Our knowledge of the aims and mentality of an urban guerrilla may give us good reason to believe that he will seek opportunities for violent demonstrations of his political views, in which death or injury is either an acceptable by-product or an actual aim. Or a case history of repeated assaults on children may justify our calling a man a child-molester without any insight into his motivation.

Sometimes, on the other hand, the fear and indignation caused by a single act of violence or sexual molestation leads us to classify a person as likely to behave in that way, without any psychological or actuarial justification for our belief. A single incident is enough to earn a man the label "murderer" or "rapist." The very word "rapist" implies a propensity for rape, and we have no accepted term that is free from this implication.*

*"Raper" is very uncommon.

Even very general labels can carry implications of dangerousness. The best examples are "criminal" and "mentally ill." When both labels are attached to the same person, it is difficult indeed to resist their effect.

So difficult is it that the only corrective is a very convincing demonstration of overreaction. Hitherto the best-known demonstration of this sort has been the Baxstrom case in New York State. Baxstrom, a felon serving a medium-length prison sentence, had been transferred from prison to Dannemora State Hospital for the criminally insane. At the end of his sentence he continued to be detained there as if he had been civilly committed, but without the usual jury review of the need for compulsory detention. With remarkable intelligence and persistence, he secured a U.S. Supreme Court decision that had the effect of transferring him and 966 other inmates of similar status to civil hospitals for reassessment. The result was that the majority were eventually freed, and of these only a small minority later committed crimes involving serious harm to others. Even those who remained in the hospital were found to be less violent to staff and other patients than had been feared.

The Baxstrom demonstration did not show, as is sometimes said, that mentally ill criminals are no more of a risk to others than men and women who do not bear that label. Not all of them, after all, were freed; and most of those who were freed were by then well past the peak age for violence. What it did suggest was that the Dannemora staff had been much too apprehensive about their future behavior; that the staff's decisions should have been subject to an effective review from outside; and that the release of the majority of the criminally insane from Dannemora at an earlier stage would probably not have resulted in a politically unacceptable number of incidents of violence.

In 1971 in Pennsylvania, the Dixon case led to a similar reassessment of 586 inmates of Farview State Hospital for the Criminally Insane, who were transferred to civil hospitals and then in many cases discharged to the community. This gave Terence Thornberry and Joseph Jacoby a rare chance not merely to replicate the Baxstrom follow-up but to carry such studies a stage further. With the objectivity and insight characteristic to the Philadelphia Center for Studies in Criminology and Criminal Law, they interviewed not only hospital administrators but also

more than half their sample of ex-inmates. They were even able
to ask the latter about offenses—detected and undetected—that
they had committed since transfer. In short, they carried out one of
the most thorough follow-ups of this sort of sample in the
literature.

They found that within four years only 14 percent of the ex-
inmates had been arrested or readmitted to the hospital for a
violent act. No doubt this is a higher percentage than is to be
expected from a comparable sample of the population at large;
but it is far below the expectations engendered by the label
"criminally insane."

Only someone who has attempted a task of this complexity and
difficulty can appreciate what they have achieved. Their book is
not only a contribution of the first importance to the literature of
dangerousness, but a model for future contributors.

NIGEL WALKER

ACKNOWLEDGMENTS

The authors owe many debts for the time, diligence, and concern expressed by the following people who are or were associated with the Center for Studies in Criminology and Criminal Law:

Marvin E. Wolfgang, Ph.D., director of the Center, who provided the initial opportunity to do this research, and the administrative structure to support it; Rhoda Piltch, who guided the finances of the project through the complexities of the university budgetary process; Barbara Naab, Patricia Coyne, Diana Sowder, Sandra Johnson, and Esther Lafair, who shared the burden of typing too many drafts of this report and all the correspondence, schedules, and supporting material which were generated by the project; Jonathan Katzenelson, Don Goldstein, and Mark Keintz who performed computer analyses at various stages of the project; Barry Mike, who did a large share of the interviewing as well as performing the duties of chief research assistant; and Bob Sloan, coding supervisor and author of a meticulously prepared code book.

Counsel for the plaintiffs in the court suit described in this book realized that an important research opportunity could grow from their efforts to secure the release of the patients. One of them,

Richard Bazelon, actively sought such a research project and acted as our legal consultant. Richard Lonsdorf, M.D., had examined some of the plaintiffs at the time of the suit and was a natural choice to be our psychiatric consultant. Both these men contributed to the direction taken by the study.

To Saleem Shah and the Center for Studies of Crime and Delinquency, NIMH, we give our thanks for financial support, helpful suggestions, and patience.

Officials of the Pennsylvania state government were always cooperative and helpful in providing information and access to data. Ralph Phelleps of the Department of Public Welfare was a steadfast door-opener through several changes of higher-level officials and policies. The administrators and staff of all the Pennsylvania state mental hospitals were always helpful after they were convinced that our data gathering would not be harmful to their patients.

We are particularly grateful for the cooperation of the staff at Farview, who accurately saw their institution and their policies as being under siege from a variety of directions, yet opened their institution and their records to us. We hope that they do not consider this report to be a deliberate attack on their institution. The study was not undertaken to attack Farview, but the findings so strongly pointed to weaknesses in policy that we felt compelled to specify those weaknesses.

We also thank the Dixon class patients, the subjects of our research, for allowing us to interview them without providing any direct compensation. To them we owe the greatest debt. Their payment will have to be the immodest hope that their participation in this research helps to bring about changes in the way mentally ill offenders are treated by the state.

Finally, we would like to thank a number of our colleagues for their thoughtful and critical comments. Leslie Sebba, Ph.D., of Hebrew University; Marvin E. Wolfgang, Ph.D., Marc Riedel, Ph.D., Richard Lonsdorf, M.D., and Barry Mike, M.A., of the University of Pennsylvania; Herbert H. Krauss, Ph.D., of the University of Houston at Clear Lake City; and Melvin Heller, M.D., and Barry Miller, Ph.D., of the Pennsylvania Department of Public Welfare. Richard Bazelon and Eileen Thornberry read and improved various portions of this book. Although we benefited from their advice, they are not responsible for the results and, of course, all errors are my coauthor's.

1   The Criminally Insane
in Pennsylvania

In 1972 there were fifteen thousand adults living in correctional or mental health facilities in the United States who were characterized as criminally insane. These offenders had become involved in criminal proceedings and, either before or after trial, had evidenced symptoms of mental illness. As such they suffer from the double stigma of being both mad and bad, and this has led many states to create maximum security mental hospitals for their treatment. This book is about one such facility, Farview State Hospital in Pennsylvania. More specifically, it is about a group of patients who were released from Farview, not because they had been "cured," but because a federal court held that their commitments had been unconstitutional.

THE HOSPITAL AND ITS PATIENTS

In the record-making time of two years, the first unit in the grand series of buildings which will comprise Pennsylvania State Hospital for the Criminal Insane at Farview has been completed.

Thus began the lead article in the 27 November 1911, edition of the *Carbondale Leader*. The opening of this building was a significant benchmark in the completion of a project begun by

1

the Pennsylvania State Legislature in 1905, when a law entitled
"An Act to Provide for the Selection of a Site and the Erection of
a State Hospital for the Treatment and Care of Criminal Insane,
To Be Called the State Hospital for the Criminal Insane..." was
enacted (Laws of Pennsylvania, session of 1905, no. 247). It was
also a benchmark in the history of the availability of specialized
care for the criminally insane in Pennsylvania. After the opening
of the State Hospital for the Criminally Insane, later renamed
Farview State Hospital, prisons and civil mental hospitals had the
option of transferring their most troubled and troublesome inmates to Farview.

The history of how the hospital for the criminally insane came
to be located at Farview is a rather curious one. The Act of 1905
created a six-member commission to "select a tract of land suitable for the purpose of said hospital, which shall be accessible by
railroad facilities from all parts of the Commonwealth." Dr. T.
C. Fitzsimmons, who was to become the first superintendent of
Farview, lobbied strenuously for building the institution close to its
eventual site. The *Carbondale Leader* reported that

Fitzsimmons' first efforts were for the State Hospital for Epi-
leptics which was located at Spring City.... It was first intended
to locate the epileptic hospital at Farview, but such powerful
influence was brought to bear that it was finally placed at Spring
City. But nothing daunted Doctor Fitzsimmons[. W]ith the
promise of a donation by the Delaware and Hudson [Canal Co.]
of six hundred acres of land in the most beautiful county in
Pennsylvania, [he] was able to get a decision that the hospital for
the criminal insane should be built at Farview (27 November
1911).

In many respects the fruits of Dr. Fitzsimmons' labor are quite
impressive, and Farview has grown considerably since its found-
ing. It has almost tripled in size from its original six hundred
acres to its current fifteen hundred acres. The core of the institution is surrounded by massive walls, within which is a large main
building and a number of smaller ones, the most recent having
been built in the 1960s. There are more than twenty patient
wards, some of which can house up to a hundred men; and, in
toto, Farview can handle a patient population of over fifteen
hundred.

The management of an institution of this size is a complex and difficult task. Accordingly, the staff has grown substantially since the days of Dr. Fitzsimmons: in 1969, when the case under study here was brought to court, the total staff numbered well over four hundred. At that time the medical staff at Farview consisted of the superintendent, who was a psychiatrist, and five physicians, none of whom had any psychiatric experience before coming to Farview. The rest of the professional staff consisted of two psychologists, two master's-level social workers, two caseworkers, one recreational therapist, five registered nurses, and twelve licensed practical nurses. Approximately four hundred psychiatric security aides constituted the bulk of the hospital's employees.

The growth of Farview and its staff was matched by the growth of the inmate population. The first patient was registered in 1911 and from the time of his admission, Farview's inmate population grew steadily to a peak of 1,403 patients in December 1961. One reason for this consistent population growth is suggested by the first patient's career at Farview. In 1950, thirty-nine years after his admission, he died while in confinement. His career was by no means unusual, and long periods of confinement were the rule rather than the exception. Indeed, of the 1,229 patients who were discharged between 1945 and 1960, the average length of stay had been six years and four months, and the most common discharge disposition was death. Two-fifths (41.5 percent) of these 1,229 subjects died during their confinement at Farview (*University of Pennsylvania Law Review* 110 (1961):100.

The reason for this policy of long-term confinement, which for many was synonymous with a life sentence,[1] is intimately linked to the conditions of commitment to Farview. Patients were not committed to Farview for specified periods of time, but were committed on an indeterminate basis. They were not to be released until, in the judgment of Farview's clinical staff, they were no longer dangerous to themselves or others, or in need of maximum security care. Working within a system which provided for indeterminate commitments, the task of Farview's staff should have been twofold: to expedite the release of these patients by providing treatment and therapy and to judge when this treatment had become effective enough to warrant release. In a situation in which an individual's freedom is indefinitely constrained until he evidences mental stability, commitment and release criteria should be carefully and explicitly developed, and the institution should provide adequate treatment programs to facilitate the individual's release. In practice, neither of these requirements for just and rational procedures were met at Farview.

COMMITMENT TO AND RELEASE FROM FARVIEW

Commitment criteria for Farview were never carefully developed and an examination of the statutes governing commitment procedures indicates that over the years these criteria became less rather than more specific. During its first years of operation Farview was to provide "for the treatment and care of the criminal insane, and such other patients as are hereinafter specified." Patients from other state hospitals for the insane could be transferred to Farview, "giving preference in all cases to those patients having known criminal tendencies" (Acts of 1905, P.L. 247). The Mental Health Act of 1923 provided that a person could be sent to Farview only if he was "an insane criminal," defined as "any person mentally ill who has been convicted on a criminal charge and the period of whose sentence had not expired or who had a criminal tendency." "Criminal tendency" was "a tendency to repeat offenses against the law or to perpetrate new offenses as shown by repeated convictions for such offenses—a tendency to habitual delinquency" (Acts of 1923, P.L. 998).

The Mental Health Act of 1951 (Acts of 1951, P.L. 533) said that Farview should be devoted exclusively to patients convicted of a crime or with criminal tendencies, retaining the earlier definition of this term. In 1963 the act of 1951 was amended to expand the class of persons who could be committed to Farview by adding "upon petition and order of court after a hearing notice of which was given to the next of kin or person responsible, if any, those persons requiring maximum supervision" (Acts of 1963, P.L. 976). Thus by 1963 any person who exhibited criminal tendencies or who required maximum supervision could be indeterminately committed to Farview.

The law in force at the time of this study and up until 1977, the Mental Health and Mental Retardation Act of 1966, provided the broadest possible selection criteria. It did not designate Farview as the place of confinement for any particular class of persons. In practice, patients came to the hospital directly from courts after being found incompetent to stand trial or, less often, after being declared not guilty by reason of insanity. A large number also came from prison, where, under the tensions of prison life, they developed symptoms of mental illness. Still another group came from civil mental hospitals in Pennsylvania, where they had proved too violent or troublesome for the staff to handle.

By the mid-1960s Farview had in many respects become an institution of last resort, where individuals who could not be handled in other state institutions were sent. No specific criteria were established to govern commitments to Farview, and state law provided for fairly simple commitment procedures. Prison inmates were usually committed to Farview when two physicians—not necessarily psychiatrists—certified to a court that the subject was mentally ill and in need of treatment. When a court hearing occurred in a case, the proceedings were at times brief and non-adversarial. Witness the following (entire transcript of a commitment hearing in 1965):

THE COURT: Proceed.

[ASSISTANT DISTRICT ATTORNEY]: If it please the Court, [subject] was in the Allegheny County Jail charged with the violation of the Uniform Firearms Act. The warden of the Allegheny County Jail asked us to see this man. He believed the man was insane. This Court appointed Dr. X and Dr. Y as the qualified physicians. He was examined by both Dr. X and Dr. Y and it was their opinion that this man is psychotic. We are recommending the commitment to Farview State Hospital. He is represented by [defense counsel]. I think [defense counsel] is aware of the fact that he is mentally ill and needs hospitalization.

[DEFENSE COUNSEL]: At that time I asked for an O.R. bond [release on own recognizance], Your Honor. I mean, he was on the street for ten years, and he was a disabled veteran and he got picked up with a couple of guns. They felt it was best to get him some psychiatric treatment right now. [The assistant district attorney] tells me the Veterans Administration doesn't have any treatment.

THE COURT: All right.

The judge's decision resulted in a six-year stay at Farview.

The procedure for transferring patients from civil mental

hospitals to Farview did not even require the involvement of a court. Because Farview was run by the Department of Public Welfare, the agency responsible for all other mental hospitals in the state, transferring a patient who was not confined under a criminal commitment was a simple administrative matter. It required only the concurrence of officials of the hospitals involved and the department.

Although these proceedings were often quite brief and handled as simple bureaucratic matters, their import was not lost on the prospective patients. Indeed, in one case a man's fear of being sent to Farview led to a suicide attempt which contributed to his transfer:

His facial expression was anxious and he claimed that he was very much afraid of this institution; claimed that inmates at the ____ Penitentiary had told many wil[d] stories about Farview; that they did terrible things to you here and when you were once committed here it was absolutely impossible to get out. He was so disturbed and frightened that he attempted suicide by cutting himself on the right side of the neck with a razor blade (from the patient's admission notes in 1951).

While the road into Farview was easily traveled, the road out was another matter. Although the commitments were indeterminate, the law did not require periodic review of each case, even by the Farview staff. A patient could be kept indefinitely and the state did not have to justify the continued confinement of the patient. Indeed, an examination of Farview records suggests that a patient's mere presence at Farview constituted prima facie evidence that he should remain.

Not only did the law not provide for routine releasing procedures, it was also silent on the criteria that were to be used in deciding on discharges. Section 418 of the Mental Health and Mental Retardation Act of 1966 authorized the director of a state mental hospital to detain a patient on indefinite commitment until, in the director's professional opinion, care or treatment was no longer necessary. However, no criteria were specified for the director to use in reaching this decision, which was left entirely to his discretion.

The patient could attempt to secure his own release through the courts by filing a habeas corpus petition, either on the grounds that the proceedings leading to his commitment were illegal or that his continued hospitalization was no longer warranted by his mental condition. In practice, it was difficult for the patient to argue successfully on the first criterion, because the commitment procedures, as we have seen, were quite flexible. To argue on the second criterion the patient had to send with his petition an affidavit from a physician supporting the patient's contention that he was no longer so mentally ill as to require continued hospitalization. Prior to the 1966 act this procedure was only available to those patients who could afford a private psychiatric examination, and there were very few patients at Farview in this position. After the 1966 act, indigent patients could request one independent psychiatric evaluation per year, which would be paid for by the state. This opportunity, however, did not guarantee a sympathetic psychiatrist, nor did it permit the patient to "shop" for one. In practice very few of these independent psychiatric reviews led to a discharge.

Given this legal situation, the patients had to rely primarily on the clinical staff at Farview to secure their freedom. Such reliance was seldom successful, as evidenced by the high proportion of patients who died in the hospital. A few illustrations will indicate the wide range of arguments mustered by the staff to justify continued confinement.

Occasionally the interest of hospital maintenance was paramount (although seldom was the staff so candid in its written evaluations):

The staff felt that in the absence of any family contacts or interests there would be no point of considering this patient for transfer to a civil mental institution. Staff also recognized the patient refers [*sic*] to remain here and recognized selfishly that the patient is one of few dependable workers on ward. Staff recommended that he be retained in this hospital (from the Farview staff evaluation of a subject in 1963).

Being hospitalized in an institution in which the prospects of release are remote may reasonably make a person angry with the hospital, especially when the criteria for release are vague and ill-defined. Yet from the perspective of well-meaning hospital physicians such anger was unreasonable, symptomatic of illness, and sufficient cause for continued confinement.

Obviously the gross signs of his psychosis have subsided. Nevertheless there are demonstrable and significant residuals of his schizophrenic illness in addition to the above including social withdrawal (avoidance of others), subtle suspicions (he would rather read, train himself in mathematics, etc. to avoid regression rather than socialize with the usual element found in this institution). A definite feeling of grandeur as evident in his speech and attitude with a tendency to project (being held here and not given any treatment whatsoever[)]. When reminded that he could request an independent psychiatric examination (of which he obviously was aware) he countered by saying he preferred to test his sanity in Court. He prides himself on his legal knowledge (from the Farview ward notes of a subject in 1964).

At a civil mental hospital to which another subject was sent from Farview, the staff inferred from the patient's impeccable behavior that his previous lengthy confinement at Farview had been justified by his attitude toward perceived unjust confinement at Farview:

HOSPITAL COURSE: At [this hospital] the patient showed no psychotic symptoms whatsoever and indeed was one of the most pleasant and cooperative patients that I have ever seen in a State hospital. The patient worked willingly, was well oriented, was able to talk with some appropriate bitterness about his treatment and confinement at Farview. The patient felt that the confinement was unjust. At Farview they seemed to feel that this feeling showed that the patient needed continued care rather than the fact that the patient was just plain angry from being kept incarcerated against his will. The patient was in the Halfway House program run by _____ and went home every weekend on passes. The patient did exceedingly well on passes (from the disposition summary of a subject in a Pennsylvania civil mental hospital in 1970).

TREATMENT AT FARVIEW
The evidence indicates that once a patient was committed to Farview he could look forward to a lengthy period of confinement. We conclude from available descriptions of Farview, however, that he could not look forward to living in a therapeutic environment. Although patients were to be committed to Farview until they achieved some degree of mental health, there were virtually no clinical facilities available to them in their search for such health.[2]

The following testimony by a former Farview patient is taken from the transcript of the court hearing in *Donald Dixon* et al. v.

Attorney General of the Commonwealth of Pennsylvania, the case which generated the subjects of this study. Counsel for the plaintiffs posed the questions, and the witness testified on behalf of the plaintiffs:

Q. I know you were at Farview for many years, but can you describe a typical day in your life at Farview?

A. Well, you get up 6:00 o'clock in the morning, get dressed, have breakfast, and you come back to the ward. If you have a job, then you go to your work where you are assigned to and you work on through until noon hour, dinnertime, and then you have dinner. Then after dinner you go back to work, and if you are working in the dining rooms, that works you up until 6:00 o'clock, then at that time you come back to the ward.

Q. How much contact did you have with the doctors on the staff at Farview during your 29 or 30 years?

A. Well, I had quite good contact, I would say, with the doctors in the wards, that passed through the wards. I'd say I had fairly good contact with them.

Q. What do you mean by contact passing through the wards?

A. Well, I would greet them every morning most of the times if I saw them coming through. I was always on good friendly terms.

Q. Did you consult with them in their offices about problems?

A. Occasionally.

Q. What does "occasionally" mean?

A. Well, once in six months, maybe once a year.

Q. And apart from this maybe once every six months or once a year consultation, was most of the contact in seeing doctors walk through your ward and greeting them in some way?

A. That is right.

Q. Were you ever part of group therapy?

A. They don't have much in the way of group therapy there at Farview. Actually Farview is a prison, that is, the guards there admit it is a prison. They defy even the doctors to say that it is not a prison, and that makes it altogether different from being a hospital.

Q. What happens during the day, Mr. _____, to a person who does not have a job?

A. Well, they're confined to the ward.

Q. And what goes on in the ward?

A. Well, they just sit on a bench or on the chair.

Q. How long do they just sit on the bench or on a chair?

A. Well, they can get up and walk around the room, but most of the time they are sitting down.

Q. Can you describe physically to the Court what a ward is like, what comprises a ward?

A. Well, there's close to a hundred individuals to a ward and all types of personalities. Some participate in games, playing checkers and chess and cards, but more or less most of them are just sitting around on the benches or chairs.

Q. Just sitting and doing nothing?

A. Just sitting and doing nothing.

Q. All day long?

A. A few of them laying on the floor.

Q. Are there guards present in these rooms?

A. Yes, there's guards present.

Q. And what do they do?

A. Well, they sit in the chair at the end of the room. There's two chairs, at each end of the room.

· ·

Q. Can you describe for the Court what recreation there is both indoors and outdoors?

A. Well, indoors, there is not much recreation indoors—in fact, there is none. But outdoors they have softball in the summertime and a little basketball. That comprises about the sports down there (Dixon case transcript, 22 July 1970, pp. 132–36).

The view that Farview is antitherapeutic is not peculiar to its patients, but is shared by many mental health experts. A psychiatrist employed at another Pennsylvania state mental hospital reported his impressions of Farview gathered during a visit in June 1968.

. . . the poverty of the wards, the lack of stimulation, the drabness, the controls—as we walked through the wards, patients would be off to the side of the center aisle and occasionally they would make an attempt to approach us and these guards—and their role was as a guard—would shoulder the patients and us, in a sense to protect us from the patients.

The air of inactivity is something I haven't seen in a hospital for a long time, of the person who was really sentenced to a chair, just sitting there, staring off into space. This of course conflicted with the working patients in the kitchen area who I say were really quite energetically involved. Activity is present in occupational therapy, in group therapy, in industrial therapy, and so on, but in a very limited degree. It exists, but it is extremely limited.

The sense of remoteness is appalling and the isolation [*sic*] (Dixon transcript, 23 July 1970, pp. 245–46).

The Dixon court concurred with these evaluations of the lack of treatment provided for Farview patients, as the following excerpt from the opinion shows:

At the time the answer was filed there were at Farview approximately four hundred psychiatric security aides who functioned primarily as guards, and the regimen for inmates of Farview consisted almost entirely of custodial care, the prescribing and administering of drugs, a modicum of recreation and, for a smaller number of inmates, assignment to jobs which were in substance housekeeping positions.

We cannot avoid the conclusion that medical-psychiatric treatment of inmates at Farview was grossly inadequate not because of lack of willingness or competency of the Superintendent, Dr. John Shovlin, or of his staff, but because of the woeful inadequacy of the funds made available by the Commonwealth of Pennsylvania or its agencies to Farview for its maintenance and staffing. It is conceded that only three percent of inhabitants of Farview received any therapeutic-psychiatric treatment (323 F. Supp. 969 [1971]).

Because the federal judiciary has been active in recent years in litigating cases involving the right to treatment for mental patients, objective standards now exist for deciding whether a mental hospital is providing adequate treatment facilities and programs. Although the right-to-treatment issue was not raised in the Dixon case, a comparison of the description of Farview provided here with the standards declared in *Wyatt* v. *Stickney* (344 F. Supp. 373 [M.D. Ala. 1972]), the most prominent case in the right-to-treatment area, shows Farview to be inadequate in staffing, living arrangements, and programming.

For example, table 1.1 presents a comparison of the number of professional staff members in a variety of classifications which Farview should have employed, under the standards established in *Wyatt* v. *Stickney*, with the number actually employed in 1969. Clearly the professional staff at Farview at the time of the Dixon case was considerably less than it should have been, in each of the categories below.

TABLE 1.1   Comparison of Farview Staff with Recommended Staff

Occupational Classification	No. of Employees Required by *Wyatt* v. *Stickney* Standards	No. Employed by Farview in 1969
Psychiatrist (3 years' residency training in psychiatry)	6	1
M.D.	16	5
Registered nurse	48	5
Licensed practical nurse	24	12
Psychologist (Ph.D.)	4	0
Psychologist (M.A.)	4	2
Social worker (M.S.W.)	8	2
Social worker (B.A.)	20	2
Patient activity therapist (M.S.)	4	1

Not only did Farview fail to provide treatment for its patients, there is considerable evidence that, in addition, life at Farview was both brutal and dehumanizing. A Pulitzer Prize-winning series of articles appeared in the Philadelphia *Inquirer* between June and December 1976 and reported the following:

A passerby driving through this anthracite region could almost mistake [Farview] for a small college or a resort hotel or a monastery.

It is none of those things. Over and over, those who have been patients at Farview and who have been lucky enough to get out describe it as a living hell on earth.

And there is a wealth of evidence from others—guards, administrators, scholars and even government investigators whose findings have been supressed—that the description is chillingly accurate.

A three-month investigation by *The Inquirer* has revealed that:

Farview State Hospital is a place where men have died during or after beatings by guards and by patients egged on by guards.

It is a place where men who have died this way have been certified as victims of heart attacks. . . .

It is a place where an unwritten code requires all the guards present to hit a patient if one guard hits him. . . .

It is a place where there is virtually no treatment aside from the use of mood-altering drugs, some of which other institutions abandoned a decade ago.

It is a psychiatric hospital without a board-certified psychiatrist.

It is a place where a man under a 30-day sentence for disorderly conduct can wait 30 years for his freedom (Philadelphia *Inquirer*, 27 June 1976, p. 1).

In the lengthy series the above passage introduced, the reporters presented many firsthand accounts by former patients, former employees, and state investigators to substantiate these allegations. At this writing, grand jury and legislative investigations are continuing into deaths of several patients that occurred under suspicious circumstances and little evidence has been presented to refute these charges.

The portrait of Farview State Hospital just presented is quite negative. We encountered no substantial material, either through personal inspection of the facilities or in the court records of the Dixon case, in which conditions at Farview were described extensively, that would portray Farview in a more favorable light. In this respect it is worth noting that during the Dixon hearings counsel for the commonwealth did not object to the negative content of the testimony quoted above, nor did he present counterevidence. Moreover, both the Dixon court and the National Institute of Mental Health (NIMH 1976) concluded that the treatment program at Farview was grossly inadequate. The Dixon court did conclude, and we concur, that this situation did not exist because the Farview staff was callous. The reasons for inadequacy of the treatment program are systemic and involve the political setting in which Farview operates, a topic to which we will return in the next chapter.

We note again that the Farview experience of the subjects of this research had ended by mid-1971 and our direct observations of the institution were concluded by mid-1974. The most recent authoritative description of Farview is contained in the 1976 NIMH Medicare certification examination. Between the collection of these data and the present writing the state has claimed that conditions at Farview have improved. In one respect improvement is readily apparent: the staff-to-patient ratio has risen to the point where there are now over four hundred staff members caring for fewer than two hundred patients. However, we know of

no recent evidence which contradicts the accuracy of the description of life at Farview, ca. 1970, that we have presented above. All
of the available evidence indicates that while the Dixon patients
were at Farview, the treatment program was woefully inadequate.

At this point Farview remains an enigma. It is a maximum
security facility that confines people until they are cured, but that
does not provide treatment facilities to cure them. It is a hospital
without a therapeutic program. It is a prison in disguise in which
the mad and bad are warehoused because they are judged to be
too difficult to handle in other institutions and too dangerous to
have in the community. In the end we conclude that the substance
of Dr. Fitzsimmons' institution lies more in its ability to contain
than in its ability to help people.

But in a larger sense the situation is worse than this sketch
implies, for Farview is by no means a unique institution in this
country. Farview and other hospitals like it have operated in this
manner for decades. "The story is the same everywhere. The
mentally ill offender is confined in a grim storehouse. Treatment
is grossly inadequate. There is virtually no therapy" (Brooks
1974, p. 397). Indeed, if there has been a national policy concerning the treatment of the criminally insane, it has been to commit
them to maximum security hospitals and forget them. How else
can one explain the ease of admission, the difficulty of release,
and the lack of therapy while in confinement?

Nevertheless, institutions like Farview are not without their proponents. Some argue that there are violent, deranged offenders
who require maximum security care because they are not easily
treated and that once released they will pose a threat to the community. As we will see in the next chapter, this is essentially the
position of the Farview staff and the *raison d'être* of the institution.
Scientifically however, it is a *raison d'être* that is seriously flawed
since it is not open to refutation. Because the patients were viewed
as dangerous they were kept in confinement for long periods of
time and the opportunity to determine if they were in fact dangerous rarely occurred. Indeed, since few criminally insane patients
were released when they were still young, the recidivism rate of
those who were released was generally low, which falaciously gave
proof to the efficacy of this approach. The ability of institutions
like Farview to resist change over the years is linked to this
inability to prove the approach wrong. Since few patients released

from Farview were dangerous, the state implicitly accepted the Farview approach as appropriate, without investigating its effectiveness, necessity, or social benefits.

One purpose of this book is to conduct such an investigation by following the careers of a group of patients who were released from Farview because a federal court intervened in the ordinary operations of that institution. As a result, we have the opportunity to evaluate the efficacy of these policies and, through that evaluation, to examine the appropriateness of the orientation that recommends the indeterminate confinement of the criminally insane in maximum security facilities.

2   The Dixon Case:
A Natural Experiment

The court case that gave rise to this research, *Dixon* v. *Attorney General of the Commonwealth of Pennsylvania* (325 F. Supp. 966 [M.D. Pa. 1971]), concerned the constitutionality of the commitment procedures that were employed to confine a group of mentally ill offenders at Farview State Hospital. In many ways the Dixon case can be viewed as a direct extension of an earlier New York case—*Baxstrom* v. *Herold* (383 U.S. 107 [1966])—which was remarkably similar to the Dixon case in terms of legal issues, the court decision, and practical outcome.

Baxstrom, a convicted felon, had been sentenced to a two-and-a-half to three-year term in a New York State prison. While serving that sentence he was certified as insane and was transferred to Dannemora State Hospital, a special facility for the criminally insane. After his three-year criminal sentence expired, the state maintained that he was still mentally ill and "dangerous," and his confinement at Dannemora was thereby continued, but under a civil commitment. This change in status—from criminal to civil commitment—took place without benefit of jury review, which lead the U.S. Supreme Court, in a decision written by then Chief Justice Earl Warren, to rule that Baxstrom had been denied the equal protection of laws under the Fourteenth Amendment.

The court ruled that since a jury trial was allowed under civil proceedings to determine whether an individual is mentally ill, Baxstrom should have been given access to similar procedures, since with the expiration of his sentence he was no longer committed as a criminal patient. He was at that time a civil patient under the custody of the Department of Mental Hygiene (Steadman and Cocozza 1974, pp. 50–51).

Moreover, the court ruled that Baxstrom had also been denied equal protection in that he was not granted a court hearing to determine if he was "dangerous," a protection that, by statute, would have been afforded a civil patient. In sum, the court's decision held that "no longer could time-expired, mentally ill inmates be the only patients in New York who did not have access to jury review on the question of mental illness and dangerousness" (Steadman and Cocozza 1974, p. 51).

The immediate outcome of the Baxstrom case was that Mr. Baxstrom and 966 other patients who were in the same legal class were transferred to civil mental hospitals in New York for reevaluation. The majority were eventually released to the community and their careers were observed and analyzed by Steadman and Cocozza (1974).

In Pennsylvania, the situation was not substantially different from the one that existed in New York before the Baxstrom decision. Prior to 1 January 1967, patients at Farview whose criminal commitments had expired were retained at Farview without judicial action under Section 309 of the Mental Health Act of 1923, later Section 348(b) of the Mental Health Act of 1953. In 1966 a new Mental Health and Mental Retardation Act was passed which provided for slightly different procedures. All the time-expired patients in Farview at that time, and those whose sentences expired after 1967, were recommitted under Section 404 of the 1966 act, reprinted here in its entirety:

SECTION 404. Commitment on Application by Relative, etc.; Physicians' Certificates; Review.—(a) A written application for commitment to a facility may be made in the interest of any person who appears to be mentally disabled and in need of care. It may be made by a relative, guardian, friend, individual standing *in loco parentis* to the person to be committed, or by the executive officer or an authorized agent of a government or recognized nonprofit health or welfare organization or agency or any responsible person.

(*b*) Such application shall be accompanied by the certificates of two physicians who have examined the person whose commitment is sought, within one week of the date of the certificates, and who have found that, in their opinion, such person is mentally disabled and in need of care. In the case of a mentally retarded person, the physician's certification shall be accompanied by the report of a psychologist. No person shall be committed hereunder if any certificate is dated more than thirty days prior to the date of commitment, except that if the mental disability consists of mental retardation, the certificates may be dated not more than three months prior to the date of commitment. The application, certificates and the report, if any, shall be signed and sworn to or affirmed.

(*c*) The director may receive the person named in the application and detain him until discharge in accordance with the provisions of this act. When application is made by any person other than a relative or guardian, the director upon reception of the person named in the application shall notify the appropriate relative or guardian of such person of the commitment.

(*d*) Every commitment made under this section except those to the Veterans Administration or other agency of the United States Government, shall be reviewed at least annually by a committee appointed by the director from the professional staff of the facility wherein the person is detained, to determine whether continued care and commitment is necessary. Said committee shall make written recommendations to the director which shall be filed at the facility, and be open to inspection and review by the department, and such other people as the secretary, by regulation, may permit (Laws of Pennsylvania, session of 1966, 50:4404).

In essence, Section 404 allowed involuntary, indeterminate commitments to be based on two physicians' certificates, did not require judicial review for such commitments, and only required annual *administrative* review of each case.

On 25 July 1969, Donald Dixon and six other named plaintiffs "individually and on behalf of all inhabitants of Farview...situated like unto them" filed suit alleging the unconstitutionality of their commitments under Section 404. The original complaint requested both a permanent injunction restraining the commonwealth from using this section to commit patients to Farview and the convening of a three-judge panel to rule on the constitutionality of Section 404.

On 2 June 1970, the court denied summary judgment and interim relief but authorized a hearing before the three-judge panel. This hearing took place in July 1970, and nine months later—on 30 March 1971—the court ruled in favor of the Dixon patients.[1]

The members of the Dixon class were in one of two legal categories when they originally arrived at Farview. A minority (14 percent) were civil commitments who had been transferred to Farview from civil mental hospitals because they were disruptive at those hospitals. The majority of the Dixon patients were criminal commitments and were in one of the four following legal statuses: (1) transferred from prison while awaiting trial, after which charges were disposed of other than through prosecution; (2) transferred from prison while under sentence; (3) committed after conviction, after sentence had been deferred pending psychiatric examination, or in lieu of sentence; or (4) committed under Pennsylvania's defective delinquent statute, the Barr-Walker Act, which provided for indeterminate sentences.[2]

Although they arrived at Farview via different legal routes, the common legal characteristic of the Dixon patients and the one that led to their suit was that they were all confined at Farview "after the original [judicial] authority for their confinement predicated on criminal convictions or charges had terminated" (Dixon decision, 1971, p. 967).[3] When the expiration of criminal commitment occurred, the Farview staff had the plaintiffs civilly committed to Farview under a two-physician certificate procedure. This recommitment was characterized by a notable absence of due process:

(a) The applications for these recommitments were not made by a relative or guardian or a person standing *in loco parentis* to these people. (b) The applicant for recommitment was the Director of Social Services of Farview or another member of the Farview staff. (c) The applications were supported by certificates of two physicians who were members of the staff of Farview. (d) The applications were submitted to the Superintendent of Farview who "received" the persons named in the application. (e) The persons thus committed were not consulted or given notice of the filing of the applications by the Director of Social Services or others on the staff of Farview. (f) No relative, guardian, or friend was consulted by the Director of Social Services or others on the staff at Farview concerning the continued confinement of these persons. (g) The persons thus committed were not represented by counsel in the proceedings leading to their recommitments. (h) These persons had no independent psychiatric diagnosis or psychological evaluation in connection with either the decision of the Director of Social Services to apply for commitment of the certifications by physicians that they were mentally disabled and in need of care. (i) No court made a finding that these recommitted persons required inpatient care. (j) There is no period fixed by the statute after which persons committed under Section 404 must be released (Dixon decision, 1971, p. 968).

After reviewing the evidence, the court ruled Section 404 to be unconstitutional on its face and in its application to the members of the Dixon class.

The issue as to whether Section 404 has been unconstitutionally applied to the plaintiffs need not detain us long. An examination of the transcript of the hearing of March 13, 1970 shows that the process of "recommitment" concededly was by way of a "paper notation," without any formal hearing or process whatsoever (Dixon decision, 1971, pp. 972-73).

Thus the Dixon court ruled, as did the Baxstrom court, that sentence-expired mentally ill offenders could no longer be denied the equal protection of laws. Any further confinement would be acceptable only after they had been afforded the constitutional safeguards available to all citizens.

Furthermore, in specifying the reason for its decision in favor of the Dixon class, the court exhibited concern for due process in the administrative handling of all the mentally ill. In *Baxstrom*, as in other cases concerning mentally ill offenders, courts have ruled on the principle of equal protection—insisting that offenders who are committed for mental illness receive the same procedural safeguards as the civilly committed mentally ill. In the Dixon case the court ruled that the process by which the plaintiffs had been committed (and all other patients committed under Pennsylvania's two-physician certificate) was unconstitutional whether applied to criminally or civilly committed patients.[4]

In declaring Section 404 unconstitutional the court went far beyond the plea for relief of 586 inmates of Farview. It eliminated the legal basis for commitment of approximately 80 percent of the patients who were in Pennsylvania state mental hospitals. Because the two-physician certificate commitment was an administratively easy way to have a person involuntarily admitted to a hospital, and because it gave the hospital nearly total control over the patient's discharge, it was the preferred commitment procedure. After *Dixon*, however, it was no longer constitutional.[5]

The immediate practical outcome of the case for the Dixon patients was their transfer to civil mental hospitals throughout Pennsylvania where, after reevaluation, decisions concerning their release to the community would be made.

A NATURAL EXPERIMENT

Although there are a variety of lenses through which one can view the mass release of the Dixon patients, the one most appropriate for the purposes of this research is that of a natural experiment. According to F. Stuart Chapin, natural experiments occur when "physical factors at the basis of social life have been limited, or held constant, or the ordinary restraining factors have been removed so that the sociologist need only observe the effects" (Chapin 1947, p. 3). Under ordinary circumstances the decision of the Farview staff to retain an inmate because he was ill and dangerous, or to release him because he was no longer so troubled, was the controlling factor in the determination of whether a patient stayed or left. Courts seldom intervened to countermand a staff decision regarding patients who had been committed to the hospital. We will call the perspective of the Farview staff the medical perspective, for it embodies solely medical or psychiatric criteria. A natural experiment was created here when the medical perspective was overruled by the court employing different criteria, which may be called the legal perspective.

The legal orientation is explicitly a constitutional one and has been described above. In essence the Dixon patients were viewed as citizens whose constitutional rights had been violated, and the court was asked to remedy that violation by releasing the members of the class from Farview.

But to the Farview staff the situation was neither that straightforward nor that legalistic. From the materials available to us the view of the staff can be typified as follows: the Dixon patients were seen as mentally ill individuals who were in need of the care and close supervision that was provided at Farview. They were seen as dangerous offenders who should not be transferred to civil mental hospitals and who should not be released to the community because of their potential for violence. Put differently, we believe the Farview staff saw the majority of the Dixon patients as having a high probability of engaging in violent behavior and, given the difficulty of predicting which individuals fell into that majority, advocated the continued maximum security confinement of the entire class.

Unfortunately, our typification of the views of the Farview staff has to be based on incomplete information. Nowhere in the records of the court case is there a clear, concise statement summarizing these views or presenting an "official" statement of the Farview position on the condition of the entire class. Yet even with this limitation, the material on the transcript of the 22-23 July 1970 court hearing is informative.

During the two years that the Dixon case was in litigation, members of the Dixon class were evaluated by the Farview staff and many of them were transferred to civil hospitals.[6] Yet, at the 22 July hearing, Mr. Bazelon, the attorney for the plaintiffs, reported to the court on the situation of 110 of the 400 members of the class[7] as follows:

These individuals were people who, at the time we had the hearing in March [1970], the Commonwealth said were *too dangerous* to be transferred from Farview. There were roughly between 100 and 110 people on that list whom the commonwealth said were *too dangerous* to be transferred, and there were brief descriptions of those people (Dixon transcript, 1970, p. 9, emphasis added).

An examination of the actual list by the authors verifies Mr. Bazelon's position, to which the commonwealth's attorney did not object. There were a total of 114 patients described in that report and in every case the hospital was opposed to the patient's transfer. The reasons were as follows: (*a*) four patients were considered too old and too sick to be moved; (*b*) two patients were in a work release program at Farview and plans for their discharge were under way; (*c*) the transfer of one patient was opposed by a relative; and, (*d*) 107 patients were considered to be too dangerous for release to a civil hospital or to the community. The primary concern of the Farview staff centered on the potential dangerousness of the subjects. This concern is reflected in the following descriptions taken from that list.

PATIENT A. Long history of disorderly conduct, assault and battery, robbery (mugging), assault 3d degree, robbery by strong arm, and finally homicide. Diagnosis—schizophrenic reaction, paranoid type. Patient is service-connected for disability and asked for transfer to a VA hospital. His application was denied on the basis that the VA did not have maximum security facilities. We consider this patient very dangerous, one who could readily act out his impulses on persons in an aggressive, assaultive manner.

PATIENT B. Throughout his period of hospitalization, patient has been widely delusioned, showing much grandiose ideation. His verbal comment includes aides bringing in guns to him, a gun hidden in his aunt's home, and preoccupation with the thought of guns. He tells staff explicitly that he will escape from any hospital if he has the opportunity to do so. Staff feels the gun references give a pretty clear indication of the feelings beneath the surface and it is highly probable that he could secure and use guns offensively if he escapes from a less secure hospital.

PATIENT C. With another patient, knifed a third patient in Farview State Hospital because of homosexual problems. He has acted out both homicidally and suicidally and will continue to do so. Utterly without control. Cut himself as late as last month (July). He is explosive, unpredictable. He could be truly dangerous in a less secure setting.

These three passages illustrate the dual concern that the Farview staff had about the pending transfer of the Dixon patients. First, the staff did not think the patients could be cared for or controlled in less secure civil hospitals since they needed the security and regimentation of Farview. Second, they saw them as potentially dangerous individuals who were likely to act out their violent impulses if released to the community. The Dixon patients were viewed as both mad and bad, and in need of maximum security care.

Although the preceding material helps to delimit the views of the staff, it refers only to the 114 patients on the list presented to the court at the July hearing. The potential dangerousness of the other members of the Dixon class is not dealt with in that report, or in the transcript of the July hearing. It is thus difficult to draw a complete picture of the views of the staff, but at least a sizable minority of the Dixon patients were seen as dangerous and in need of maximum security care.

A second source of information on this issue can be found in a report that the Farview staff prepared about the fifty-three members of the class who were still at Farview at the time of the July hearing. The report contained brief descriptions of each of these fifty-three patients, as well as a summary statement:

In noting the above, we specially wish to stress that there has been but limited acting out behavior on the part of this group of patients because of the strict, maximum security care received at Farview State Hospital. There is a high expectancy that patients will control their acting out behavior.

Patients understand that violent and assaultive behavior will not be tolerated. They know that limits are set and that any violation of the limits will call for imposed controls. It is our *considered professional opinion that if we take away the maximum security controls, the patients will not be able to contain their impulses within acceptable limits* (Dixon transcript, 1970, p. 61, emphasis added).

Again the same situation exists. A portion of the Dixon class is clearly described as requiring maximum security care, in this case because of their presumed inability to contain their impulses. The position of the Farview staff concerning the impulsiveness and dangerousness of the entire Dixon class is not discussed, however.

Finally, we refer to a portion of the testimony presented by Dr. John Shovlin, the superintendent of Farview at the time of the Dixon case. In describing Farview to the court, Dr. Shovlin indicated that there was one minimum security ward at the hospital. He went on to say that

... this ward can, I think rightfully, be considered to be a minimum security ward, presently housing approximately 30 patients. We have tried over a period of years to use this facility more and more, that is, transfer as many patients out to this facility as possible, which has a capacity of 65 patients. But our staff felt that a majority of these patients, of course, were *untrustworthy* in the sense that they would attempt to *escape or may injure themselves or someone else* (Dixon transcript, 1970, pp. 260–61, emphasis added).

Although the referent for Dr. Shovlin's term "majority of these patients" is unclear, it seems to encompass the entire Farview population, including the Dixon patients. Since fewer than half of the beds on the minimum security ward were in use at the time of this testimony and the thirty patients residing there represented only 4 percent of the total population at Farview (Dixon trans-script, 1970, p. 260), Dr. Shovlin's descriptions of the staff's feelings seem quite accurate. Patients at Farview were viewed as untrustworthy and unstable, as having a high potential for violent behavior, and as requiring the type of maximum security avail-able at Farview. Given this material, and our own conclusions based on discussions with the Farview staff and the systematic examination of hospital records, we believe that the prevailing opinion of the clinical staff at Farview was that the Dixon patients were dangerous and in need of maximum security confinement.

This view is inferentially seen in data gathered during the course of this research. The Dixon patients were held at Farview for an average of fourteen years before release under the Dixon case. During this period of confinement few attempts were made by the Farview staff to transfer the patients to less secure, civil hospitals. Although some members of the Farview staff explained this by the reluctance on the part of civil hospitals to receive transfers from Farview, evidence in the files of the Dixon pa-tients, which we gathered systematically, indicates that transfer attempts initiated by Farview were few and far between. The policy of confining these patients for a long period of time and not seeking their transfer to less secure facilities is quite consistent with the perception that the patients were untrustworthy, poten-tially dangerous to themselves and others, and in need of maxi-mum security care.

The clinical view is quite different from the legal view described earlier. Proponents of the legal perspective saw the Dixon pa-tients as a group of individuals whose constitutional rights had been violated and, regardless of their potential dangerousness, urged the court to release them to civil mental hospitals where their confinement could be reevaluated. On the other hand, the clinical staff at Farview appeared to see the Dixon patients as mentally ill offenders, with a high potential for dangerous be-havior, who required maximum security care. In the end the decision of the Dixon court endorsed the legal perspective. Al-though the court was sensitive to the medical view and concerned with the health of the patients, its decision declared the confine-ment of the Dixon patients to be unconstitutional, and it ordered the entire class transferred from Farview despite the prediction of potential dangerousness.

Since the decision of the court was in almost complete agreement with the legal view, the result, from a methodological perspective, is the creation of a natural experiment. By following the careers of the Dixon patients after their release from Farview one can with a minimum of contamination assess the accuracy of the clinical view. By acting to continue the confinement of the subjects at Farview, the clinicians in effect predicted that the Dixon patients would be dangerous and unable to control their impulses if released from the maximum security of Farview. Yet the court's decision, based on an entirely different set of criteria, ignored this prediction, thereby allowing for the empirical testing of the accuracy of the prediction. As Chapin would have it, we need only observe the results of this mass release, for once not having to concern ourselves with the contaminating influence of the discharge action being based on the variable whose predictive validity we are trying to assess.

PREDICTIONS: CLINICAL, STATISTICAL, AND POLITICAL

In the previous section we stated that the Farview staff predicted that a majority of the Dixon patients would be dangerous if released from maximum security confinement. There are many, no doubt, who would object to this conclusion and, based on their own experiences at state mental hospitals, would conclude that the Farview staff made no predictions about the future behavior of the Dixon patients.[8] They would argue that these patients were kept at Farview because bureaucratic inertia resulted in the failure to make positive decisions to release, and not because future behavior was predicted. This position has some validity. Though confinement of the Dixon patients was due in large part to the results of a predictive process, this process was a good deal different from the techniques traditionally discussed in the literature on prediction.

By and large that literature has focused on the continuing controversy over the relative value of clinical versus statistical prediction. In brief, clinical predictions are made by trained psychiatrists or psychologists based on information gathered from clinical interviews and testing. Statistical predictions, on the other hand, are made on the basis of numerical combination and analysis of data about the subject. (See Meehl 1954 and Sawyer 1966 for detailed discussions of this literature.) We are not suggesting that the Farview staff made rigorous clinical or statistical predictions about the future behavior of the Dixon patients. Indeed, the available evidence indicates that neither of these types of prediction were made at Farview.

We would submit, however, that there is a third type of predictive exercise which was in fact performed by the Farview staff. This type of prediction, which we will call political prediction, is based, not on the characteristics of the individual, but on the assumed characteristics of a group to which the individual belongs. In essence, group predictions are projected onto the members of the group. If the majority of the group is predicted to be violent, then all the members of the group, simply because of their membership in the group, are predicted to be violent.

All statistical prediction involves assigning to members of a group characteristics of the whole group. For example if 25 percent of the members of a group commit an offense, the probability of any members of the group committing an offense is said to be .25. When the process is properly conducted the probability of group events, and the deduced individual event, is based on grouping subjects together on the basis of variables known to be associated with offending. In political prediction, groups are created on the basis of criteria which are assumed, but not demonstrated, to be correlated with offending. The legal status "mentally ill offender" is just such a category. All those classified as mentally ill offenders are predicted to be dangerous by virtue of their legal status, a variable whose statistical association with dangerousness is assumed, but not known. The logic of this type of prediction is as follows: (l) It is assumed that the legal classification "mentally ill offender" contains a high proportion of persons who would be dangerous if released from a security hospital to a less secure setting. (2) Accurate prediction of which individuals in the class would and which would not be dangerous if released is difficult, if not impossible. (3) The consequences of mispredictions, especially false-negatives, are perceived as negative and quite severe. (4) Therefore, the decision maker, in order to protect himself and his institution from these negative consequences, predicts that all, rather than some, of the class will be dangerous and recommends that release be denied them all.

Previous explanations of the phenomenon of overprediction of dangerousness have tended to be eclectic, citing a number of variables which may, singularly or in combination, lead to such overprediction. Monahan, for example, has discussed a number of these factors, including the following: (1) lack of corrective feedback—officials who erroneously predict dangerousness usually have no way of learning of the error to correct subsequent predictions; (2) illusory correlation—"Predictor variables that in fact bear no relationship to dangerousness will continue to be used because those who believe in them will find (illusory) support for their beliefs by selectively attending to the data: They will see only what they wish to see" (1975a, p. 24); (3) low base rates—predictions without many false-positives are difficult to make for any phenomenon which occurs infrequently, and dangerousness is no exception. (See Monahan 1975a, pp. 20–25 for a more detailed discussion of these reasons as well as the presentation of others.)

While these factors no doubt contribute to the overprediction of dangerousness, we think there is a more general, systematic explanation that, in the first place, explains why nonscientific factors such as those discussed by Monahan are allowed to exist, and which, in the final analysis, explains why clinicians routinely predict that most criminally insane offenders will be dangerous after release. This explanation is intimately linked to the general political and social setting in which maximum security mental hospitals operate and, because of this, we have labeled the phenomenon of overprediction "political prediction." The factors that lead clinicians to utilize political predictions in their decisions concerning the release of the criminally insane exist at two levels. The first concerns the general political order, as exemplified by the policies of the state government and legislature, and the second concerns political consequences that can befall clinicians who make decisions about the release of mentally ill offenders.

Many acts of the state government, both acts of commission and omission, have led to the adoption of political prediction. In the first place, the government has never provided maximum security hospitals with the professional staff required for treating the criminally insane. At Farview, for example, the psychiatric, psychological, social work, and nursing staffs have all been judged to be inadequate (see chapter 1). Such a situation makes it virtually impossible to use clinical or statistical prediction in decisions to release patients, since these types of predictions require highly trained professionals, working with adequate resources. The decision maker is therefore forced to rely on less sophisticated prediction methods which invariably lead either to overprediction or underprediction. In the case of the criminally insane the political pressures demand that if errors in the prediction of violence are to be made, they are made in the direction of overprediction.

The use of the indeterminate sentence, combined with a lack of treatment resources, goes a long way to insuring this guarantee. Patients are confined at Farview for indefinite periods of time, and can only be released when the clinical staff decides that they are no longer mentally ill and dangerous. The clinical staff, however, is well aware of the fact that the state has not made adequate resources available to facilitate the treatment of these patients. Because of this the policy of the state government can be viewed as a paradox: the criminally insane should be hospitalized until cured, but the state will not facilitate their cure and release by providing treatment programs. This paradox is not unique to Pennsylvania, nor are we the first to note its existence. Others have described the combination of indeterminate sentences and the lack of treatment as mechanisms for ridding society of undesirables.

> . . . by taking the criminal off the streets while at the same time promising rehabilitation, the indeterminate sentence makes it easy for society to ignore the underlying social causes of crime. To put it another way, indeterminate sentencing allows society to isolate the fruits of its inadequate social policies when they are disruptive but simultaneously to ignore the problem as a whole since the most unpleasant results (crime and criminals) are effectively removed (Prettyman 1972, pp. 18–19).

Clinicians have no difficulty in concluding that the implicit policy of the state is one which encourages the continued confinement of these patients. This policy—exemplified in the combination of the indeterminate sentence and the lack of treatment facilities—places a higher value on protecting the community than on rehabilitating and discharging the patient. It suggests that criminally insane patients should be released only when the clinician is virtually certain that the patient will not be dangerous, but as numerous studies have shown, certainty in the prediction of postrelease dangerousness is impossible to achieve.[9] As a re-

sult, the clinician is forced to rely on the overprediction of dangerous behavior. This is the "safe" approach, and the only approach
that is consistent with the paradoxical policy implicit in state law.

The likelihood that political prediction about the dangerousness of the criminally insane will be made is enhanced by the
reward system which exists for clinicians who make decisions
about the release or retention of these patients. This reward
system is a logical extension of the state's overall policy which
recommends the long-term confinement of the criminally insane.
Indeed, the reward system can be viewed as the mechanism by
which policy is implemented.

Positive rewards for correctly predicting which patients will not
be dangerous and then releasing them are virtually nonexistent.
In a setting in which the state's policy is to protect the community
from the criminally insane, large inmate populations are not
politically undesirable and, in some respects, can be viewed as an
indication of the successful implementation of the policy. Thus,
there are few rewards for decisions that will reduce the hospital
population but simultaneously increase the risk of erroneously
releasing patients who become dangerous. In fact, administrators
of maximum security hospitals are more likely to be rewarded for
running large, "quiet" institutions. Ironically, the indeterminate
sentence and its attendant discretionary discharging authority is
one of the mechanisms by which the administrator can achieve
this goal. "In most instances, the indeterminate sentence is used
as an instrument of inmate control. The staff and the releasing
authority simply play God with the offender, wielding the variable
sentence as a weapon" (Prettyman 1972, p. 19).

Although the clinician will gain few positive rewards for releasing mentally ill offenders who will not be dangerous, he will
experience negative consequences for releasing criminally insane
offenders who in fact become dangerous. The political and administrative consequences for *erroneously* predicting that a patient will not be dangerous after release are probably the most
serious that can befall the clinician. This point has been made by
a number of previous researchers. Monahan has concluded that:

The correctional official or mental health professional who predicts that a given individual will not commit a dangerous act is
subject to severe unpleasantness should that act actually occur.

Often he will be informed of its occurence in the headlines ("Freed Mental Patient Murders Mother") and he or his supervisors will spend many subsequent days fielding reporters' questions about his professional incompetence and his institution's laxity (1975a, p. 22).

While we agree with Monahan's position, we would not limit the interrogators to members of the media, but would include politicians, judges, and legislators as well. As Steadman has said, "There may be no surer way for the forensic psychiatrist to lose power than to have a released mental patient charged with a serious crime in the district of a key legislator" (1972, p. 264). Prettyman, in discussing the effect of the indeterminate sentence on the prediction of dangerousness, has made a similar point:

In practice, the psychiatrist becomes more of a jailer than a healer. While he is supposed to treat the inmate, he also knows that he will have to testify in court at various times about his "patient" and that his recommendation to the releasing authority will virtually determine the inmate's release date. This puts the psychiatrist in an inherently untenable role, *brings political pressure to bear on his decisions,* and restricts his freedom to work for the best interest of his patients (1972, p. 19, emphasis added).

Two cases from the files of the Dixon patients can be used to illustrate how decisions about the release of the criminally insane can be affected by the likelihood of negative reactions from political figures. In the first case, the following exchange of memos occurred:

Memo to Hospital Administrator, February 12, 1970:[10]
    Patient presented to staff on January 30, 1970.
    Referred for your decision.
Administrator's response:
    He should have a trial at a civil mental hospital.
Memo to Hospital Administrator, February 20, 1970:
    Were you aware that the D.A. suspects [patient] of murdering a girl at a local carnival and they are anxious to get to see him? See Social Work Not[e]s for running account of this. Do you still want him transferred?
Administrator's response:
    After reconsideration he should remain here until further stabilized.

The second illustration follows the same format:

Memo to Hospital Administrator, January 16, 1965:
  Patient presented to staff on January 12, 1965.
  Referred for your decision.
Administrator's response:
  Suitable for transfer to ——— S.H.
  [a civil mental hospital].
Memo to Hospital Administrator, January 25, 1965.
  You OK'd transfer to ——— S.H. on pt. I don't know whether
  you reviewed the older files or not. If you do, you will note the
  strong objection of Judge X to the transfer. We, at one point,
  decided to cancel an earlier recommendation for transfer.
    If transfer and elopement occurred, we might be "in the
  middle" with the Court.
    So on my attached letter to the family I am asking them to
  take the responsibility to discuss transfer with the Court, rather
  than having us open up the case again. . . . I wish you would
  again "rethink" this particular case.
Administrator's response:
  I agree wholeheartedly with your suggestion.

As a result of the "rethinking," the patient spent an additional
six years at Farview.

To avoid these negative political consequences, the prediction
that a patient will not be dangerous after release is rarely made.
Instead, the clinicians at maximum security hospitals routinely
overpredict the rate of dangerousness among their patients.

Because psychiatrists cannot accurately predict who will become
violent, they frequently err. Rather than random errors, however,
their inaccurate predictions are consistently on the safe side. They
overpredict. They assume that since some patients are dangerous,
the one under consideration might be. The result of this practice
is that as many as 20 harmless persons are incarcerated for everyone who will commit a violent act (Steadman and Cocozza 1975,
p. 35).

This is the sense and meaning of the term *political prediction*
as it is used in this research. It refers to the gross overprediction
of violence among the criminally insane, which is not primarily
caused by the shoddy work of uneducated, misinformed clinicians,
but is part and parcel of society's handling of the criminally
insane. It is quite consistent with the state's policy of confining

the mentally ill offenders until they are cured, but of confining them in hospitals that do not provide treatment facilities. It is also quite consistent with the reward system that exists for the clinicians who are responsible for making these decisions. Because these explanatory factors exist in the political realm, we have labeled these predictions political.

Our position is that this type of prediction is commonly employed in decisions concerning the release of the criminally insane. Moreover, we contend that political predictions were made by the Farview staff concerning the Dixon subjects. Because the state maintained a policy of continued confinement for the criminally insane, and because negative consequences would follow the erroneous prediction of nondangerousness, the Farview staff predicted that most of the Dixon patients would be dangerous after release and accordingly retained these patients at Farview. One of the major foci of this research will be the empirical assessment of the validity of these predictions and, through that assessment, an evaluation of the efficiency and necessity of long-term indeterminate confinement of mentally ill offenders.

Before the specific research questions that will orient the empirical analysis are presented, a methodological note about the evaluation of political predictions is needed. One could take the position that political predictions, because of their unscientific nature, are not "real" predictions and therefore need not be subjected to empirical validation. Our position, however, is that political predictions are real predictions, that is, they are statements about expected future behavior, and further, that decisions concerning the confinement or freedom of mentally ill offenders are made on the basis of these predictions. Indeed, political prediction is the most common type of prediction used in decisions concerning the release of the criminally insane. Because they have such an important impact on the handling of the criminally insane, it is essential that the validity of these predictions be assessed with the same rigor that is applied to the assessment of more scientific approaches. This in no way implies that one would expect political predictions to be valid and accurate estimates of future behavior. Indeed, when one considers the low levels of accuracy of other more systematic attempts to predict criminal and violent behavior conducted under politically insulated conditions, the obvious hypothesis about such nonscientific, politically sensitive predictions is that they are, by and large, poor estimates of future behavior.

Continuing to accept the existence of such predictions without adequate assessment, however, places us in the awkward position of being unable to estimate exactly how poor the predictions are. Such an ostrichlike position serves neither the advancement of scientific knowledge nor informed decision making. The resulting ignorance, however, does help to perpetuate a system of prediction which may be badly flawed and which may result in the institutionalization of many patients who do not require such care. Because political predictions are predictions about future behavior, and because they lead to decisions that affect the lives of individuals, they should be examined with care and diligence.

THE ORIENTATION OF THE RESEARCH

Indeed, one of the two major research questions that will orient the present study concerns the political prediction that the Dixon patients required maximum security care and, if released, would engage in dangerous, violent behavior. We are interested in determining whether such a prediction was justified and, whether it was or not, how valid and accurate it was.

The first part of this issue—the justification for the prediction—involves an examination of the extent and nature of the violent behavior that the Dixon patients committed before the prediction was made. Although prehospitalization violence is important and will be analyzed, our primary emphasis will be on violence that occurred during confinement at Farview. If serious assaultive acts occurred frequently during the confinement of the Dixon patients, the Farview staff would be justified in predicting that such behavior would continue, perhaps even intensify, in less secure settings. At least the predictions about future behavior would be consistent with past, observed behavior. If violent behavior at Farview was not common, however, the justification for the prediction of postrelease violence would be questionable because of the dissonance between the past, observed, behavior and the future, expected, behavior.

If the rate of violence at Farview is in fact found to be low, alternate interpretations emerge. One would suggest that the Dixon patients are not prone to violence; the other that they are, but the strict security at Farview contains these propensities. This

dilemma can be resolved by examining the rates of assaultive behavior at the civil hospitals to which the Dixon patients were
transferred. Low rates of assault in these less secure settings
would argue against a containment model in which Farview is
seen as "keeping the lid on," while high rates would provide
support for the actions of the Farview staff.

The data on behavior at the transfer hospitals can be viewed as
bridging the two aspects of our question about political predictions—justification and validity. The prediction, as we have presented it, is twofold—that the Dixon patients would be disruptive
and unmanageable at less secure hospitals and would be dangerous if released to the community. The data on the rate and
seriousness of assaultive behavior at the civil mental hospitals will
allow us to assess directly the first aspect. The second aspect will
be examined by an analysis of postrelease recidivism and rehospitalization, especially for violent offenses.

In both cases our hypothesis is that the Dixon patients, by and
large, would not be assaultive. This hypothesis is based in part on
the existing literature on postrelease violence (see Thornberry 1974
for a discussion of this literature), and on the nonscientific nature
of political predictions. Since these predictions are not based on
association with variables known to be related to violence among
such a population, one would expect them to be inaccurate. We
take it to be an important research task, however, to document
their accuracy and to estimate the extent of the error. An associated task involves specifying those variables which are in fact
associated with postrelease violence and which may form the basis
for a prediction process which is more accurate than political
prediction. These tasks will constitute the first of the major
orientations of this work.

The second orientation concerns the appropriateness of the
legal perspective that was put forth at the time of the Dixon case
and which was endorsed by the court in its decision. The court
ruled that the patients should be transferred from Farview because they had been confined there unconstitutionally. Essentially
we are interested in determining if such a decision was in the best
interests of the patients and if it is a decision with which the
members of the class agreed.

Darold Treffert has written a provocative paper which presented "a series of case reports of psychiatric patients who have

'died with their rights on', i.e., *situations where scrupulous con-cern for the patient's* [legal and constitutional] *rights oversha-dowed or outweighed reasonable concern for the patient's life"* (1974, p. 1, emphasis in original). Such cases represent what Treffert called "dubious and hollow legal triumphs." Although the number of cases Treffert presented is rather limited, they do raise intriguing and complex issues relevant to the Dixon case.

The court ordered all the Dixon patients transferred to civil mental hospitals for reevaluation. Furthermore, unless the staff members at the civil hospitals could demonstrate a compelling reason for maintaining the subjects in confinement, the court felt the Dixon patients should be released to the community.[11] We are interested in the extent to which this order was consistent with the interests of the patients. This is not to imply that the court was insensitive to this issue. The transcript of the July hearing indicates that the judges were quite concerned with it, but given the relatively rare nature of the situation—the Baxstrom case being one of the few similar precedents—should the court have ordered the release of 586 long-term, mentally ill patients who had exhibited violent behavior in the past?

There are two aspects to this matter. The first concerns the increased possibility of danger to the staff and patients at civil hospitals and to the general public. Since this is essentially the same question as the validity of the political predictions of the Farview staff, however, it need not detain us here.

The second aspect is related to Treffert's concern and involves the extent to which the court order was in the best interest of the Dixon patients. In view of the patients having been at Farview for such long periods of time, probably resulting in the development of "institutionalized personalities," was it appropriate to order their release from Farview? Conceivably many of the Dixon sub-jects might have preferred to remain at Farview where the living conditions were stable and familiar, albeit spartan. Even if they preferred to leave Farview, they may not have been mentally able to cope with the freedom of the civil hospitals and the even greater freedom of the community. If the final result of the order was to transfer patients who preferred to remain at Farview to com-munity settings where they ended up living alone, in dingy board-ing houses, unemployed and on welfare, without the medical and psychiatric care provided at Farview, and with few of life's amenities one would have to question the extent to which the Dixon patients "won" their court case.

The second major theme of this work will be an analysis of this issue—the extent to which the Dixon patients are dying, or at least living poorly, with their rights on. In this analysis we will examine the attitudes of the Dixon patients toward Farview, civil mental hospitals, and the community; describe their postrelease treatment and residential and employment histories; and study their social and psychological adjustment. This analysis is intended to provide answers to theoretical issues such as the social adjustment of long-term mental patients and the ability of patients to make the transition from maximum security settings to the freedom of community living. The analysis will also be concerned with the more practical issue of suggesting guidelines and procedures for the release of patients in similar situations in the future.

In sum, there are two major themes that will be used to orient and guide the data analysis. Essentially they are the two sides of the same coin—(1) the validity of the political predictions that were made at the time of the Dixon case and (2) the consequences which resulted from the domination of the legal perspective, and the release of the patients, in a circumstance where the medical perspective had traditionally been dominant.

3   Methodological Issues

IDENTIFYING THE SUBJECTS

The first methodological task that confronted the project concerned sampling and the selection of subjects. Our original intention was to study all the members of the Dixon class and as large a control group as possible. Since we had received the official list of plaintiffs in the Dixon case from the State Department of Public Welfare (DPW), we had assumed that the composition of the Dixon class was given and only the composition of the control group was left to be determined. At the outset of the project, however, we found that the list of 551 Dixon patients that the DPW had sent to the court in its report of final disposition was inaccurate. Ten of the men named on the list had never been patients at Farview, thirty-one had been transferred before the Dixon complaint was filed, and seventy-six Farview patients who were *de jure* members of the Dixon class, and were treated as such by Farview, did not appear on the list.

This finding forced us to create a definition of the Dixon patient and to determine which Farview patients fitted the definition. For our purposes a Dixon patient is an individual (1) who was held at Farview for some period between 25 July 1969 (the date the complaint was filed) and 22 April 1971 (the date of the

38

court order), and (2) who was held at Farview under Section 404 of the Mental Health and Mental Retardation Act of 1966, or its statutory precedents, while the suit was pending, and; (3a) whose maximum sentence, if held under criminal sentence, had expired on or before 22 April 1971, or (3b) whose maximum sentence would have expired on or before 22 April 1971 if the subject had been sentenced. (This last group includes subgroups who were never sentenced, such as those who were found incompetent to stand trial, and in these cases the statutory maximum sentence the individual could have received for his offense was used as the actual maximum.)

One of the authors reviewed the file of every patient who was transferred from Farview in the years 1969, 1970, and 1971 to identify subjects who met these criteria. Based on this search, the final list, after correcting erroneous inclusions and omissions, contained 586 men who, for the purposes of this research, will constitute the "Dixon patients."

The purpose of having a control group was to determine the effect of new policies instituted as a result of the Dixon case, which, for any Farview patient whose criminal commitment expired and whom the state wished to keep hospitalized, required a new court commitment after evaluation at a civil mental hospital. The question we had hoped to answer by studying the post-hospital experience of the control group is "What would have happened if the Dixon patients had been released immediately on expiration of their criminal commitments and there had been no legal issue for a Dixon case?" Such a control group could be used to validate any prediction procedures developed from the experience of the Dixon patients.

Because Farview is the only maximum security mental hospital in Pennsylvania, this meant the control group had to be drawn from among its patients or from a similar hospital in a neighboring state. The differences in criminal codes, mental health statutes governing admission and discharge, varying institutional, political, and adminstrative policies, and the difficulty in acquiring the cooperation of another state bureaucracy—all of which could affect the comparability of the data—led us to decide against cross-state comparisons and to focus on Farview patients.

Thus the control group was defined as all patients who met the criteria for inclusion in the Dixon class except that they were transferred from Farview between 23 April 1971, immediately after the conclusion of the Dixon case, and 31 December 1973, six months before the beginning of the field research.

Based on the Department of Public Welfare reports to the Dixon court, we anticipated that a control group of at least sixty subjects would be generated by this definition. Unfortunately, for research purposes, the reports on which our estimate was based were incorrect and only twenty-two men met the criteria for control group membership. The majority of the subjects who were originally thought to be eligible for the control group were in fact members of the experimental group, that is, they were Dixon patients. As a result, the control group that does exist is too small for statistical analysis and data related to these subjects will not be presented. Where appropriate, and where data exist, material from previously published sources will be used for comparative purposes. The data to be described and analyzed below refer only to the 586 members of the Dixon class.

ACCESS TO DATA

The wide range of substantive issues to be investigated called for a number of different research methods. Since we sought information across time and about different issues, the resulting research strategy included abstracting information from hospital and police records and interviewing patients, patients' relatives, and hospital staff. Early in the formulation of this strategy it became apparent that the research required entry to state agencies and access to patients, patients' records, and hospital staff members.

This entry and access were problematical because the authors of this report are university-based researchers with no official relationship to the Pennsylvania government and with no legal right to the records which were crucial to the conduct of this inquiry. Yet the Pennsylvania DPW provided us with complete access to the required data. This access was granted for at least two reasons. The first and most important reason was simply that the officials of the DPW shared our intellectual curiosity about the consequences of the Dixon case. They too wanted to know if the released Dixon patients were dangerous, if they could be treated in civil hospitals, and if they could adjust to community living, and they therefore fully supported our research.

In addition to this curiosity, however, the officials of the DPW were confronted with a major policy issue that was directly related to the topic of this research. Our work was conceived and conducted between March 1972 and January 1975, a period of intense controversy in Pennsylvania regarding the disposition of mentally ill offenders. Since the Dixon case resulted in a 50 percent reduction of Farview's inmate population, officials in the state government questioned whether this would be a suitable time to close Farview completely and to decentralize the treatment of Farview-type patients. Preliminary plans were made to establish regional security units at five of the state's civil mental hospitals, to transfer Farview's remaining patients to them, and to use the regional facilities for direct transfer from civil hospitals, courts, and prisons.

When we approached DPW officials in the spring of 1972 with a plan to study the consequences of the Dixon case for the patients, the civil hospitals that received the patients, and the community at large, the officials expressed enthusiasm for the proposal. This research offered them the opportunity to acquire, from a disinterested university-based research team, data which would answer questions they had about the consequences to the civil hospitals and the community which might attend decentralizing the care of mentally ill offenders.

They agreed to aid our research in whatever way they could. The officials understood from the outset that the results of our research would be analyzed and publicized as warranted by the data and not by any political considerations, and in no way did they interfere in our research. Having agreed to help us in the conduct of the study, DPW officials opened every door we asked within the agency, aided us in locating the Dixon patients who had been released, and secured access to state police records for us. Their cooperation was complete, and without it this research could not have been conducted. In return we hope that the information presented below will be useful to these officials in their future policy decisions.[1]

HOSPITAL RECORDS

Patient records at Pennsylvania state mental hospitals are very useful for research purposes. These records contain large quantities of information about the patient's background, behavior, and treatment; information that accumulates with the passage of years of hospitalization and is retained intact for many years after the patient is discharged or dies. Trained record librarians are in charge of the organization and location of these records, so that even after many years of entries by many different staff members, the records are surprisingly accessible, complete, and informative.

Our first step in using them was to gather relevant background and behavioral data on the subjects from the files at Farview. After a preliminary screening of the records to determine organization and content, a coding form, presented in appendix 2, was constructed. This form provided structure for the collection of information on such variables as demographic characteristics and family background, offense and hospitalization histories, psychiatric and psychological evaluations and behavior in the hospital. For two three-week periods during the summers of 1973 and 1974, one of the authors worked at Farview with two teams of five assistants extracting this information from patient files and completing the coding form.

In addition to the Farview records, the records of the civil mental hospitals to which the subjects were transferred, "transfer hospitals," were also examined for relevant information. From the fall of 1973 through the summer of 1974 the research staff visited all seventeen transfer hospitals to complete transfer hospital record summaries on all subjects. The transfer hospital summary is much briefer than the Farview summary and focuses on behavior in the hospital and behavior after discharge. This form is presented in appendix 3.

Data were collected from the files of all subjects with only two exceptions: a 50 percent random sample of subjects was selected for coding information about attempts to secure the transfer of subjects before the time of the Dixon case and for independent psychiatric evaluations. Farview patient records were so voluminous and the time involved in scanning the complete record so great that we decided a sample of records would suffice for these two variables which were peripheral to the main concerns of the study.[2]

Two sets of data collected from the hospital files require more detailed explanation. They refer to the measures that will be used to gauge the level of violent behavior that occurs in the institution. The first measure is based on the official incident reports which are completed by staff members who observe incidents which resulted—or may have resulted—in injury to patients or staff members. Incident reports are signed by the reporting official's supervisor and by a high-ranking member of the administration. Each incident report usually contains a description of the incident, including who initiated the incident, the names of participants, the extent of injuries, and any medical treatment administered.

Although our subjects were mental patients, we are assuming some degree of volition in their violent acting out, and we accepted as intentional every violent act which was not reported as accidental by the staff. We excluded from the analysis every report of a subject's falling, tripping, or otherwise injuring himself or another person that was recorded as an accidental event by the staff. Furthermore, to take account of the varying lengths of hospitalization of the subjects, the data analysis will primarily focus on annual rates of incidents.

Though records of injuries reflect the most serious violent behavior occurring in the hospital, they provide only a coarse measure of all violent behavior and give little indication of behavior viewed as indicating potential for violence. Therefore a second measure—employing the ward notes of the subjects—was constructed for more subtle indications of in-hospital violence.

Physicians on the Farview staff enter ward notes in each patient's file at regular, though infrequent, intervals. The contents of these narrative reports vary, but they usually contain statements regarding changes in the patient's physical and mental condition; his activities; requirements for change in medication, ward or work assignments; and observations of his behavior. The last item, physicians' notes about behavior on the ward, provides our indicator of in-hospital violence.

Content analysis of a sample of ward notes, conducted with the aid of our psychiatric consultant, yielded fifty common phrases which either describe violent behavior or are considered by many clinicians to be indicative of violent potential. These phrases exist on three logical levels in their relation to violence. First are statements of observed violence, for example, "fights" or "attack." Second-level phrases are generalizations about the subject's violent nature based on observation of behavior, for example, "dangerous" or "homicidal." At the third level are statements of nonviolent behavior which clinicians commonly believe to be suggestive of violent potential, for example, "paranoid" or "suspicious."

The research staff read all the ward notes for all the subjects and noted the presence of each of the fifty phrases when they appeared. Based on these data, the second index of violent behavior during hospitalization is the rate of notations of these fifty phrases. Initially it was hoped that the observed frequencies of the various entries could be statistically combined into more refined indexes of different aspects of violent behavior and violent propensities. Both cluster analysis and factor analysis, however, failed to yield any systematic groupings or patterns of entries. This absence of empirically demonstrable groupings could have been a statistical artifact, due largely to the effect of the many zero and near-zero cell entries on the factor and cluster procedures. Whatever the reason, no strong factors emerged. In the absence of natural groupings we have combined the fifty phrases into seven mutually exclusive groups based on their meanings and connotations. They are as follows: (1) overt violence toward others, (2) potential for violence toward others, (3) self-injury, (4) property destruction, (5) management problems, (6) angry and antiauthoritarian attitudes, and (7) psychotic symptoms. The items contained within these groups are specified in appendix 4.

Although incident reports and ward notes will be employed to measure in-hospital assaultiveness, the validity of these measures needs to be assessed. A variety of institutional factors may create pressures among recording officials to underreport the number of violent incidents, even assuming that they have accurate and complete knowledge about all these events. For example, too many official reports of violent incidents on a ward might be interpreted as indicating that those in charge are not able to control their patients. Moreover, some incidents may occur which should have been prevented by staff and which, if reported accurately, would reflect badly on the staff or, in the extreme, make staff legally liable for injuries. Add to these examples of intentional distortion, honest errors and incidents about which the staff has no knowledge, and the resulting picture raises questions about the validity of these data.

Although these factors may distort our perception of in-hospital violence, we have decided to use these measures for two reasons. The first is that they are, quite simply, the only measures available. In the absence of other sources of data, we are forced to use these records, being constantly aware of their limitations, or not conduct the analysis at all. We have opted for the former. Second, we are more interested in serious assaults that may have occurred during confinement than in minor scuffles that probably erupted among the patients. It is our contention that serious assaults are likely to be reported in incident reports and ward notes while the underreported events are likely to involve minor disturbances. Thus the invalidity of the records is most likely to affect the behavior we are least interested in observing. For these reasons we have decided to utilize incident reports and ward notes as indicators of in-hospital violence.

POLICE RECORDS

A major focus of this study is a follow-up of the criminal careers of the Dixon patients. Although records at Farview contained information on prior arrest and incarceration for most subjects, a more complete and accurate picture of the arrest histories of the subjects was required for our purposes. Upon request of the secretary of welfare, the Pennsylvania State Police conducted a record search during the summer of 1974 for the arrest histories of all the Dixon subjects. The state police were able to identify 96 percent (N = 564) of the 586 subjects. They then forwarded to us police record summary sheets for these subjects, including reports of arrests before and after hospitalization at Farview, or statements of "no record."

Because we knew that out-of-state arrests which occurred after the release of these patients were not likely to appear on Pennsylvania State Police records, and suspecting that these records would not be complete even for in-state arrests, we sought other sources of arrest information. It is common practice for criminal justice and mental health agencies to share information on previous clients. Frequently when a person is arrested, particularly if he is charged with a serious offense, and his history of mental hospitalization is discovered, the arresting agency or presentence investigator contacts the hospital requesting a summary of the defendant's record. Whenever requests of this nature were encountered during the process of completing the record summaries at Farview and the transfer hospitals, the information was coded in as much detail as possible. When the available information was incomplete we sent letters to the prosecuting agency that made the initial request and, through the Pennsylvania State Police, made requests to out-of-state police agencies based on the partial information we possessed. This informal process yielded 23 percent of the total number of arrests we recorded for the Dixon patients after discharge.

There are serious deficiencies suggested by our supplementary information sources in using state police records. Not all police agencies in the state report all arrests to the state police. Furthermore, the state police have no way of knowing the extent of underreporting by other agencies, but it seems reasonable to assume that underreporting occurs most frequently for minor offenses that do not result in conviction or incarceration. Conviction for a felony resulting in imprisonment in a state institution will almost certainly appear in state police records. This conclusion is supported by our search of the state prison population list. We found several subjects incarcerated in state prisons during the summer of 1974, but none whose status was not accurately reflected on the police "rap sheet." Therefore we feel quite comfortable with the coverage of serious in-state offenses provided by our data sources, but acknowledge that out-of-state arrests and arrests for minor offenses are quite possibly underenumerated by our techniques.

Although police arrest data are flawed as indicators of unlawful behavior, they are the official records closest to the event. As cases are filtered through the levels of criminal justice processing—police, courts, corrections—knowledge about criminal behavior is lost. Therefore, an arrest by the police has been accepted for the purposes of our analysis as the best available measure of criminal behavior and will be treated as though it were sufficient evidence of guilt. This assumption tends to inflate the apparent criminality of the subjects, a systematic bias in the opposite direction of our hypothesis that the level of crime among the released subjects was low.

In seeking a composite measure of involvement with the law to be used in subsequent multivariate analyses, the police data allowed for several possibilities: the number of arrests, number of arrests for violent offenses, and two summary scales. The first of these, the legal dangerousness scale (LDS), developed in the assessment of the impact of the Baxstrom case in New York, incorporates several aspects of criminal activity and institutional responses (Steadman, n.d., and Steadman and Keveles 1972). The factors are presence of a juvenile record, number of previous incarcerations, number of violent crime convictions, and classification of the current offense. Scores on the LDS range from 0 to 15, with higher scores indicating more prior involvement with the law.

The second scale is a standardized measure of the severity of offenses developed by Sellin and Wolfgang (1964), in which a numerical weight is assigned to each offense committed by the subject. The original scores range from 1 (least serious) to 2,600 (most serious). Application of the Sellin-Wolfgang seriousness weights required a modification of the original scheme, in which the component parts of each offense are scored and then these subscores are summed, yielding the seriousness score for that offense. Because we only had information on type of offense provided by police "rap sheets," and not the component parts of injury, theft, and damage, we were limited to using average weights for each offense type. These average weights, given in appendix 5, are based on the scores of 10,850 offenses[3] scored in an earlier study (Wolfgang et al. 1972). For each subject a total seriousness score was computed by adding the seriousness scores for all his prior offenses resulting in arrest.[4]

TABLE 3.1   Correlations among Various Offense Measures

	AVO	AAO	LDS	TSS	Mean r[a]
AVO	. . .	.421	.355	.643	.483
AAO	.421	. . .	.431	.744	.553
LDS	.355	.431	. . .	.514	.436
TSS	.643	.744	.514	. . .	.643

Note: AVO=arrests for violent offenses

AAO=arrests for all offenses

LDS=legal dangerousness scale score

TSS=total seriousness score for all arrests

[a]The average coefficients were computed by first converting the correlations to Z coefficients, then averaging the Z scores, then converting back to r (see Guilford 1956, pp. 325–26).

All four measures of prior criminal activity were found to be moderately intercorrelated (table 3.1). Because the total seriousness score has the highest average correlation with all of the measures, it will be employed as the representative indicator of involvement with the law prior to the Dixon offense.[5] The other measures will be analyzed in zero-order relationships and in situations in which they are particularly relevant, but the total seriousness score will be the primary measure employed.

PATIENT AND RESPONDENT INTERVIEWS

Because police and hospital records could provide only the institutional perspective on patient careers, such records yield an incomplete picture. Only the patients can furnish their opinions, perceptions of their experiences, and indications of personal needs and desires. Therefore our research strategy called for interviewing as many subjects as possible.

Construction of an interview schedule proceeded after we defined the major issues to be covered: residential history following confinement, employment history, social services and treatment received, social and psychological adjustment, attitudes toward Farview and transfer hospitals, victimization, and self-reported delinquency. A copy of the interview schedule and the actual measures of these issues can be found in appendix 6.

The issue which was most difficult to measure was that of social adjustment, because it is a broad and relatively ill-defined concept. A review of the literature on adjustment measures, however, revealed a number of scales which covered the issues subsumed under this concept and which had been used in previous research on former mental patients. One such scale, the Katz Adjustment Scale (KAS), developed by Martin Katz and Samuel Lyerly (1963), seemed to be especially well suited to our purposes as it offered a number of appealing qualities. (1) The items contained in the scale were aimed at a low educational level, an important consideration in our case given the level of functioning of many of our subjects. (2) The KAS had been used in previous studies of patients released from civil mental hospitals as well as with a normal population, thereby providing comparative data. (3) It was shown by Katz and Lyerly to have high discriminant validity between well-adjusted and poorly adjusted subjects (1963, pp. 518–22). (4) The scoring system developed for the KAS in relation to the formulation of the subscales was found to have high reliability across different groups of subjects (Katz and Lyerly 1963, pp. 527–29). (5) Finally, the KAS contained provisions for external measures of validity since relatives or friends of the subject also evaluated the adjustment of the subject. In a sense, then, the KAS contains two sets of adjustment measures—one provided by the subject and one provided by a close observer of the subject's behavior. This feature was considered quite important in this project since at the outset we anticipated difficulties in obtaining recordable responses from a large number of subjects, given their allegedly serious mental deficiencies. As indicated below, however, this fear proved to be groundless. Nevertheless, the data generated by the respondents are important, additional sources of information on adjustment.

For these reasons the Katz Adjustment Scale was incorporated, with one modification, in the interview procedure. The original scales were to be administered as checklists to be completed by subjects after brief instructions. Since we anticipated serious difficulties with any self-administered device, the scale items were read aloud by the interviewers, who then recorded the responses on the interview schedule.

Constructing the interview schedule, however, was a small problem compared to locating subjects who were not hospitalized at the time of our attempts to interview them. Our plans called for noting from transfer hospital records the most recent addresses of discharged subjects and their relatives. By August 1973, however, when interviewers first went into the field, as many as four years had passed since the subjects had been in contact with the transfer hospitals. In addition, subjects had little reason to wish to be found by our interviewers. The only inducement we had to offer was the opportunity for them to talk to an interested person, but one who was powerless to assist them in any significant way. Furthermore, men who had been as enmeshed in the workings of the criminal justice and mental health systems as had the Dixon class had every reason to be suspicious of anyone inquiring about them.

Given these impediments, interviewing 269 of the subjects, 52 percent of those who were alive at the time of the interviews, was a substantial accomplishment. In table 3.2 the specific reasons why we had difficulty in completing interviews are indicated. Our inability to locate subjects accounted for more failures to interview than did all other reasons combined. Interestingly, in view of their allegedly serious mental illness, the proportion of eligible subjects who could not be interviewed due to physical or mental impediments is low (12 percent). Of course, the fact that we were able to elicit recordable responses to rather simple questions is not a very sensitive indicator of mental well-being. Yet initially we were very much concerned that we would be confronted by a large number of incoherent or catatonic men. Our fears proved nearly groundless as we were consistently surprised by the men's reasonably successful attempts to understand and to respond meaningfully to our questions.

TABLE 3.2   Results of Interviewing

	All Subjects	Living Subjects
Interviewed	45.9%	52.2%
	(269)	(269)
Not interviewed[a]	42.0	47.8
	(246)	(246)
Dead	12.1	. . .
	(71)	
Total	100.0	100.0
	(586)	(515)

[a]Reasons for not completing interviews among eligible subjects: could not locate, 56.5% (139); outside Pennsylvania, 15.9% (39); refused, 13.8% (34); mental impediment, 7.7% (19); physical impediment, 4.5% (11); relative refused access, 1.6% (4).

Once a subject was located we tried, with varying degrees of success, to explain why we wanted to talk with him and what we would do with the answers he gave, stressing the confidentiality of the information. A consent form containing this information was read aloud to each subject as he read along and interviewers were candid in answering any questions posed about the study.

Since not all subjects were located and interviewed, we are confronted with the possibility of a selection bias distorting the findings to be presented below. To examine this potential bias, we have compared interviewed and noninterviewed subjects in relation to a number of variables. Variables on which the two groups are not significantly different are race, type and seriousness of the Dixon offense, category of original commitment to Farview, number of previous hospitalizations, education, and escapes from the transfer hospital.

On the other hand, the subjects who were interviewed had

stayed longer at Farview on the average (15.7 vs. 13 years), were younger at the time of transfer (45 vs. 49 years of age), had lower total seriousness scores, had stayed longer at the transfer hospitals, and were more likely to have been diagnosed as mentally retarded or schizophrenic. In addition 58 percent of the subjects who were still institutionalized at the time of the interviewing were interviewed, while 38 percent of the subjects already released to the community were interviewed.

Although the interviewed and noninterviewed subjects differ on a number of variables, this is primarily due to the inclusion of the older subjects who had died in the noninterviewed group. When these subjects are removed from the analysis, most of these differences diminish and two, age and length of stay at Farview, are no longer significant. The two groups still differ in terms of length of stay at the transfer hospital, being institutionalized at the time of the interview, mental diagnosis, and total seriousness score. These first two differences would be expected since it was a good deal easier to find and interview institutionalized subjects, but the differences in diagnosis and total seriousness score are not readily explicable. In general, though, there were few strong selection biases determining which of the subjects still living were interviewed. The most important of these was whether the subject was an inpatient at the time we attempted to locate him.

One of the advantages of the Katz Adjustment Scale is the provision for the responses of friends and relatives on items similar to the questions contained in the subject interview schedule. We incorporated these supplemental interview schedules in the research design in the following manner. At the conclusion of each interview we asked the subject to nominate someone who knew him well and whom we could interview concerning the subject's current behavior. If the subject refused, we pursued the matter no further. If he agreed, an attempt was made to locate and interview the person named. These "respondent" interviews were conducted privately and the respondent was told that the subject had agreed to our interviewing him.[6] Subjects who were still hospitalized at the time of the interview were asked to nominate a staff member who was familiar with their daily activities.

These respondent interviews were conducted differently for hospitalized and nonhospitalized subjects. The first difference was in the content of each schedule. Both hospital and community respondent interviews contained a 205-item checklist describing the subject's emotional and physical condition, but the community respondent's schedule contained four additional sections which did not apply to inpatients. These sections concern social functioning, free-time activities, anticipation of social functioning before subject's arrival, and satisfaction with subject's level of free-time activities. In addition, the hospital respondent's schedule was employed as a self-administered checklist, whereas community respondents answered the questions verbally after they were read aloud by the interviewer.

Respondent interviews were completed for 41 percent of the living subjects. As in the case of the subject interviews, more were completed for hospitalized patients (56 percent) than for subjects in the community (23 percent). The explanation, once again, was the ease of locating institutionalized subjects and the respondents named by them. A full accounting of our attempts to complete respondent interviews is contained in table 3.3.

HOSPITAL ADMINISTRATOR INTERVIEWS

The impact of the influx of nearly six hundred allegedly dangerous offenders on the civil mental hospitals was understandably a concern of state officials and civil hospital staff members. We felt that recording the details of individual patients' experiences in the civil hospitals would provide an incomplete picture of the impact of the mass transfer. We therefore conducted semi-structured interviews with at least two administrators at each of the seventeen civil mental hospitals which received Dixon patients. These interviews consisted of a series of general questions regarding problems anticipated and experienced by the hospitals, special preparations made by the hospitals, comparison between the Dixon patients as a group and other patients, and impressions about the desirability of the new procedures for the transfer of Farview patients instituted as a result of the Dixon case.

The criterion for selection of staff members for our interview was that they had been employed by the hospital during the period of the Dixon case litigation (1969–71) and that they had been in an administrative position giving them an overview of the impact of the Dixon patients on the hospital. Among the thirty-seven staff members interviewed were superintendents, clinical directors, nursing supervisors, social work directors, and ward physicians.

TABLE 3.3   Results of Respondent Interviews

	All Subjects	Living Subjects
Respondent interview completed[a]	36.3%	41.4%
	(213)	(213)
Respondent interview not completed[b]	51.5	58.6
	(302)	(302)
Subject dead	12.1	. . .
	(71)	
Total	100.0	100.0
	(586)	(515)

[a]Of the 213 respondent interviews completed 62% (132) were with hospital employees and 38% (81) were with community residents.

[b]Reason for not completing respondent interviews included the following: subject not located or living outside Pennsylvania, 58.9% (178); subject denied permission, 18.2% (55); other (e.g., respondent not located), 9.9% (30); subject could not name a respondent, 7.3% (22); respondent refused, 4.3% (13); respondent claimed ignorance of subject's activities, 1.3% (4).

The usual pattern of these interviews was that two staff members were interviewed separately at each hospital to provide at least two perspectives on the issues and a measure of response reliability. There were some deviations from this pattern, as in the case of one hospital where five administrators had been assembled in anticipation of our arrival. Concern about response variation proved groundless, however, since little variability appeared in the response either within or among the hospitals. The data acquired through these staff interviews will be presented in chapter 6.

In sum, the data to be analyzed in this project come from a variety of sources. Official data were collected from the files of Farview, the transfer hospitals, and the Pennsylvania State Police. Structured interviews were conducted with Dixon patients and respondents nominated by the Dixon subjects, while unstructured interviews were conducted with staff members of the various transfer hospitals. By analyzing data from each of these sources separately and in combination, we hope to provide a clear and complete empirical assessment of the impact of the Dixon decision.

The Dixon Patients:
       Characteristics and Backgrounds

We can begin the empirical assessment of the Dixon case by describing the social, medical, and legal backgrounds of the Dixon patients. We are interested in establishing who they are and where they came from so that the findings which follow can be placed in the proper sociological perspective. As such this chapter is essentially descriptive and is not concerned with hypothesis testing, which will be dealt with in the following five chapters.

In some ways the description that follows could be viewed as a history of all patients admitted to Farview, which opened its door in 1911. Only three years later the first of the Dixon patients arrived, and by the time World War II began, 10 percent of the Dixon class were in residence at Farview. Half of the 586 subjects were incarcerated by 1957 and only 4 percent arrived during the 1970s (see fig. 4.1). Although the Dixon patients cannot be viewed as a representative sample of the Farview population, the point remains that they represent a large portion of the Farview population, both numerically and temporally.

SOCIAL HISTORIES
At the time of their admission to Farview, the men[1] in the Dixon class were of approximately the same age as populations admitted

to other total institutions (table 4.1). Their average age was thirty-three years, and 40 percent of the subjects were between twenty-five and thirty-four years of age. Admissions to federal prisons tended to be somewhat younger than the Dixon patients, al-

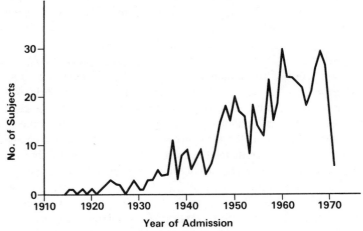

Fig. 4.1. Year of admission of Dixon patients to Farview.

TABLE 4.1   Age on Admission (Males)

Age (yr)	Dixon Patients	Federal Prisons	State and County Mental Hospitals
12–17	1.2%	3.9%	6.1%
	(7)	(499)	(16,775)
18–24	19.8	31.7	15.9
	(116)	(4,039)	(43,703)
25–34	40.8	34.7	21.0
	(239)	(4,413)	(57,759)
35–44	25.8	17.8	20.8
	(151)	(2,266)	(57,061)
45–64	12.5	11.9	36.2
	(73)	(1,513)	(99,463)
Total	100.0	100.0	100.0
	(586)	(12,730)	(274,761)
Mean	32.7	. . .[a]	. . .
Median	31.3	29.3	. . .

Source: Federal prisons: Hindelang et al. (1975), table 6.29. State and county mental hospitals: NIMH (1975), table 1.1.

[a]Ellipses indicate data unavailable.

though the modal age category is still twenty-five to thirty-four and only two years separate the median ages of the two groups. Patients admitted to mental hospitals were older than the Dixon patients, but this was due mainly to the impact of geriatric cases. If these were removed, the distribution would be relatively similar to the one for the Dixon patients. We can conclude that the Dixon patients are not particularly different from either prisoners or mental patients in terms of age at time of admission.

But this similarity does not extend to length of stay and age on release. Half of the Dixon patients stayed at Farview for more than twelve years, and the average for the group was slightly over fourteen years (table 4.2), which is longer than the average time served on a "life" sentence in the United States. By the time of the Dixon decision, the class averaged forty-seven years of age and 12 percent had reached the normal retirement age of sixty-five. These subjects were long-term inmates—the residual accumulation of men admitted over a fifty-five-year time span and not discharged either at the expiration of their prison sentences or subsequently, until the intervention of the Dixon decision.

TABLE 4.2   Length of Stay at Farview and Age on Transfer from Farview

Length of Stay		Age at Transfer	
Years	Subjects	Age (yr)	Subjects
0–4	22.9% (134)	17–34	21.3% (125)
5–11	26.6 (156)	35–49	37.7 (221)
12–20	25.4 (149)	50–65	29.0 (170)
21–54	25.1 (147)	65–80	11.9 (70)
Total	100.0 (586)	Total	100.0 (586)
Mean	14.08	Mean	47.10
Median	11.62	Median	46.36
SD	11.08	SD	13.90

The family life and backgrounds of these men are quite different from the typical pattern found in the general population. Seventy-one percent of the Dixon patients never married and only 12 percent were actually married at the time of their admission to

Farview. Among the 263 subjects who were interviewed, only 50 percent reported living with both parents while they were growing up and 9 percent indicated that they did not live with a relative.

As is true of most institutional populations in this country, members of minority groups and the poorly educated are over-represented in the Dixon class. Forty percent of the subjects are black—a figure that is a good deal higher than the proportion of blacks in the general Pennsylvania population (9 percent in 1970). Similarly, two fifths of the Dixon patients did not advance beyond the sixth grade and the average grade completed was the seventh (table 4.3).

TABLE 4.3   Education

Highest School Grade Completed	Subjects
None	3.1% (16)
1–6	39.9 (209)
7–8	32.8 (172)
9–11	16.2 (85)
Completed high school	6.7 (35)
Some college	1.0 (5)
College graduate	0.4 (2)
Total	100.0 (524)[a]
Mean	6.76
Median	7.05
SD	3.09

[a]The educational attainment of sixty-two subjects was unknown.

The occupational achievement of the Dixon subjects, and to a lesser extent their fathers, is also clustered at the lower end of the social hierarchy (table 4.4). Among subjects who were interviewed, 10 percent reported that during the time they were growing up, their fathers were unemployed and the majority reported their

TABLE 4.4 Occupation before Hospitalization

Occupation	Dixon Patients	Fathers of Interviewed Subjects[a]
Professional, manager	1.9%	6.3%
	(11)	(15)
Farmer	2.1	6.3
	(12)	(15)
Clerical, sales	3.0	4.2
	(17)	(10)
Craftsman	6.9	18.2
	(39)	(43)
Operative	8.0	35.2
	(45)	(83)
Service worker	9.0	11.5
	(51)	(27)
Laborer	59.0	7.7
	(334)	(18)
None or unemployed	10.1	10.6
	(57)	(25)
Total	100.0	100.0
	(566)[b]	(236)

[a]The question asked for the occupation of the father or the head of the household if the subject did not reside with his father.

[b]Occupations of twenty-two subjects were unknown.

fathers to hold either skilled or semiskilled positions. When compared to their fathers, the Dixon subjects exhibit a rather marked degree of downward mobility. The majority of the subjects (59 percent) worked as unskilled laborers, while only 14 percent were professionals, managers, farmers, white-collar workers, or craftsmen. The comparable figures for their fathers are 8 percent and 35 percent, respectively. But job classifications alone reveal only a part of the poor employment patterns of the Dixon patients which, according to hospital files, were commonly intermittent and frequently interrupted by episodes of institutionalization for mental illness and criminal offenses.

Finally, in terms of their social history, we can report that the Dixon subjects were predominately Pennsylvanians. Two-thirds of the class was born in the commonwealth and of those who were not, most (20 percent) were born in the South, with only 5 percent of the Dixon patients being foreign born. The subjects who were born out of state were Pennsylvania residents for an average of eighteen years before they were institutionalized on the Dixon commitment,[2] and over 90 percent of the subjects were residents of Pennsylvania at the time of that commitment.

The social histories of the Dixon patients indicate that by and large they were drawn from the lower end of the status hierarchy. They tended to be undereducated and unskilled and were more likely to be members of minority groups than one would expect given the population of Pennsylvania. Although not markedly older than other institutional populations at the time of admission, they spent considerable amounts of time in confinement at Farview and were quite old at the time of release.

HISTORY OF MENTAL ILLNESS

The two components of the label "criminally insane" suggest histories of arrest and imprisonment, on the one hand, and mental illness and hospitalization on the other. Both elements are present in the backgrounds of these patients.

Although most subjects came to Farview from penal institutions, 43 percent had been patients in mental hospitals at some time prior to their admission to Farview on the Dixon commitment[3] (see table 4.5). The average number of prior hospitalizations for the entire class was 0.9 and for the 43 percent who had been hospitalized the average was 2 inpatient episodes. Three-quarters of that group had been hospitalized three or more times, and one patient had a record of seventeen different hospitalizations.

These previous hospitalizations averaged twenty-eight months per episode, but the range of duration was enormous (two days to thirty years). Subjects with previous hospitalizations were, on the average, twenty-six years of age at the time of their first previous admission. For all subjects the average age at first admission, considering the Dixon hospitalization as the first admission for subjects with no previous admission, was twenty-nine.

With this rather extensive history of hospital care for mental disturbance, it is not surprising that the subjects were diagnosed as having severe mental illnesses on admission to Farview. The data are presented in table 4.6. The most common diagnosis was schizophrenia—36 percent of the subjects were considered to be paranoid schizophrenics, and 28 percent were diagnosed as suffering from other forms of schizophrenia. The next most frequent

TABLE 4.5 Number of Previous Hospitalizations

No. of Hospitalizations	All Dixon Patients	Those with Prior Hospitalizations
None	56.7% (332)	. . .
1	21.0 (123)	48.4
2	11.6 (68)	26.8
3	5.5 (32)	12.6
4	1.5 (8)	3.2
5	1.9 (11)	4.3
6	1.0 (6)	2.4
7+	1.0 (6)	2.4
Total	100.0 (586)	100.0 (254)

Mean   .92
Median   .38
SD   1.57

TABLE 4.6 Mental Diagnosis at Time of Admission to Farview

Diagnosis	Dixon Patients
Psychoses with organic brain syndrome	12.4% (71)
Schizophrenic, paranoid	36.1 (200)
Schizophrenic, other	28.4 (163)
Other psychoses	10.3 (59)
Other	12.7 (73)
Total	100.0 (573)

category was psychosis with organic brain syndrome, accounting for 12 percent of the subjects. Overall, almost 90 percent of the subjects were diagnosed as being psychotic.

OFFENSE HISTORIES

In addition to exhibiting extensive histories of mental disorders, the Dixon patients easily fit the implications of the "criminal" half of the criminally insane label. Not including the Dixon offense, 81.4 percent of the subjects had been arrested before the Dixon commitment and the average number of arrests for the entire group was 5.3 (table 4.7). In other words, the 586 Dixon patients were arrested 3,135 different times during the years they were free in the community.

TABLE 4.7   Arrests Prior to Dixon Offense

No. of Arrests	Subjects	Excluding "Some, Many"
None	18.6% (109)	19.1%
1	14.3 (84)	14.8
2–4	25.9 (152)	26.8
5–10	23.9 (140)	24.6
11+	14.2 (83)	14.6
"Some, many"[a]	3.1 (18)	. . .
Total	100.0 (586)	100.0 (568)
Mean	5.35	
Median	3.17	
SD	6.82	

[a]Farview records indicated a history of arrests without giving specific numbers or details for some cases. These cases were excluded here from calculations of statistics.

Examining the data for the subjects for whom we have detailed information, we see that two-thirds of them can be classified as recidivists and 39 percent can be considered chronic offenders—those who committed five or more offenses (see Wolfgang et al. 1972, chapter 6, for a discussion of this concept). This rate of offensivity is remarkably high, even considering the age of the Dixon subjects.

By the time the Philadelphia birth cohort of 1945 was eighteen years of age, 6 percent of the whole cohort and 18 percent of its delinquent members (that is, those who had been arrested at least once) were classified as chronic offenders (Wolfgang et al. 1972, pp. 88–89). In following up a 10 percent sample of this cohort through the age of twenty-nine the rate of chronic offenders only increased to 14 percent for the cohort and 31 percent for its delinquent members (Collins 1977). Yet prior to the Dixon commitment, when the subjects averaged thirty-three years of age, 39 percent of the Dixon subjects had become chronic offenders. Moreover, if the Dixon offense is added to the prior offenses, the proportion of chronic offenders increases to 46 percent.

In addition to committing a relatively large number of offenses, the Dixon patients were also frequently arrested for committing serious types of offenses. Table 4.8 presents information on violent and sex offenses. Forty percent of the Dixon patients were arrested for committing at least one violent offense and 16 percent were violent recidivists. Thirteen percent had been arrested as sex offenders and 4 percent committed more than one such offense.

TABLE 4.8   Prior Arrests for Violent and Sex Offenses

No. of Arrests	None	1	2–5	6+	Total	Mean	Median	SD
Violent[a]	59.2% (347)	24.2 (142)	15.4 (90)	1.2 (7)	100.0 (586)	.76	.34	1.36
Sex[b]	87.4% (512)	8.4 (49)	3.9 (23)	0.3 (2)	100.0 (586)	.24	.09	.76

[a]The following offenses are included: criminal homicide, manslaughter, forcible rape, assault, threats.

[b]The following offenses are included: attempted rape, sodomy, indecent assault, corrupting the morals of a minor (when the offense involved sex), fornication, adultery, and incest.

The relative seriousness of these offense careers can also be seen in the total seriousness scores and the legal dangerousness scores of the subjects (table 4.9). The mean total seriousness score, which represents the sum of the seriousness scores attached to all offenses committed by an individual, is 922.5. Referring to appendix 5, we see that the average prior offense history of the

Dixon patients accounts for approximately as much social injury as one rape (seriousness score, 1,096) or three robberies (seriousness score, 380 each), or one aggravated assault plus one burglary (seriousness score, 637 + 258). Although all of the prior offenses of the Dixon patients are not of major gravity, in combination they add to the equivalent of serious, major offenses. The mean legal dangerousness score of the Dixon patients is 5.57, which is quite similar to the score for the Baxstrom patients released in New York (6.17). These scores lie in the middle range of the LDS scoring system as reported by Steadman and Cocozza (1974). All in all, these summary measures are consistent with the previous data on number and type of previous offenses and indicate rather extensive criminal histories on the part of the Dixon patients.

TABLE 4.9   Seriousness and Legal Dangerousness Scores

	Dixon Patients	Baxstrom Patients[a]
Total Seriousness Score		
Mean	922.5	. . .
Median	500.0	. . .
SD	1115.7	. . .
N	(586)	
Legal Dangerousness Score		
Mean	5.57	6.17
Median	4.90	5.02
SD	5.04	4.60
N	(586)	(199)

[a]The data for the Baxstrom patients were supplied in a personal communication from Dr. Henry J. Steadman, 4 June 1976.

The data available on the court dispositions of these previous arrests are rather incomplete because we were dependent on state police "rap sheets" and did not have access to court records. However, we did find information that at least 64 percent of the subjects had previously served jail or prison sentences and the entire group averaged 2.6 prior incarcerations.

The members of the Dixon class clearly conform to both aspects of the dual label—criminally insane. They have extensive police records, have committed many serious offenses, and have been frequently incarcerated. At the time of their admission to Farview, they were diagnosed as suffering from serious mental disorders and the social histories reveal rather high rates of previous hospitalizations.

COMMITMENT TO FARVIEW

The Dixon patients arrived at Farview through one of two major channels. The majority (86 percent) had been enmeshed in the workings of the criminal justice system before their transfer to the hospital and are therefore criminal commitments, while a relatively small proportion (14 percent) were civil commitments, coming to Farview from other hospitals. Given these different pathways we will dichotomize our discussion to explore the distinctive processes which resulted in their hospitalization at Farview, returning afterward to a comparison of the two groups.

For the criminal commitments, the question of why the Dixon patients came to Farview is two-pronged—the first dealing with the behavior which resulted in their arrest and the second with the response of the criminal justice system to that behavior. The offenses for which they were arrested—the Dixon offense—cover the gamut of criminal behavior, with thirty-eight different offense types being represented. Although the range is quite extensive, the offenses tend to be violent—half of the offenses (54 percent) are so classified and 6.5 percent were for homicide (table 4.10). The stereotype of the sexual nature of the offenses committed by the criminally insane is not verified by the Dixon patients. Seven percent were charged with rape and another 5 percent committed other sex offenses. Indeed, the Dixon patients were far more likely to be property offenders (29 percent) than sex offenders, and within the property group the modal offense was burglary.

Although violent offenses predominate, the data in tables 4.10 and 4.11 clearly indicate that the most serious offenses of homicide and rape are not the typical ones. For example, half of the violent offenses were for assault—either aggravated or simple. Moreover, the average seriousness score is 508, and 37 percent of the offenses had scores in the 200s. Thus the typical offense, with a score of 508, would be much closer to an assault or a robbery than to a homicide, which has a score of 2,734.

Even though the Dixon offenses are, in general, classified as violent, we should not lose sight of the fact that a significant minority of the Dixon class spent a considerable amount of time at Farview for committing rather trivial offenses. At the extreme, one subject was confined for thirty-one years on the charge of violating a 600-year-old common law statute—being "a person not of good name." This point is made more systematically when we see that 12 percent of the Dixon offenses had seriousness scores of less than 100, and 21 percent had scores of less than 200 (table 4.11). An examination of the table and appendix 4 indicates the relatively trivial nature of offenses that appear in this range of seriousness scores.

TABLE 4.10   The Dixon Offenses

Major Offense Type	Subjects
Violent	53.7%[a]
	(271)
Homicide	6.5
	(33)
Rape	7.1
	(36)
Robbery	13.3
	(67)
Aggravated assault	13.7
	(69)
Other assaults	12.3
	(62)
Threats	0.8
	(4)
Sex	4.6
	(23)
Property	28.9
	(146)
Other	12.9
	(65)

[a]The base for computing these percentages is the total of 505 criminal commitments. Eighty-one Dixon patients had been civilly committed and therefore, by definition, could not have a "Dixon offense."

Of course no one is committed to an institution for many years for being a vagrant in the same sense that courts sentence offenders to prisons for committing specific felonies. The commitment decision may well have been influenced by knowledge of the patient's mental illness and prior criminal record. Nevertheless, for a substantial number of the Dixon patients, the event which precipitated a series of law enforcement and judicial responses resulting in a long period of incarceration under maximum security conditions was not extremely serious.

Turning to the second aspect of the question, the reactions of

TABLE 4.11   Seriousness of the Dixon Offense

Seriousness Scores	Typical Offense with This Score	Subjects
<100	Disorderly conduct	12.1% (61)
100–199	Larceny	9.1 (46)
200–299	Burglary	37.2 (188)
300–399	Robbery	13.3 (67)
400–499	Narcotics	1.0 (5)
600–699	Aggravated Assault	13.7 (69)
1,000–1,099	Rape	7.1 (36)
2,700–2,799	Homicide	6.5 (33)

Mean   507.7
SD   646.8
N   505

the criminal justice system, the majority (60 percent) of the patients who had been criminally committed came to Farview after they had been convicted of an offense and after they had begun to serve a prison sentence. These subjects were considered to have become mentally ill while serving a prison sentence. The next largest group—30 percent—came to Farview from detention centers after they were judged to be incompetent to stand trial and in need of psychiatric care. The remaining 9 percent of the subjects were in one of three categories: they had been tried and convicted but sentence had been deferred pending psychiatric evaluation (4 percent); they were sent to Farview on indeterminate sentences as "defective delinquents" (3 percent); or they were found by a court to be "not guilty by reason of insanity" (2 percent).

The second major pathway to Farview was via a civil commitment and 14 percent of the Dixon class were committed in this manner. All of these patients were confined in a civil mental hospital before their transfer and were sent to Farview because they were thought to be violent or unmanageable by the staffs at the civil hospitals. This initial commitment to the civil hospitals was not predicated on criminal charges, but when the number of prior offenses committed by these subjects is examined, we see that the patients who were civilly committed have offense histories that are similar to those who came under criminal commitment. For example, 73 percent of those at Farview under civil commitments had been arrested in the past, while 83 percent of those at Farview under criminal commitments had a prior record.

The reasons for transferring the subjects from prisons and civil mental hospitals to Farview were abstracted from patient files at Farview. The two most common reasons given were behavior that was directly symptomatic of mental illness (for example, delusions, bizarre behavior, defective judgment), and violent behavior in the institution. When these reasons are divided by civil and criminal commitments (table 4.12) we find that patients civilly committed were more often transferred for being management problems and being violent in the civil hospitals, whereas subjects transferred from prisons were more often transferred because they exhibited symptoms of mental illness. These findings are consistent with the different purposes served by Farview for civil mental hospitals and prisons. Mental hospitals send patients who upset other patients and staff by their violent and obstreperous behavior. Prisons send inmates whose symptoms of mental illness and attitude make them unsuitable for confinement under regular prison conditions.

Although there is some overlap in these categories which is not entirely consistent with the purposes that Farview was supposed to serve—for example, the reasons for transfer for 38 percent of the civilly committed patients were direct symptoms of mental illness, which is not sufficient for transfer to Farview—this is primarily a function of the manner in which the data were recorded. A number of reasons were usually presented with no indication of priority. As a result it is impossible to present a clearer picture of this relationship. For example, one reason for transferring a patient from a civil hospital may have been his violent behavior, while another reason was his mental illness. We would have preferred to be able to state the priority of these reasons but often it was not reported. As it stands, the results are consistent with the function that Farview served—the prisons were more likely to cite mental illness as the reason for the transfer while

TABLE 4.12   Reasons for Transfer to Farview

Reason[a]	Criminal Commitments	Civil Commitments
Direct symptoms of mental illness (e.g., delusions)	74.0% (374)	38.3% (31)
Violence in prison or hospital	37.8 (191)	55.5 (45)
Offensive attitudes (e.g., opposition to authority, unsociability)	22.2 (112)	11.1 (9)
Preprison or prehospital history (e.g., criminal offenses, mental hospitalization)	20.0 (101)	19.8 (16)
Nonviolent behavior in prison or hospital (e.g., management problem)	16.0 (81)	42.0 (34)
Physiological conditions (e.g., mental retardation)	14.1 (71)	8.6 (7)
No. of cases on which percentages were calculated	505	81

[a]The categories are not mutually exclusive. Many subjects had several transfer reasons recorded.

the civil hospitals were more likely to cite violent and disruptive behavior.

ACCUMULATIVE DISADVANTAGE

The social marginality of the Dixon patients as a group is readily apparent. In a society which values high educational attainment, professional and craft skills, mental health, marriage, and avoidance of conflict with the law, the Dixon patients would be considered failures or deviants on every criterion. Furthermore, the cumulative impact of these negative qualities is probably greater than would be expected based on their simple "sum."

In their work on social stratification in science, Cole and Cole introduced the concept of "accumulative advantage": "In science as in other areas of life, those who are initially successful have greater opportunities for future success" (1973, p. 119). Since the Coles found the concept of accumulative advantage to have utility in explaining the accomplishments of scientists, its converse "accumulative disadvantage," or the accumulation of failures, may be useful in understanding the careers of chronic "losers" such as the Dixon patients.

Half the subjects had left school before completing the eighth grade. Half came from broken homes. Two-thirds had police records as juveniles and their average age at first arrest was twenty. By the time the typical subject had arrived at Farview at age thirty-two, he had failed to learn a marketable job skill, had been arrested five times, served two prison sentences, and had been a patient in a civil mental hospital. He ended up in Farview, literally the end of the road for many who had preceded him, because he was believed to be both mentally ill and dangerous. If ever there was a group that suffered from accumulative disadvantage, it is the Dixon patients. There is scarcely a positive note in their backgrounds to alleviate the devastating components of their personal histories entitling them to the dual label—criminally insane.

Nor was their stay at Farview likely to have any ameliorating effect. At Farview the Dixon patient endured fourteen years of isolation—locked away from the support of family and friends, away from jobs and schools, under conditions that were unlikely to be therapeutic. One should not expect that this experience would serve as a counterweight to their accumulative disadvantage. Indeed, given the general reputation that Farview has in the state prison and hospital systems, one can view any confinement at Farview as a major disadvantage in its own right since one has to be "pretty bad" to be sent to Farview—or so the conventional wisdom goes.

For the Dixon patients, however, the federal court interrupted an almost unbroken string of defeats by ruling in their favor. Since the modal category of release from Farview before the Dixon case was death (*University of Pennsylvania Law Review,* 1961, vol. 110), the court's decision literally gave many of these patients a new lease on life. We will see in the following chapters whether this decision produced positive changes in the lives of these patients or if the accumulative disadvantage of the histories recounted here will continue apace.

5   The Farview Experience

A major theme of this study focuses on the consequences of the domination of the legal perspective over the medical perspective in the Dixon case. The medical opinion is inextricably intertwined with the political prediction that the Dixon patients required maximum security care because they were potentially dangerous, while the legal opinion is based on remedying the unconstitutionality of their commitment. In relation to the former, we are interested in assessing the validity of the political prediction made by the Farview staff, and in relation to the latter we are concerned with the consequences of the court's decision to release so many criminally insane offenders to civil hospitals for reevaluation.

These are rather complex questions which we will begin to address in this chapter by analyzing data relating to the behavior of the Dixon patients while they were confined at Farview and their attitudes about that institution. The behavioral area of concern is that of violent or assaultive acting out. If the Dixon patients were extremely violent during their stay at Farview, there would be good reason for the staff to recommend their continued confinement. If, on the other hand, the patients were not often assaultive and did not commit serious acts when they were assaultive, there would be less reason to keep them in confinement and more support for the court's actions. That is, if the Dixon patients were not disruptive, were not hard to manage, and were not posing a threat to the staff and patients, it would appear that it was not necessary for them to be held in a maximum security setting.[1] The first portion of this chapter will address this issue by examining data concerning the Dixon patient's behavior while at Farview, as that behavior is reflected in incident reports and ward notes.

BEHAVIOR AT FARVIEW

Incident reports accumulated in the files of the Dixon patients over the years of their stay at Farview, being filled out whenever a patient was involved in an incident that resulted in injury to himself or another patient, or damage to property. As such they reflect overt behavior rather than inferences or suppositions about likely behavior. Moreover, since injury or property damage are usually required before an incident report is filed, it is unlikely that very trivial events are included in these reports. The incident reports, then, can be viewed as a measure of actual behavior, probably of a nontrivial nature.

Based on the actions and views of the Farview staff one would expect the Dixon patients to be highly aggressive and disruptive while in confinement, but the incident report data do not confirm this notion (table 5.1). Over half of the subjects—56.3 percent— had no incident reports in their files even though the average length of stay at Farview was over fourteen years. The Dixon class

TABLE 5.1 Distribution of Incidents at Farview

No. of Incident Reports	Subjects		Cumulative %
	N	%	
0	330	56.3	56.3
1	129	22.0	78.3
2	61	10.4	88.7
3–4	32	5.5	94.2
5+	34	5.8	100.0
Total	586	100.0	
Mean	1.08		
SD	2.24		
Median	0.39		

as a group accumulated 630 incidents during their confinement, an average of only 1.1 per subject, and very few subjects had large numbers of reports during their Farview career. Approximately 22 percent had more than one report and only 6 percent had five or more reports. Based on these simple data one would not conclude that the Dixon patients were highly disruptive while institutionalized. Indeed, over half of the subjects never engaged in behavior serious enough to warrant the filing of an incident report.

But to look simply at the marginal distributions is only to skim the surface of the analysis, since a number of other variables could affect the likelihood of aggressive behavior. One set of variables is temporal in nature and includes the subject's age and the length of time he was institutionalized. It is possible, for example, that young patients or newly admitted patients were more aggressive but as they aged and became accustomed to the institution the frequency of disruptive outbursts decreased.

When the relationship between age and annual incident rates is examined, this is what appears to have happened (figs. 5.1 to 5.3).[2] The youngest subjects had the highest annual rates—approximately 0.36 per year for the subjects between eighteen and twenty—but even these rates were not exceptionally high. It took approximately ten twenty-year-old subjects to generate 3.5 incidents during a year's time. After the teenage years the annual rates dropped rather sharply, and by the age of thirty they leveled out to an annual rate that fluctuated between 0.10 and 0.02. In general, then, no age group is exceptionally disruptive, but there was an inverse relationship between age and the frequency of incident reports.

The same pattern is repeated when the incident reports are divided along the dimension of who is reported to have initiated the incident, where initiation is defined as making the first aggressive gesture. Incidents which were initiated by the subject occurred in the same pattern as incidents initiated by another inmate (figs. 5.2 and 5.3).

Figures 5.4 to 5.6 present the distributions of violent incidents by the number of years spent in confinement at Farview. These distributions are similar to those based on age, with one notable difference—the curve for the total incident rate is U-shaped. The highest rates are associated with those who had been at Farview for

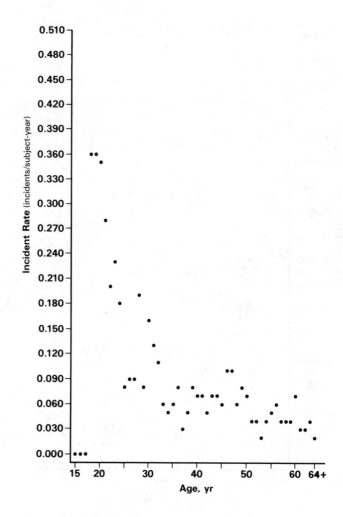

Fig. 5.1. Total incident rate, by age of subject.

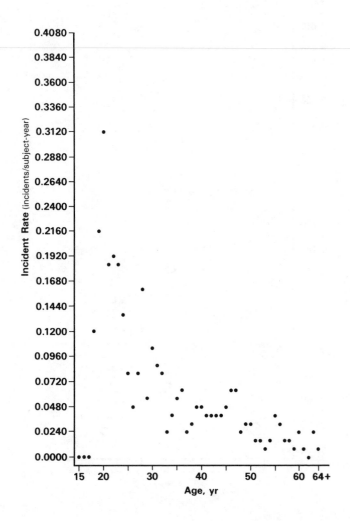

Fig. 5.2. Subject-initiated incident rate, by age of subject.

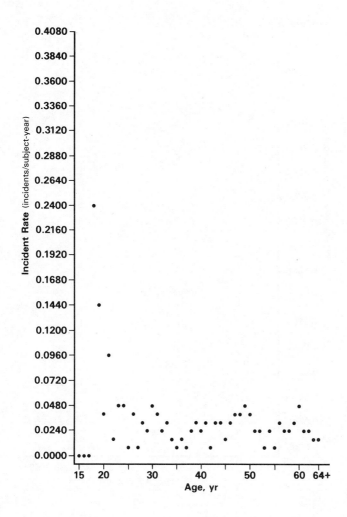

Fig. 5.3. Nonsubject-initiated incident rate, by age of subject.

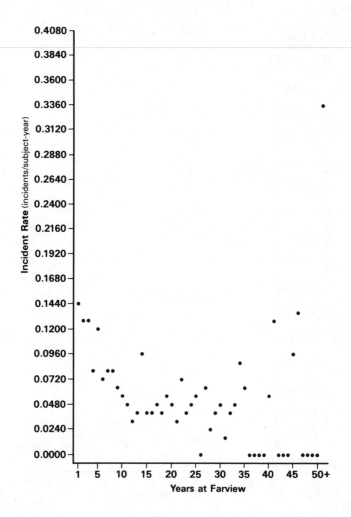

Fig. 5.4. Total incident rate, by year at Farview.

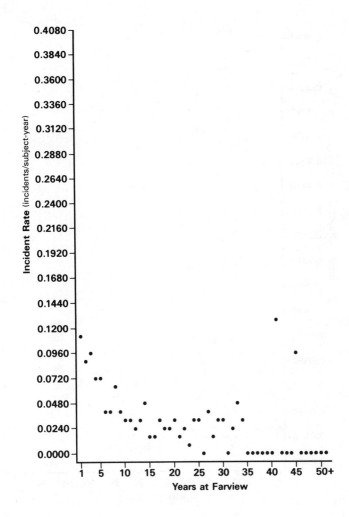

Fig. 5.5. Subject-initiated incident rate, by year at Farview.

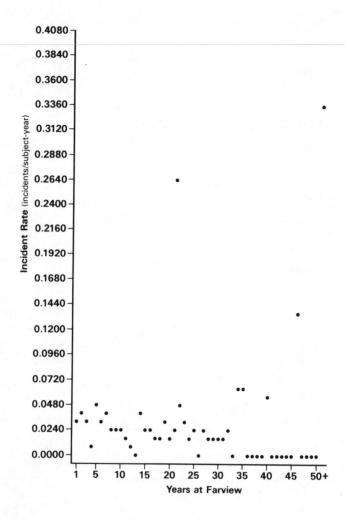

Fig. 5.6. Nonsubject-initiated incident rate, by year at Farview.

the least and for the greatest amounts of time. The early years were typified by a decreasing rate—those who had been at Farview between one and three years had an annual incident rate of approximately 0.13, but by the time the subjects had spent ten years in confinement the rate diminished to 0.05. Between the tenth and thirty-fifth year of confinement the rate remained consistently low—varying from 0.09 to 0. After the thirty-fifth year the pattern became erratic, fluctuating from rates of zero to rather high rates, which is probably due to the decreasing number of observations. Thus, with the exception of the U-shaped curve, which is probably an artifact produced by the small number of observations in the last few years, an inverse relationship again appears between a temporal variable, here the length of time in confinement, and incident rates.

For subject- and nonsubject-initiated events the curves are essentially flat, especially for nonsubject-initiated incident rates (figs. 5.5 and 5.6). For subject-initiated events the U-shaped pattern is somewhat evident, with decreasing incident rates through the earlier years of confinement and erratic fluctuations in the later years.

In general, the Dixon patients cannot be classified as exceptionally violent patients on the basis of the incident reports. Over half of the patients never engaged in such incidents and the average Dixon patient had one incident report in his folder.[3] Age was inversely related to involvement in incidents and, with the exception of somewhat erratic patterns at the end of the stay, length of confinement was also inversely related to involvement. There was no age group or length-of-stay group that was inordinately disruptive, although the younger—and probably less institutionalized—patients had a higher annual rate than their older colleagues.

It is possible that an examination of the frequency of incident reports is inappropriate for our purposes since it misses the qualitative aspects of the incidents themselves. If these reports reflected behavior that resulted in serious injury or major property damage, then the fact that they were infrequent would be relatively unimportant. If the reports were only filed for events that would be classified as attempted murder or aggravated assault, for example, the fact that the annual rates were rather low would be inconsequential to the decision of the Farview staff to keep the Dixon patients confined.

TABLE 5.2   Type of Incidents Involving Subjects

Type[a]	No. of Incidents		%	
Assault initiated by subject	127		20.2	
Against other inmate		61		9.7
Against guard		57		9.4
Against both		7		1.1
Fights among inmates	147		23.3	
Verbal assaults initiated by subject	6		1.0	
Assaults initiated by other inmates	188		29.8	
Provoked by subject		44		7.0
Unprovoked by subject		144		22.8
Initiated by guard	30		4.8	
Incidents not involving others[b]	132		20.9	
Total	630		100.0	

[a]These categories are mutually exclusive. Incidents involving combinations of assaults and property destruction were classified under the most serious component of the event, assault.

[b]This category primarily refers to self-injury, property destruction, or a combination of these two elements.

The data in table 5.2 indicate the types of behaviors that are reflected in these incident reports. Our earlier assumption about the nontrivial nature of these reports is supported by these data. Only 1 percent of the reports are based on verbal assaults—arguments, threats, and the like—the other 99 percent being based on overt behavior. Three-quarters of the incidents involve physical assaults of one type or another but only 20 percent were initiated by the subject. In 23 percent of the cases there was a fight among inmates but the initiator was unknown, and in 30 percent of the cases the assault was initiated by another inmate, making the subject the victim rather than the offender in the incident. In addition to these assault categories, the other major type of incident is one in which the subject was the only person involved. Of these 132 incidents, the most common type (78, or 59.1 percent) involved self-injury and property destruction. This category almost always referred to a situation in which the subject put his fist through a window. Finally, 4.8 percent of the incidents refer to cases where the subject was injured while being subdued by a guard, usually because the subject refused to obey an order.[4]

The picture that emerges from these incident reports is one in which physical violence is the mode but not one in which the Dixon patient was always the offender, disrupting the hospital by assaulting guards and other inmates. Indeed, the Dixon subject was about as likely to be the victim of the assault as he was to be the offender. The incident reports portray Farview as an institution not unlike prisons and other total institutions in which assaults are common but in which the probability of being an offender or a victim are about equal.

Although the incident reports are primarily concerned with assaults, the assaults that occur do not seem to be very severe, as can be seen in table 5.3. In the vast majority of the incidents (86.5 percent) there was only one person injured and in only one incident were there as many as seven people injured. The person most likely to be injured was the subject, and in 5 percent of the incidents other patients were injured while in another 5 percent guards were injured. Although the subject was as likely to initiate the event as anyone else, he was far more likely to be injured.

Turning to the extent of the injuries, we again see evidence that these assaults were relatively minor. Only 7 percent of the injured patients required hospitalization in the medical ward for their injuries, 67 percent were treated and returned to their wards, and 26 percent required no treatment. For other patients and staff members, the number of cases is rather small, but in both cases the majority of the injured were either not treated or treated and returned (86 percent of other patients, 97 percent of staff), while 14 percent of the other patients and 3 percent of the staff required hospitalization. No one died as a result of the events recorded in the incident reports.

To summarize this section we can say that events judged to be of sufficient seriousness to warrant the filing of an incident report did not occur very frequently in the careers of the Dixon patients, even though those careers spanned fourteen years in confinement. Half of the patients had no incidents and the average for the entire class was 1.1.[5] Incident rate varied inversely with both age and length of institutionalization, but at no time were the annual rates inordinately high.[6] The events described in the incident reports were predominately assaultive, but the subject was as likely to be a victim as an offender. Finally, the assaults that occurred were not, by and large, extremely serious. Although injuries occurred, the number of persons injured was likely to be

TABLE 5.3 Injury Resulting from Incidents

	No. of Subjects	%
No. of people injured		
0	31	4.9
1	546	86.5
2+	54	8.6
	(631)	
Was subject injured?		
Yes	582	92.2
No	49	7.8
	(631)	
No. of others injured		
0	596	94.4
1+	35	5.5
	(631)	
No. of staff injured		
0	598	94.9
1+	33	5.2
	(631)	
No. of subjects		
Not treated	35	25.9
Treated and returned to ward	331	67.0
Transferred to medical ward	128	7.1
	(494)	
No. of other patients		
Not treated	15	42.8
Treated and returned to ward	15	42.8
Transferred to medical ward	5	14.3
	(35)	
No. of staff		
Not treated	18	54.5
Treated as outpatients	14	42.4
Hospitalized	1	3.0
	(33)	

NOTE: The number of subjects on which the percentages are based is indicated in parentheses and varies depending on the variable under investigation. Also, for some variables there is missing information, further decreasing the size of the base. For example, although 582 subjects were injured, information on the extent of the injuries is available in only 494 cases.

one, and in the majority of all injuries, the injury was sufficiently minor so that the person required no treatment or was treated and returned to his ward.

The second source of data concerning in-hospital assaultiveness came from the ward notes that were placed in the files of the

Dixon patients. These notes contain the comments of the Farview medical staff on changes in the patient's physical and mental condition, and observations about the patient's behavior and attitudes. Our concern was with the comments that described violent behavior or that described traits that are considered by clinicians to be indicative of potential violence. Whenever these comments were encountered they were encoded in a standardized format.[7] As such, this measure includes information on the staff's perceptions concerning the likelihood of the patient's being violent or disruptive, as well as reports of actual violence. Table 5.4 presents the relative occurrence of these types of ward note behavior codes.

TABLE 5.4   Types of Behavior Codes

Type	Total Entries	%	Mean No. of Entries
Overt violence toward others	767	14.2	1.31
Potential for violence for others	443	8.2	0.76
Self-injury	85	1.6	0.14
Property destruction	44	0.8	0.08
Management problems	323	6.0	0.55
Antiauthoritarian attitudes	1,751	32.4	2.99
Psychotic symptoms	1,990	36.8	3.40
Total	5,403	100.0	9.22

The 586 Dixon patients accumulated 5,403 behavior code entries in their files—an average of 9.2—during the fourteen years of their stay at Farview. Of these entries, 14 percent reflected overt violence toward others (including such codes as "assaultive," "homosexual attack," "hits"), while another 8 percent involved a potential for violence toward others ("aggressive," "dangerous," "threatens"). The mean frequencies for these two categories are 1.3 and 0.8, respectively, and in combination the mean is 2.1, indicating that over their fourteen-year stay at Farview an average of two such entries were made in each subject's file.

The modal category in table 5.4 is that of psychotic symptoms (disturbed, paranoid, psychotic, and so on), which accounts for 37 percent of the entries, appearing an average of 3.4 times. The next most frequent category is antiauthoritarian attitudes (antisocial, hostile, sullen, and so on), which accounts for 32.4 percent of the total and appeared an average 3.0 times in a patient's ward notes. Finally, three other categories appeared rather infrequently—self-injury, 1.6 percent; property destruction, 0.8 percent; and management problems, 6.0 percent.

The entries in the ward notes, then, fall into two major groupings. The largest concerns negative attitudes and psychotic symptoms, which in combination account for 69.2 percent of the entries, and the other grouping centers on observations about violent behavior or the potential for violence, accounting for 22.4 percent of the entries. Although the ward note entries are far more common than incident reports—the means are 9.2 and 1.1, respectively—they do not offer strong support for the notion that the Dixon patients were assaultive in the hospital. Only 14.2 percent of the entries reflect overt violence toward others—a rate of 1.3 per subject over the fourteen years of residence at Farview—a rate quite comparable to the rate of 1.1 for the incident reports. The ward note entries do provide stronger support for the notion that the Farview staff saw the Dixon subjects as potentially violent. Over three-fourths of the entries are comments concerning the patients' attitudes, symptoms, and potential for violence, while only 22.6 percent of the entries focus on the subject's actual violence, self-injury, property destruction, or problematic behavior.

Analysis of the relationship between the temporal variables of age and length of stay at Farview and the ward note entries provides scant support for the decision to confine the Dixon subjects for fourteen years. Looking first at the age of the subject (fig. 5.7) we see a strong inverse relationship between age and frequency of ward note entries. The teenage years and the early twenties have annual rates on the order of 3.0 per year, but after the age of twenty-three the annual rates fall below 2.0 and by the age of thirty-three the rates all fall below 1.0. Only among the youngest subjects are the annual rates of ward note entries even relatively high, and by the mid-twenties the rates decrease substantially and continue to do so until the time of release.

The comparable data for year of stay at Farview are presented in figure 5.8 and contain a very similar picture. The annual rates decrease rather uniformly from the first to the last year of residence at Farview, and only for the first year is the rate above 1.0. By the fifth year the rates are below 0.64 and after the tenth year, with one exception, they fall below 0.46.

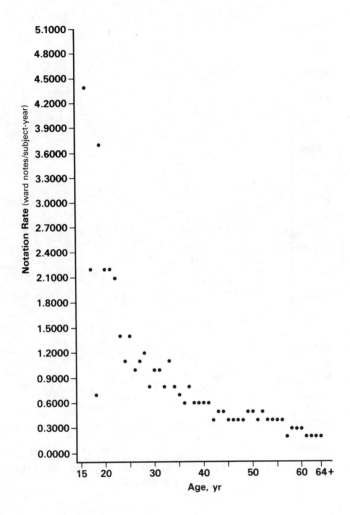

Fig. 5.7. Ward note entries, by age of subject.

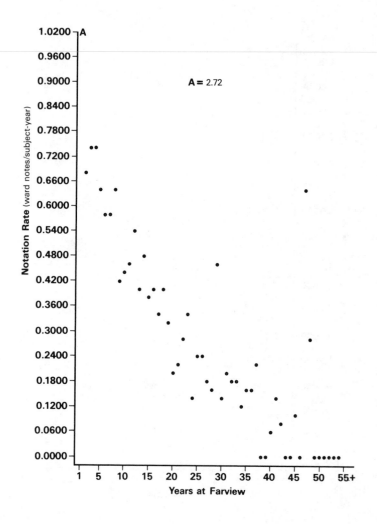

Fig. 5.8. Ward note entries, by year at Farview. *A*, above range.

While the absence of an adequate control group makes conclusions about the magnitude of ward note entries difficult, our
interpretation is that these data do not support the decision of the
Farview staff to keep the Dixon patients in confinement for
fourteen years. The vast majority of such entries deal with the
potential for violence, while entries reflecting overt violence toward
others constitute 14 percent of the total and only appear in the
files of the subjects an average of 1.3 times. In addition, a strong
inverse relationship exists between the temporal variables of age
and length of stay and annual rates of ward note entries. Even if
the overall average of 9.2 is considered high, the annual rates
were high only for the subjects in their early twenties or for the
subjects who had only spent a few years at Farview. After that,
the rate of ward note entries became rather low and remained so
throughout their confinement. Given this situation, one cannot
use these data to justify the continued confinement of the Dixon
patients at Farview, and certainly not to justify a policy that led to
confinement for an average of fourteen years. This conclusion is
quite consistent with the one presented after the discussion of the
data on incident reports. In general, we have uncovered no evidence of frequent, repetitive, prolonged, or serious violent behavior by a substantial number of the Dixon patients during their
stay at Farview.

ATTITUDES ABOUT FARVIEW
The second area of concern in this chapter is the attitudes that
the Dixon patients held about Farview—did they view it as a
hospital capable of providing care and treatment or did they see it
as an essentially antitherapeutic environment? The basic information on this topic was collected in two sets of open-ended
questions—one set dealt with what the patients liked and disliked
most about Farview and the other set asked about good and bad
results of their stay at Farview.[8]
Looking first at the reasons why the Dixon subjects liked
Farview, we see that the modal response was "did not like it"—
41 percent of the subjects indicated that they had no reasons to
like Farview and even with interviewer probing could not indicate
one thing "they liked most about Farview" (table 5.5). The most
frequently used positive responses were "living conditions," 37.8
percent, and the "ability to work," 18.5 percent. The specific

TABLE 5.5   Reasons Subjects Stated for Liking Farview

Reasons	No. of Responses	% of Responses	% of Subjects[a]
Did not like it	102	30.4	41.0
Ability to work at Farview	46	13.7	18.5
Living conditions	94	28.0	37.8
Treatment and programs	30	8.9	12.0
Relations with others	22	6.5	8.8
Institutional order	16	4.8	6.4
Other	26	7.7	10.4
Total	336	100.0	
No. of subjects responding	249		

[a]Percentages do not sum to 100 since the subjects could give more than one reason.

responses in both of these categories indicate that what the subjects liked was the ability of these activities to break up the routine life at the institution and to provide at least a few of the amenities of life. For example, the category "living conditions" contains such specific responses as television, recreation, movies, the canteen, and other privileges; while the "working conditions" category contains such reasons as working on the farm and working outside. On the other hand, only a minority of the subjects indicated that they liked the treatment and programs at Farview (12 percent), relations with others (8.8 percent), or the institutional order at Farview (6.4 percent).

In general, a majority of the Dixon subjects reported at least one favorable characteristic of Farview, but the proportion of subjects giving some positive response to the question "What did you like about Farview" is not the most important issue. Farview is a *hospital* filled with seriously troubled people. Ideally the patients in a hospital would see some value in the treatment provided. Instead, after spending an average of fourteen years at that facility, two-fifths of the subjects could not express any reason for liking the institution and the reasons that were presented tended to be ones that alleviated the boredom of institutionalization. On the other hand, positive reasons, related to the therapeutic purpose of a mental hospital, such as the quality of treatment and the availability of programs, were infrequently mentioned.

Although reasons for liking Farview are not abundant, the respondents were not as reticent about reporting reasons for disliking Farview, as the data in table 5.6 attest. A much smaller

TABLE 5.6   Reasons Subjects Stated for Disliking Farview

Reason	No. of Responses	% of Responses	% of Subjects[a]
None	42	10.2	17.4
Cruelty of security aides	98	23.8	40.7
Inadequacy of medical care	21	5.1	8.7
Other patients	26	6.3	10.8
Food	27	6.6	11.2
Institutional order	141	34.2	58.5
Other	57	13.8	23.7
Total	412	100.0	
No. of subjects responding[b]	241		

[a]Percentages do not sum to 100 since the subjects could give more than one reason.

[b]The number of subjects responding to this question differs slightly from the number responding in table 5.5 and in the following tables because of some nonresponse. The responses are based on essentially the same set of subjects, however.

percentage of the subjects—17.4 percent—indicated that they had no reason for disliking Farview, and concomitantly, a larger number of reasons were presented. The two most frequently mentioned reasons concerned the harshness of institutional life at Farview. Almost three-fifths of the subjects indicated that they disliked the institutional order—the confinement, punishments, lack of freedom, dehumanization, and kindred elements that they experienced as part of their confinement. Moreover, 40.7 percent expressed their dislike for the brutality of the guards. It is important to note that nowhere in the interview schedule was there any question asking about brutality or abuse at Farview. Yet, even without such cuing, 40 percent of the interviewed subjects indicated that such conditions existed. Following are some verbatim examples of these responses:

"The guards would knock you down and kick you if you talked."
"They once beat up a guy so bad his mother couldn't recognize him. They said a patient beat him up."
"Beatings and stompings of patients."
"Beatings they gave to the men. They beat me up about once a month or so."

In addition to these two categories, the subjects also indicated their dislike for the medical care (8.7 percent), the other patients (10.8 percent), and the food (11.2 percent). These complaints, especially the latter two, are common to any total institution and are not unexpected, but they are overshadowed by the responses concerning the harshness and brutality that typified Farview for the Dixon patients.

The question of the accuracy and validity of interview data is always at issue, but it is especially salient here. Are the guards as brutal and is Farview as harsh as the Dixon patients say? In the absence of direct observational data it is impossible to provide a thorough answer to this question. But three partial answers can be given. First, this information is quite consistent with information collected by other investigators, especially those of the Philadelphia *Inquirer* (see chapter 1). Second, based on our interviewing experiences, we do not believe that half of the patients interviewed were fabricating this information. To do so would require a conspiracy on a grand scale indeed. Third, regardless of the absolute amount of brutality present at Farview, it occurs frequently enough to be noted by 40 percent of the subjects as one of the reasons for disliking Farview. From the perspective of this chapter, this is perhaps the most important conclusion. It is inconceivable that an institution that is viewed as negatively as Farview was can have a therapeutic effect on its patients.

The other set of questions used to elicit attitudes about Farview concerned the subjects' perceptions about the effect of their stay at Farview on their lives. The questions were "What good results came out of your being at Farview?" and "What bad results came out of your being at Farview?"

TABLE 5.7   Positive Results Stemming from Stay at Farview

Results	No. of Responses	% of Responses	% of Subjects[a]
None	98	49.7	53.3
Improved mental condition	23	11.7	12.5
Change in attitude	33	16.8	17.9
Ability to control behavior	21	10.6	11.4
Learned skills	15	7.6	8.2
Other	7	3.6	3.8
Total	197	100.0	
No. of subjects responding	184		

[a]Percentages do not sum to 100 since the subjects could give more than one reason.

Table 5.7 presents the responses to the first of these questions. Again the modal category is "none," with 53.3 percent of the subjects being unable to verbalize a single response when asked about the positive effect that Farview had on their lives. The other responses that were presented indicate that Farview did have a positive effect for some of the Dixon patients: 12.5 percent indicated an improved mental condition, 17.9 percent a change in their attitudes, 11.4 percent a greater ability to control their behavior, and 8.2 percent said they had learned some skills. In general, some of the Dixon patients indicated that their stay at Farview had some salutary effect on their lives but half of the subjects responding to the question could not indicate a single positive result stemming from their stay at Farview.

When asked to respond to the question of what negative effects their stay at Farview had on them, the modal category was again "none"—with 37.7 percent of the patients responding in this fashion (table 5.8). The other responses fell into two major groupings, the first concerning violence. The effect of the brutality of the guards and the "horrors" they saw at Farview was mentioned by 18.3 percent of the subjects, while another 7.8 percent mentioned fighting and the effects of fighting. The second major grouping concerned the social costs of being confined at Farview. The modal category in this grouping was a feeling of a lost or wasted life (17.3 percent) followed by the opinion that Farview had an adverse effect on one's mental condition (14.1 percent), and the feeling of lost social contacts and a decrease in social status (8.9 percent).

TABLE 5.8   Negative Results Stemming from Stay at Farview

Results	No. of Responses	% of Responses	% of Subjects[a]
None	72	33.8	37.7
Feeling of lost life	33	15.5	17.3
Brutality of guards	35	16.4	18.3
Adverse effect on mental condition	27	12.7	14.1
Fighting and the effects of fights	15	7.0	7.8
Loss of social contacts and status	17	8.0	8.9
Other	14	6.6	7.3
Total	213	100.0	
No. of subjects responding	191		

[a]Percentages do not sum to 100 since the subjects could give more than one reason.

The overall conclusion about the attitudes of the Dixon patients toward Farview has to be that their attitudes were negative. The patients were more apt to dislike than like Farview and they could verbalize more negative consequences than positive consequences resulting from their stay at Farview. In addition there was a general lack of enthusiasm for Farview's treatment program. Only when they were asked about the positive results of their stay at Farview did subjects mention the salutary effect of treatment with any frequency, and even in this case less than half of the patients responded in this fashion. Coupled with their lack of enthusiasm for the treatment provided was the frequency with which the Dixon patients saw their stay at Farview as a brutalizing and dehumanizing experience. Because the Dixon patients saw Farview in such a negative light, it is impossible to conclude that Farview was a therapeutic environment for these patients.

Two major conclusions can be drawn from the data presented in this chapter. The first is that the Dixon patients were not particularly disruptive while they were at Farview. Neither the incident reports nor the ward notes contain evidence that the Dixon subjects engaged in repetitive or serious assaultive behavior while at Farview. The second is that the Dixon patients did not view Farview as a therapeutic environment. Indeed, they were more likely to see it as a violent, brutal, and dehumanizing institution.

Viewed from the general research question of this study, the attitudinal data presented here do not challenge the wisdom of the court's decision to transfer the Dixon patients to civil hospitals for reevaluation. If the Dixon patients had been favorably disposed toward Farview, the court's decision to transfer the patients may have been at the very least unnecessary interference in a situation which the patients viewed as bearable or even therapeutic. This appears not to be the case as not even a sizable minority of the Dixon class was positively oriented toward Farview.

The behavioral data presented here raise serious questions about the Farview staff's decisions concerning the confinement of the Dixon patients. Why were these patients kept at Farview for an average of fourteen years and why did the staff recommend, at the time of the Dixon case, that at least a large minority of them should continue to be kept in confinement? Clearly it is not on the basis of observed violent behavior while at Farview. This analysis, based on the files which contain the results of these observations, uncovered no support for the assertion that the Dixon patients were exceptionally disruptive. With the possible exception of the youngest inmates and those newly admitted, the rates of assaultive behavior were quite low. Given this, it would seem that a more defensible policy would have been to advocate relatively short stays at Farview where the maximum security care would be available during the early periods of confinement when assaults were highest. After this period the patients could have been transferred to civil hospitals where treatment facilities were more abundant. As it is, we can find no validity for justifying long periods of confinement on the basis of in-hospital assaultiveness.

Finally, the data in this chapter are consistent with our earlier claim that the Farview staff made the political prediction that the Dixon patients would be assaultive after release. Such predictions require a disjunction between past events and the probability of future behavior since they are predictions about an individual's behavior based on the likely behavior of members of the group to which he belongs, and not on his own past behavior. If the incident reports and ward notes had indicated frequent assaultive behavior at Farview, the staff could reasonably have predicted that such behavior would continue, or perhaps intensify, in less secure settings. Although the data did not indicate high rates of violence, the prediction was still made. This disjunction between the evidence concerning past behavior and the prediction leads us to label it extrascientific, in this case political. We believe that the predictions were based on the political consequences of misprediction and not on a demonstrated relationship between past behavior and future behavior.

6   The Dixon Patients
in Civil Mental Hospitals

In our opinion the Dixon patients were not sufficiently violent during their stay at Farview to justify long-term, maximum security confinement solely on the basis of their in-hospital behavior. An alternative theoretical perspective, based on a containment orientation, is available, however, under which continued confinement of individuals who were not violent *during confinement* could be justified. The argument is as follows. Most of the Dixon patients had engaged in serious violent behavior before their confinement at Farview. This prior behavior, plus the negative attitudes displayed by many of the subjects during confinement, strongly indicates a propensity for committing violent offenses. Only the constant surveillance and the threat of immediate and inevitable punishment which exist at a maximum security hospital are capable of containing such behavior. Once these restraints are removed, an increase in assaultive behavior would occur.

Unfortunately for the resident of an institution where this perspective predominates, there is no behavioral pattern which can be exhibited that would indicate that the patient would be a good risk for release or transfer to a less secure setting. An inmate who is violent in the face of or in opposition to the harsh regimen of the security hospital confirms the staff's judgment

94

that he would be even more violent if transferred. The docile, compliant inmate is viewed as untrustworthy. His calm exterior is perceived as a false image of the potential for violence brewing just beneath the surface. Indeed, just such a perspective seems to be presented in Dr. Shovlin's testimony which was quoted above:

Patients [at Farview] understand that violent and assaultive behavior will not be tolerated ... it is our considered professional opinion that if we take away the maximum security controls, the patients will not be able to contain their impulses within acceptable limits (Dixon transcript, 1970, p. 61).

If this containment model correctly describes the interaction between personality and social setting, and if the Dixon patients were potentially violent persons, transferring them to the comparative freedom of civil mental hospitals should have resulted in widespread eruption of serious violence. Statements concerning the comparative freedom of Pennsylvania's civil mental hospitals are not merely theoretical or rhetorical. We have viewed the wards of Farview and of all the civil mental hospitals and conclude that Farview is far more secure both physically and in its operations than any ward at any of the other hospitals. Although some Dixon patients were housed in "closed" wards at the civil hospitals, the majority were not, and for those who were the restraints were not so severe as at Farview. To examine the validity of this containment model, we will consider the amount and patterns of violence found among the Dixon patients after their transfer to civil mental hospitals.

Following the pattern developed in the previous chapter we will also investigate the attitudes of the Dixon patients concerning the transfer hospitals. Again we will be particularly interested in examining the issue of whether the court's decision to transfer the patients could be considered precipitous. One could argue, for example, that since the Dixon patients had spent such long periods of time at Farview they had found a home there and that it was antitherapeutic to transfer them from their familiar environment. To examine this possibility, the interview solicited information on residential preferences and the opinions of the subjects concerning the differences between hospitals.

BEHAVIOR AT THE TRANSFER HOSPITALS

The distribution of violent incidents after transfer (table 6.1) re-

veals that few (19 percent) of the subjects were involved in serious
violence in their new institutional homes. Only 5 percent were involved as initiators or victims of more than two violent incidents
and fewer than 3 percent of the subjects were so frequently involved
in violence as to be considered persistently violent.

TABLE 6.1   Distribution of Incident Reports at the Transfer Hospital

No. of	Subjects		
Incident Reports	N	%	Cumulative %
0	441	81.7	81.7
1	61	11.3	93.0
2	10	1.9	94.8
3–4	14	2.6	97.4
5+	14	2.6	100.0
Total	540[a]	100.1	
Mean 0.50			
SD 1.99			

[a]Seventeen subjects are excluded because they were transferred to a hospital where
incident reports were not filed in patients' records.

Although much of the analysis of violent behavior at the transfer hospital parallels the analysis of behavior at Farview, some
issues are not as salient for the transfer hospital data. For example, since the subjects spent an average of fourteen years at
Farview but only a year at the transfer hospital, an analysis of
changing rates of violence by age is not possible. However, by
enumerating the duration of stay in months instead of years, it is
possible to analyze changes in rates of violence during the brief
period the subjects did stay at the transfer hospitals.

A containment theory of violence would suggest that the highest incident rates would occur immediately after transfer from
the security facility unless the subjects had been constrained by
special controls on admission to the transfer hospitals, which
were subsequently reduced. The Dixon patients were not generally constrained by procedures any more severe than housing them
on locked admission wards at those hospitals where this practice
was standard for all new admissions. Therefore, the generaliza-
tion that transfer from Farview resulted in immediate substantial
reduction of external restraints for the Dixon patients is valid.

Nevertheless, the result of this transfer was that neither the
rate of all incidents (fig. 6.1) nor the rate of subject-initiated
incidents (fig. 6.2) was higher in the first months after transfer
than in subsequent months. The first months after transfer the

subjects averaged 0.03 incidents per month, or three incidents per one hundred subjects. During most of the following months, for a period of over four years, the subjects remaining in the civil hospitals exhibited rates of incidents between 0.01 and 0.04 incidents per month.

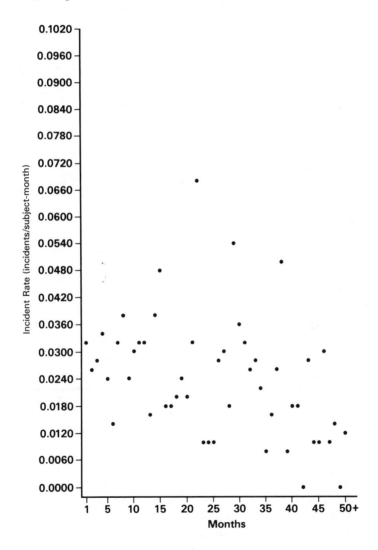

Fig. 6.1. Total incident rate, by month at transfer hospital.

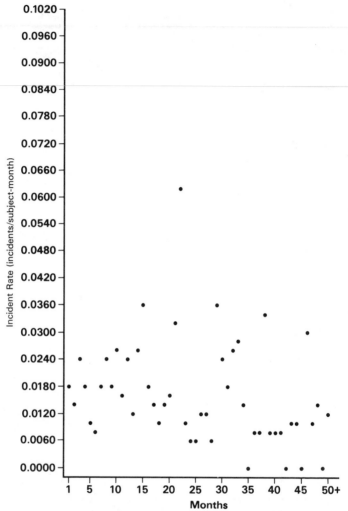

Fig. 6.2. Subject-initiated incident rate, by month at transfer hospital.

All three plots of incident rate change, including nonsubject-initiated incidents (fig. 6.3), appear as a series of low-valued random scatterings. There appears to be no systematic change in incident rates over time in the transfer hospitals.

The distribution of types of incidents at the transfer hospital (table 6.2) looks at first glance to be somewhat different than the

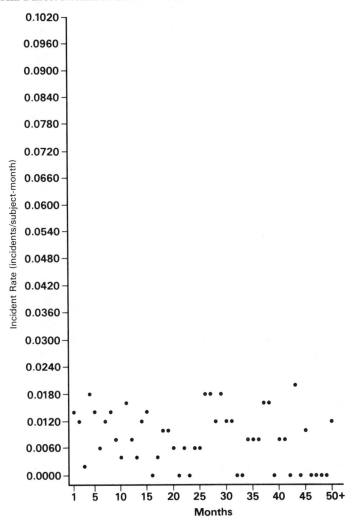

Fig. 6.3. Nonsubject-initiated incident rate, by month at transfer hospital.

distribution at Farview. Subject-initiated assaults comprise a larger percentage at the transfer hospital (48 percent vs. 20 percent) and solitary incidents account for a smaller percentage (6.5 percent vs. 20 percent). However, much of the difference in the first type of incident may be explained by more complete reporting of violence at the civil hospitals. At Farview 23 percent of the incidents were described as fights in which the initiator was not specified, while at the civil hospitals this category included only 10 percent of the cases.

TABLE 6.2   Type of Incidents Recorded at Transfer Hospital

Type	No. of Incidents	%	
Assault initiated by subject	140	48.1	
Against another inmate	118		40.5
Against guard	18		6.2
Against both	4		1.4
Fights among inmates	30	10.3	
Verbal incidents	3	1.0	
Assaults initiated by other inmates	97	33.3	
Provoked by subject	18		6.2
Unprovoked by subject	79		27.1
Subject injured while being subdued	2	0.7	
Incidents not involving others (self-injury and/or property destruction)	19	6.5	
Total	291	99.9	

The reduction in the proportion of solitary incidents (that is, self-injury and property destruction) is intriguing. It suggests that the less restrictive environment of the civil hospital causes less stress on the individual, reducing the level of noninstrumental violence. Consistent with this speculative view is the proportionate reduction in violence directed at staff (from 10 percent to 6.2 percent).

Comparing the incident rates at Farview and at the transfer hospitals, the rates are higher at the latter institutions. During their last year at Farview the Dixon patients averaged 0.06 incidents per patient. During their first year after transfer (after weighting the rate by actual time in the hospital for subjects who remained less than one year) they averaged 0.35 incidents per patient. This is over a fivefold increase in the rate of violent incidents from the year before to the year after transfer, lending support to the containment theory of violence, even though the absolute level of the rate was still low.

Detailed evidence about the incidents diminishes the force of the containment argument, however. The small number of cases where treatment was required reveal that the incidents reported seldom involved serious injuries (table 6.3). Of the 114 subjects injured in incidents at the transfer hospitals, 3.5 percent were

TABLE 6.3 Injuries Resulting from Incidents

	No. of Subjects	%
No. of people injured		
0	116	39.9
1	160	55.0
2+	15	5.2
	(291)	
Was subject injured?		
Yes	114	39.2
No	177	60.8
	(291)	
No. of other patients injured		
0	228	78.4
1	63	21.6
	(291)	
No. of staff injured		
0	276	94.8
1+	15	5.2
	(291)	
No. of subjects		
Not treated	20	17.5
Treated and returned to ward	90	78.9
Transferred to medical-surgical ward	4	3.5
	(114)	
No. of other patients		
Not treated	30	47.6
Treated and returned to ward	32	50.8
Transferred to medical-surgical ward	1	1.6
	(63)	
No. of staff members		
Not treated	5	33.3
Treated as outpatients	10	66.7
Hospitalized	0	0.0
	(15)	

injured so severely that they had to be transferred to the medical-surgical ward. The corresponding figure at Farview was 7 percent. Among the sixty-three other patients injured, only one was transferred to the medical-surgical ward for treatment while at Farview 14 percent (seven of the thirty-five cases) were transferred. The higher proportion of incident reports at the transfer hospitals describing events not resulting in serious injury suggests that the threshhold for reporting violence was lower there and that the higher rate of incident reporting may be at least partly a function of a greater sensitivity to violence. This argument is tenuous, however, because both the validity and reliability of the reporting process are less than perfect.

The ward notes, the second source of information on in-hospital violence, supplement the findings based on incident reports (table 6.4). As at Farview the two most common types of entries referred to angry or antiauthoritarian attitudes and psychotic symptoms. Together, these two categories account for 78 percent of all entries. Although the description of angry and antiauthoritarian attitudes was the most common, only 31 percent of the subjects were so described. The description of greatest interest, overt violence toward others, accounted for 7 percent of the entries and was found in only 9.7 percent of the patients' ward notes. Thus the ward notes also reveal that violence, even of a nonserious nature, was an uncommon event for the vast majority of subjects. Overall only 38.3 percent of the subjects were ever described with any of the fifty terms on the violent behavior list.

TABLE 6.4   Types of Behavior Codes

	Ward Note Entries		Subjects with One or More Entries	
Type	No.	%	No.	%[a]
Overt violence toward others	97	7.2	51	9.7
Potential for violence	139	10.3	64	12.1
Self-injury	22	1.6	13	2.5
Property destruction	5	0.5	3	0.6
Management problems	30	2.2	23	4.4
Antiauthoritarian attitudes	638	47.5	163	30.9
Psychotic symptoms	412	30.7	122	23.1
Total	1,343	100.0	202	38.3

[a]Percentages are based on 528 subjects transferred to sixteen hospitals where ward notes were written.

The distribution of the ward notations over time, unlike the distribution of incidents, does show a pattern of higher rates in the first three months than in the later months after transfer (fig. 6.4). The rates taper off from a high of 0.24 entries per month in the first month to half that rate in the fourth month. The first impression, generated by the ward note data, in view of low rates of actual violence, is that the Dixon patients were psychotics who rebelled against authority. Even these qualities became less pronounced—or were not perceived as significant— after the subjects were hospitalized for a few months.[1]

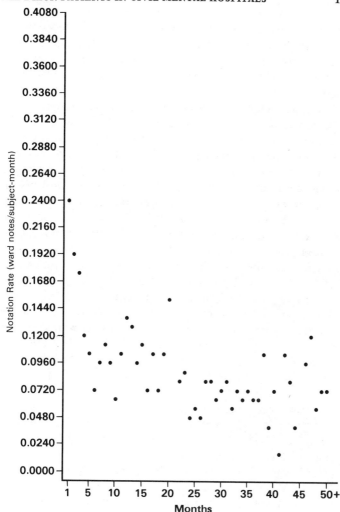

Fig. 6.4. Ward note entries, by month at transfer hospital.

IMPACT ON THE TRANSFER HOSPITALS

A third and final source of data on the subjects' behavior at the transfer hospitals comes from a series of informal interviews conducted by one of the authors with staff members at each of the seventeen civil hospitals. At each institution at least two staff members who were present between 1969 and 1971 and whose position allowed them to view the overall impact of the transfer of the Dixon patients were interviewed. Because the interviews were loosely structured and because two opinions, although independently stated, do not represent the possible range of opinions staff members could have had, conclusions derived from these interviews might be taken as weakly based. However, there was so little response variation, both within and between hospitals, that some confidence in these findings seems warranted.

Before the subjects arrived, few of the hospital administrators anticipated special problems. In a few cases they expressed concern about readmitting patients whom they had previously sent to Farview because the patients had been assaultive. Most respondents, however, expressed little anxiety over the potential dangerousness of Farview transfers, reporting that they had previously received patients from Farview without significant problems or that their fears were alleviated by the receipt of extensive records on the Dixon transfers. Those that expressed their own or other staff members' concern said the concern was alleviated after the subjects arrived and failed to live up to their bad reputations.

Several of the staff members interviewed revealed limited knowledge or even misinformation about the Dixon case. They had been led to believe, apparently by statements in the Farview records, that Farview was voluntarily transferring the subjects. At least one interviewee said that, had he known that the subjects were being transferred under the pressure of a legal suit, he would have been more concerned.

But ignorance did not characterize most of the staff members interviewed. One hospital superintendent made a special effort to attend the Dixon case hearings and another one prepared, with his staff, a set of guidelines and information about the case.

None of the hospitals made any structural or staffing changes in anticipation of receiving the Dixon patients and none reported finding such changes to be necessary or desirable after the subjects had arrived. Most of the hospitals used routine admission procedures, including initial assignment to a closed admissions ward. The few hospitals that had court or security wards used these wards for initial screening and observation. Compared to the advance excitement generated in New York by the Baxstrom case—where at one hospital, aides were given training in the martial arts—the Dixon case caused hardly a ripple.

Of the staff members interviewed only one offered a negative report when asked whether the Dixon patients seemed different from other patients in the hospital. She said that some of the subjects were young and bullied the other patients. Most respondents reported no differences. The few negative comments mentioned concerned such qualities as "more institutionalized personalities" and "greater than usual difficulty placing them in the community." A few respondents said they were "good patients" and "cooperative."

When asked directly whether the Dixon patients were more or less violent than other patients, only one respondent said they were more aggressive than other patients. Two said they were better, or less violent, and all the rest reported no differences.

Many of the respondents had difficulty recalling which patients and former patients were members of the Dixon class or were transferred from Farview. Most subjects quickly became part of the general patient population and, in retrospect, were not readily distinguishable as Dixon patients by the staff members interviewed. There were exceptions to this pattern as a few respondents recalled individual patients who were sent back to Farview, but such patients were few and were viewed as exceptions by the respondents.

The picture of violent behavior in the transfer hospitals is thus rounded out by these interviews. The Dixon patients were not more violent than other patients in the civil hospitals, they did not cause major disruptions in any of the institutions, nor were they especially troublesome in any other way. The only burden they created was the requirement that they be quickly processed, in sizable numbers in some instances, to conform to the court order.

ATTITUDES ABOUT THE TRANSFER HOSPITALS

The preceding data reflect the opinions of hospital staffs about the patients. It is only fair to let the subjects reciprocate. To the question "What did you like most about the transfer hospital?" the modal response (30 percent of all responses) was some aspect of the living conditions (for example, good food, clean housing, recreation, and so forth) (table 6.5). Freedom of movement was the second most frequently selected item. The major difference between these responses and the responses to the same question about Farview was the shrinkage of the response category "none" from 30 percent of responses about Farview to 9 percent of

TABLE 6.5   Reasons Subjects Stated for Liking the Transfer Hospitals

Reason	No. of Responses[a]	% of Responses	% of Subjects[b]
None	37	9.0	15.6
Closer to home	11	2.7	4.6
Living conditions	124	30.1	52.3
Freedom of movement	84	20.4	35.4
Treatment and programs	69	16.7	29.1
Absence of mistreatment	10	2.4	4.2
Relations with others	30	7.3	12.7
Work	28	6.8	11.8
Everything	10	2.4	4.2
Other	9	2.2	3.8
Total	412	100.0	

[a]Number of subjects responding, 237. The number of subjects responding to questions varies because some subjects refused to answer particular questions or because some questions were not appropriate to ask subjects in certain circumstances. The Subject Interview Schedule (appendix 6) contains instructions to exclude certain questions depending on the institutional transfer history of the subject.

[b]Percentages do not sum to 100 because the subjects could give more than one response.

responses about the transfer hospital. In the minds of the subjects there was more to like about the civil hospitals than Farview.

The subjects also had negative comments about the civil hospitals, although not in the volume recorded about Farview. Forty-six percent of the subjects responded "nothing" to the question "What did you dislike most about the transfer hospital?" (table 6.6). This compares with 17 percent giving the same response about Farview. The most common complaint, given by 28.6 percent of the respondents, concerned the institutional order of the hospital (that is, being confined, the routine, and so forth). Though living in the transfer hospital had negative features, they were not so pronounced in the minds of the subjects as the unpleasant qualities of Farview.

To elicit direct information about the subjects' preferences for various living arrangements, a series of questions were asked in which the respondent could rank the attractiveness of Farview, the transfer hospital, or the community. The stimuli that were used to elicit these rankings concerned general living conditions and the availability and quality of medical treatment and care. Here, we will only compare the subjects' preferences for Farview or the transfer hospital, and the data are presented in table 6.7.

TABLE 6.6 Reasons Subjects Stated for Disliking the Transfer Hospitals

Reason	No. of Responses[a]	% of Responses	% of Subjects
None	106	39.6	45.9
Cruelty of aides	12	4.5	5.2
Inadequacy of medical care	21	7.8	9.1
Other patients	11	4.1	4.8
Food	20	7.5	8.7
Institutional order	66	24.6	28.6
Everything	10	3.7	4.3
Other	22	8.2	9.5
Total	268	100.0	

[a]Number of subjects responding, 231.

By consistent margins of about 3:1 the subjects preferred the food, living conditions, psychiatric treatment, and medical care at the transfer hospital. They reported seeing their families more often at the transfer hospital and said the physicians and aides were better there than at Farview. Programs were perceived as more helpful at the transfer hospitals and patients had more freedom to move about the hospital.

The bottom line of course is the question "Where would you prefer to live?" The vast majority of the subjects (71 percent vs. 20 percent) responded in favor of the transfer hospital, with 10 percent undecided. It did make a difference to the Dixon patients where they lived; they much preferred the civil mental hospitals to Farview.

The data presented in this chapter offer little support for a containment perspective as the basis for the continued confinement of the Dixon patients at Farview. Based on that perspective one would expect frequent and serious episodes of violent behavior at the transfer hospitals once the restraints of the maximum security hospital were removed. There is little evidence to support this expectation.

Although the incidence of reported violence did increase after the subjects were transferred, the monthly rates of both incident reports and ward note entries were low and the contents of these two data sources do not reflect serious assaultive behavior. The incident reports indicate that few people were injured and those who were, by and large, did not require major medical attention. The ward notes contained far more entries about negative atti-

TABLE 6.7 Preference Rankings of Transfer Hospital and Farview on Living
            Conditions, Staff, Treatment, and Residence

Question	Farview Preferred	Transfer Hospital Preferred	Equal Preference
Is the food you eat better at Farview, the transfer hospital, or home?	27.0% (63)	60.5% (141)	12.4% (29)
Are the living conditions better at Farview, the transfer hospital, or home?	23.9 (55)	66.1 (152)	10.0 (23)
Is the psychiatric treatment better at Farview, the transfer hospital, or home?	21.0 (43)	66.3 (136)	12.7 (26)
Is the medical treatment better at Farview, the transfer hospital, or home?	20.3 (43)	66.5 (141)	13.2 (26)
Where did you see your family more often?	22.1 (43)	73.8 (144)	4.1 (8)
How would you compare the doctors at Farview with the doctors at the transfer hospital?	16.6 (36)	47.6 (103)	35.9 (78)
How would you compare the aides?	8.8 (18)	63.7 (130)	27.5 (78)
Would you say the programs were most helpful to you at Farview, the transfer hospital, or home?	15.6 (35)	57.6 (129)	26.8 (60)
Did you have more freedom to move about the hospital and do different things at Farview, the transfer hospital, or home?	12.0 (28)	79.0 (184)	9.0 (21)
If you could choose to live at Farview or at the transfer hospital, which would you choose?	19.7 (47)	70.6 (168)	9.7 (23)

tudes and psychotic symptoms than about violent behavior.
Moreover, the interviews conducted with the civil hospital ad-
ministrations corroborate these data. They did not view the Dixon
patients as violent nor were the hospitals required to take any
special precautions to provide security for their staff members
and other patients.

All in all we have found no consistent evidence to justify the
continued confinement of the Dixon patients at Farview. They
were not violent during their stay at Farview nor were they disruptive at the transfer hospitals. Indeed they seemed to have blended

in quite well with the general population at the civil mental hospitals.

The opinions of the Dixon subjects are quite consistent with this view. Not only is there little evidence for keeping them at Farview, their attitudes clearly indicate that they prefer not to be there. If the cooperation of the patient is necessary for any effective therapy to take place, and the psychiatric literature indicates it is, their transfer from Farview can be viewed as therapeutic. The vast majority of the Dixon patients disliked Farview and clearly preferred to be at the transfer hospitals. The data on in-hospital assaultiveness indicate that there is little reason not to grant them their preference, as the Dixon decision in fact did.

7   Discharge from the
       Transfer Hospital

Having examined the behavior and attitudes of the subjects while at Farview and the transfer hospitals, the focus of this study now shifts to the lives of the Dixon patients in the community. Since not all of the Dixon subjects were discharged to the community, however, there is an interstitial stage in the analysis which centers on the decisions made at the transfer hospitals to discharge or retain particular patients. Essentially these decisions were discretionary in that the staff at the transfer hospitals were vested with the authority to evaluate the patients and then to decide on their release or retention. This discretion was not unbounded though, since the Dixon court specified the following procedures and guidelines to be followed in the evaluations.

1. Every member of the class was to be discharged or recommitted within sixty days of the order.
2. Before seeking a new commitment the civil hospital was ordered to evaluate the person, aid him in contacting relatives, develop a treatment program, and discuss the treatment program with him and his family.
3. Before seeking an involuntary commitment the civil hospital was ordered to explore with the patient and his relatives the

possibility of a voluntary commitment involving the least restraint acceptable to the hospital.

4. If the hospital sought an involuntary commitment, the procedure must have included the right to counsel, appointment
of counsel for indigent subjects, independent expert examination also paid for by the state, a full hearing in which the
subject could present evidence, subpoena witnesses, and cross-
examine opposing witnesses, and a standard of proof that
"the evidence found by the factfinder must establish clearly,
unequivocally and convincingly that the subject of the hearing
requires commitment because of manifest indications that the
subject poses a present threat of serious physical harm to other
persons or himself." No recommitments to Farview could be
authorized unless the state proved that the subject could not
be committed to any other facility. All commitments would
specify a maximum period of confinement, not exceeding six
months, within which the hospital could release the subject
without further court approval. Finally, the results of any
commitment hearings would be reviewable in state appellate
courts.

It is apparent from these stringent criteria that the court fa-
vored the expeditious release of the Dixon patients to the community. By not ordering a direct release from Farview, however,
and by permitting the state the opportunity to continue the involuntary confinement of any subject who appeared likely to be
dangerous, the court demonstrated concern for the welfare of the
subjects and the safety of the community.

It is through this attempt at balancing the rights of the individual and of the community that the court allowed the discretion of
the transfer hospital staff to enter into the discharge decision.
Such discretion raises a number of empirical questions concerning the likelihood of being discharged, the characteristics of
patients who were actually discharged, potential biases that exist
in virtually all discretionary decisions, the underlying policies of
the staff, and so forth. The aim of this chapter is to examine
these issues in as much detail as the data will allow.

We can begin by examining the likelihood of ever being discharged to the community from the transfer hospitals. Sixty-
five percent of the Dixon patients, 368 members of the class, were
discharged, while 30 percent were not, following clinical evalua-

tions. The remaining 4 percent escaped from the hospitals and did not return. Because our concern in this chapter is with the staff's discretion to release patients, the subjects who escaped will not be included in the analysis. These patients stayed in the transfer hospitals less than three months, on the average, too brief a period—as indicated by the mean period of stay of all discharged subjects—for the staff to have made a decision concerning discharge.[1] The analysis will therefore focus on two groups—those who were discharged by the staff and those who were not.

The patients who were discharged left the hospitals rather quickly. Half of them were released within six months, three-quarters were released by the end of the first year, and only 10 percent remained in the hospitals for more than two years (fig. 7.1). The mean length of stay was 9.1 months and the median was 5.6 months, indicating the skewed nature of the distribution.

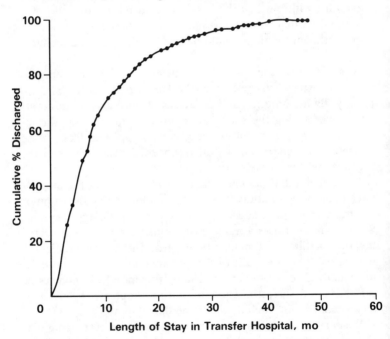

Fig. 7.1. Cumulative discharges from transfer hospitals, by length of stay.

The image that one receives about the Dixon patients based on these simple data is quite different from the image one would receive by examining comparable data based on the Farview commitment. Apparently the staffs of the various transfer hospitals did not share the opinion of the Farview staff that these were dangerous, mentally ill offenders who required secure hospitalization. On the contrary, the transfer hospital staff seemed to view the Dixon patients as mental patients who could and should reside in the community.[2]

This view was not universal, however, since one-third of the Dixon patients were never discharged.[3] The analysis in this chapter will attempt to uncover those variables that are most capable of distinguishing between the groups who were and were not discharged.

ZERO-ORDER RELATIONSHIPS

Since these variables include both quantitative and qualitative measures, we will divide the analysis accordingly, starting with the quantitative material. Table 7.1 presents this information, including t tests and two-tailed probabilities.

The two variables that are related to the age of the subjects are both associated with the decision to discharge. Patients who were never discharged, when compared to those who were, were significantly older at the time they were transferred from Farview to the civil hospitals or, put differently, they were older when they arrived at the transfer hospital. Relatedly, the patients who were not discharged had spent more time at Farview than those who were discharged—on the average five years more. There was a strong tendency on the part of the transfer hospitals to discharge younger, less institutionalized patients, who presumably were better able to deal with community living, and to retain the older ones, who were in greater need of treatment and care.

There was also a tendency for the transfer hospitals to discharge patients who had a more extensive record of previous criminal behavior. All of the measures except the seriousness score of the Dixon offense are in that direction, and five of the seven differences are significant. The discharged patients had more arrests, more arrests for violent and sex offenses, higher LDS scores, and higher total seriousness scores.

TABLE 7.1   Discharge from Transfer Hospitals by Quantitative Variables

| Variable | Never Discharged | | Discharged | | | |
	Mean	SD	Mean	SD	t	p
Age						
Age at transfer from Farview, yr	51.01	14.78	45.24	12.64	4.65	.001
Length of stay at Farview, yr	19.24	12.75	12.64	9.44	6.71	.001
Previous criminal behavior						
Arrests for all offenses	4.19	6.39	5.60	6.58	−2.30	.022
Arrests for violent offenses	0.47	0.96	0.86	1.49	−3.12	.002
Arrests for sex offenses	0.15	0.51	0.28	0.85	−1.79	.074
LDS score	4.24	4.57	6.01	5.11	−3.99	.001
Dixon offense seriousness (× 100)	5.76	7.23	4.74	5.98	1.57	.116
Total seriousness score (× 100)	6.93	10.53	10.06	11.37	−3.11	.002
Previous hospitalizations						
No. of	0.82	1.43	0.98	1.67	−1.07	.286
Behavior at Farview						
Incident rate[a]	0.12	0.38	0.12	0.27	0.04	.965
Subject-initiated incident rate	0.07	0.29	0.05	0.16	0.76	.446
Behavior at transfer hospital						
Incident rate	0.39	1.21	0.27	1.08	1.15	.251
Subject-initiated incident rate	0.25	1.02	0.18	0.92	0.80	.422
No. of escapes	0.35	1.03	0.35	1.04	0.01	.989

[a]These and other rates in this table are annual rates.

The two groups did not differ in the number of times they were previously hospitalized nor did they differ in terms of their behavior at Farview. The annual rates of incident reports, both total and subject-initiated, are almost identical for the two groups. Thus, the behavior the patients exhibited at Farview did not affect the likelihood of their eventual discharge.

More surprisingly, the violent behavior of the subjects in the transfer hospital apparently did not affect the discharge decision.

The annual rate of incidents and the annual rate of subject-initiated incidents for the two groups are not significantly different. The frequency of escapes is also unrelated to discharge decisions. Of the discharged group, 18 percent escaped and returned; of those never discharged, 15 percent escaped and returned. Thus, the aggressive behavior of the patients in the civil hospital, as we have measured it, was not highly related to the staff's decision to release patients to the community.

In addition to the quantitative data just discussed, a number of qualitative variables were also analyzed. Some of them were not significantly related to the decision to discharge.[4] They are as follows: the subject's legal status on admission to Farview, type of Dixon offense, the subject's psychiatric diagnosis at Farview and at the transfer hospital, and the security designation of the ward to which he was assigned at the transfer hospital.

Two of the qualitative variables were significantly related to discharge—the first being race. White subjects were less likely to be discharged than nonwhites (table 7.2). Over three-fourths of the black subjects were discharged by the transfer hospitals but only three-fifths of the whites were. Although there is no obvious explanation for this finding, it is not peculiar to this study. Stone notes that blacks are underrepresented at "some state institutions for the sexually dangerous," and are not overrepresented at Patuxent and other state and county hospitals for the criminally insane (Stone 1975, p. 35). Stone's suggested explanation for this finding is that since white psychiatrists often define black, criminally insane patients as untreatable they are less likely to commit and retain black patients. Whatever the explanation, the black Dixon subjects were more likely to be discharged than the white ones.

One of the most striking variables in explaining differences in the rates of discharge is the transfer hospital itself. There were

TABLE 7.2   Race and Discharge from Transfer Hospital

	Black	White
Never discharged	29.9%	37.2%
	(50)	(118)
Discharged	77.1	62.8
	(168)	(199)

NOTE: $\chi^2 = 11.59$; $p < .001$.

seventeen civil hospitals to which the Dixon patients were transferred and they had discharge rates ranging from 35.3 percent to
87.5 percent, with a relatively even distribution within this range
(table 7.3). The overall rate, as indicated earlier, was 65.5
percent.

TABLE 7.3 Discharge Rates by Transfer Hospital

Hospital	% Never Discharged	% Discharged
Retreat	64.7	35.3
	(11)	(6)
Warren	56.5	43.5
	(13)	(10)
Norristown	55.2	44.8
	(16)	(13)
Wernersville	44.4	55.6
	(8)	(10)
Dixmont	41.7	58.3
	(5)	(7)
Torrence	35.7	64.3
	(5)	(9)
Mayview	35.5	64.5
	(22)	(40)
Danville	35.0	65.0
	(7)	(13)
Holidaysburg	33.3	66.7
	(5)	(10)
Allentown	31.3	68.8
	(5)	(11)
Clarks Summit	30.0	70.0
	(6)	(16)
Woodville	27.3	72.7
	(6)	(18)
Harrisburg	25.0	75.0
	(6)	(18)
Haverford	25.0	75.0
	(5)	(10)
Philadelphia	23.4	76.6
	(46)	(151)
Somerset	14.3	85.7
	(1)	(6)
Embreeville	12.5	87.5
	(2)	(14)

Race and transfer hospital assignment can now be added to the
quantitative variables that were found to be associated with the
decision to discharge. Dixon patients who were younger, who had
a greater incidence of previous criminal behavior, who were

black, and who were transferred to certain civil hospitals were more likely to be discharged than their counterparts. Our next task is to uncover the interrelations among these variables and to isolate those that are more closely related to discharge.

THE TRANSFER HOSPITAL

Since the transfer hospital variable is of a different nature than the others, we can begin by examining its impact on discharge decisions. The first task is to see if there is an apparent explanation for the large differences in discharge rates among the various hospitals.

Only a few variables that characterize the civil mental hospitals were collected and are available for analysis (table 7.4). It is possible that hospitals located in urban counties would have discharge patterns that are different from those in rural counties because of differences in staff, patient backgrounds, community awareness, and other variables. Yet the expected rural-urban differences did not materialize, as can be seen in the Spearman correlation coefficients of .103 and .208 between the independent variable, percent of county urbanized, and the dependent variables, percent discharged, and mean length of stay.

The practical concern of the size of the patient population and

TABLE 7.4 Spearman Rank-Order Correlations for Transfer Hospitals

Dependent Variables	Independent Variables[a]		
	Urbanization[b]	No. of Dixon Patients Received	Hospital Population[c]
% discharged			
Spearman r	.103	.494	−.154
Z	0.414	1.975	0.6144
p	NS	.05	NS
Length of stay at transfer hospital			
Spearman r	.208	.315	−.368
Z	0.834	1.260	1.47
p	NS	NS	NS

[a]The hospitals were ranked from highest to lowest discharge rates, lowest to highest length of stay, most to least urbanized, and greatest to least number of Dixon patients and total number of patients.

[b]The variable "urbanization" is operationalized as the proportion of the population listed as urban dwellers in the county in which the hospital was located. Data from 1970 Census of Population, Pennsylvania, Number of Inhabitants PC (1)–A40 Pa, table 9, pp. 40–24, 40–25.

[c]As of 30 June 1971.

resulting problem of overcrowding could also affect the discharge policies at the various hospitals. In general the number of Dixon patients transferred to the hospital and the total population of the hospital were not related to the two dependent variables. The number of Dixon patients originally transferred to the hospital was associated with the proportion of subjects eventually discharged, but this association was not particularly strong—the Spearman rank-order correlation is .494 and the Z score just reaches significance at the .05 level. The other three associations are not statistically significant. In general, these variables were not very useful in explaining the diversity of discharge rates among the transfer hospitals.

The only variables that contribute to the explanation of this diversity are the age-related ones. The hospitals with the lowest discharge rates received the oldest subjects, in terms of age at transfer from Farview and length of stay at Farview, and the hospitals with the highest discharge rates received the youngest (table 7.5). Both differences are significant, and the inverse relationship is unbroken for age at transfer from Farview while for length of stay the positions of the last two groups are reversed but the general pattern is still evident.

TABLE 7.5   Age of Subjects by Discharge Rates of Transfer Hospital

Discharge Rate of Transfer Hospital[a]	Age at Transfer from Farview		Length of Stay at Farview (in years)		
	Mean	SD	Mean	SD	No.
Very low	50.5	14.1	18.3	11.7	87
Low	48.4	14.3	15.7	11.0	108
High	46.0	13.5	12.1	11.0	73
Very high	45.8	12.9	14.0	10.5	264
F	3.150		5.250		
p	.05		.01		

[a]To facilitate the data analysis, the seventeen hospitals have been divided into four groups based on the discharge rate of the Dixon patients. The first four hospitals listed in table 7.3 constitute the first group, with the lowest discharge rate, the second four and the third four are the next two groups, and the last five constitute the last group, with the highest discharge rate.

The variable of race and the variables relating to offense histories, however, are not related to the discharge rates of the transfer hospitals. The hospitals with high discharge rates were no more likely than the hospitals with low discharge rates to receive patients who were black or who had extensive back-grounds of criminal behavior.

The discharge policies at the various civil hospitals seem to have been based on the type of patients they received from Farview. The hospitals with the lowest discharge rates received the oldest patients, while those with the highest rates received the youngest. It is therefore conceivable that the significant dif-ferences found in the previous section are spurious and can be explained by the discharge policies at the different transfer hospitals. Yet this is not the case. The association between the independent variables—race, age at transfer from Farview, length of stay at Farview, and previous offense history—and the dependent variable—whether or not the subject was discharged from the transfer hospital—remains significant when the transfer hospital group is held constant.

To illustrate this, table 7.6 shows the relationships between age at transfer from Farview and ever/never discharged, when the discharge rate of the hospital is controlled. In each of the four groups those who were never discharged were older than those who had been discharged. The results are statistically significant and replicate the zero-order relationship seen earlier. Even though the hospitals with the highest discharge rates originally received the youngest subjects, among those whom they received, the youngest subjects were released and the oldest were retained.

TABLE 7.6   Mean Age at Transfer from Farview by Discharge Status and Discharge Rate of Transfer Hospitals

| Discharge Status | Discharge Rate of Hospitals | | | |
	Very Low	Low	High	Very High
Never discharged	52.7	51.8	48.6	50.0
	(48)	(39)	(22)	(60)
Discharged	47.7	46.6	44.9	44.6
	(39)	(69)	(51)	(204)

NOTE: Entries are the mean age of patients transferred to hospitals in each discharge rate group. For example, patients who were transferred to hospitals with the lowest discharge rates and who were never discharged averaged 52.7 years of age at the time of their transfer from Farview. The number of subjects is given in parentheses.

The same pattern holds true for the other variables. When the discharge rate of the transfer hospitals is held constant, those discharged were likely to have spent less time at Farview, to have had more extensive criminal careers, and to be black. The different discharge rates at the transfer hospital cannot explain these results on the individual level.

The Primacy of Age

Because the relationships between several variables and the likelihood of being discharged persist among hospitals with the same discharge rates, that is, they are not spurious, these variables may be ordered according to their importance in explaining the likelihood of a patient's being discharged. Because the dependent variable is dichotomous, a stepwise discriminant function analysis will be employed for this purpose.

This technique first chooses the independent variable that best discriminates between the groups of the dependent variable—in this case those who were and those who were not discharged—and enters that variable into a predictive equation. It next chooses the independent variable that, in combination with the first variable, best discriminates between the groups and enters it into the equation. It proceeds in this matter, adding one variable at each step, until all the variables that contribute additional discrimination between the two groups are entered. The importance of the variables can be determined by the order of entry and the magnitude of the F value. The F values are partial F ratios which measure the discrimination introduced by the variable after taking into account the discrimination achieved by the variables previously entered.

The variable of the length of stay at Farview is most highly associated with the likelihood of being discharged ($F = 41.42$, $p < .001$). Of the other three, only race adds significantly to the discrimination ($F = 5.80$, $p < .05$) (see table 7.7). Age at transfer from Farview does not enter into the equation, but this could be an artifact since it is so highly correlated with length of stay at Farview—$r = .667$. In a separate analysis, when length of stay is suppressed, age at transfer from Farview is the first to enter the equation ($F = 22.55$, $p < .001$) and the other two variables reverse order, both having significant F values.

All four variables still contribute to the explanation of discharge decisions—the young, the black, and those with higher total seriousness scores are more likely to be discharged than the old, the white, and the less serious offenders. But the two

TABLE 7.7 Stepwise Discriminant Function Analysis for Discharge from Transfer Hospital

Entry Order of Variables	F Value at Entry	p[a]
Length of stay at Farview	41.42	.001
Race	5.80	.050
Total seriousness score	2.25	NS
Age at transfer from Farview	0.79	NS
Age at transfer from Farview	22.55	.001
Total seriousness	12.37	.001
Race	4.10	.050

[a]Degrees of freedom vary from 1 and 533 to 1 and 530, depending on the step.

variables related to age are the most important and are best able to discriminate between the two groups. When length of stay at Farview is not suppressed it explains the lion's share of the difference, as can be seen in both the F and p values in table 7.7.

The data in table 7.8 indicate the predictive accuracy of the discriminant function analyses. Here the results of three separate discriminant function classifications—or predictions—of discharge decisions are presented. Each model incorporates a different combination of three or more of the variables age, length of stay at Farview, total seriousness score, and race. In all three models over 70 percent of the patients would be placed in the correct groups based on the weights derived from the analyses. But this is only an optimistic way of reporting that close to 30 percent of the predictions would be wrong. Clearly the variables at hand do not explain all of the variation in discharge procedures. Other variables not included in this study are of importance and would have to be analyzed in any complete study of discharge patterns. But for the time being, and for the purposes of the Dixon case research, we are left with the primacy of age in explaining the decisions of the civil hospital staff to discharge patients.

TREATMENT VERSUS SECURITY

This finding closely parallels the one of the Baxstrom case research: "The longer patients were housed as criminally insane patients, the less likely they were to be released to the community from the civil hospital" (Steadman and Cocozza 1974, p. 134).[5] In both Pennsylvania and New York, the clinicians at the civil mental hospitals were reluctant to release to the community

TABLE 7.8   Group Membership Predictions Based on Discriminant Function Analysis

| | Actual | | | |
| Predictions | Not Discharged | | Discharged | |
	N	%	N	%
	Model A			
Not discharged	50	30.8	37	10.1
Discharged	118	70.2	330	89.9
Total	168	100.0	367	100.0
Correct predictions			380	71.03%
	Model B			
Not discharged	46	27.4	26	7.1
Discharged	122	72.6	341	92.9
Total	168	100.0	367	100.0
Correct predictions			387	72.34%
	Model C			
Not discharged	46	27.4	31	8.4
Discharged	122	72.6	336	91.6
Total	168	100.0	367	100.0
Correct predictions			382	71.40%

NOTE: Model A includes length of stay at Farview, race, total seriousness score, and age at transfer from Farview; Model B includes age at transfer from Farview, total seriousness score, and race; Model C includes length of stay at Farview, race, and total seriousness score.

patients who were old and who had spent long periods of time in the maximum security mental hospital.

But these same age variables played a much different role in relation to the discharging policies at the original maximum security hospitals. In those settings, the staffs were reluctant to release patients who were young and who had spent short periods of time in confinement. The Dixon patients, for example, were, on the average, forty-seven years of age and had spent fourteen years at Farview when the court ordered their transfer (see Steadman and Cocozza 1974, chapter 5, for comparable figures).

Combining the different role that age plays in the maximum security and civil hospitals, we see the criminally insane patient existed in a Catch-22 world. While at Farview he was told, in effect, that he was too young to be released; but once he was transferred to a civil hospital he was told that he had become too old to be eligible for release. We would interpret this difference between Farview and the civil hospitals in the following manner. The maximum security hospital was primarily concerned with security and social control. Treatment facilities at Farview were meager and the concern of the staff was to minimize the likelihood of postrelease violence. As a result they tended not to release young patients whom they viewed as the most prone to violence. As a patient aged and matured, however, the staff at the maximum security hospital would be more likely to release the patient because the risk of his being violent was perceived to have decreased.

The civil hospitals were not oriented to security and social control to the same extent, however, and were more concerned with providing treatment and care. The younger, less institutionalized patients were seen as not requiring the care of state hospitals but were seen as capable of residing in the community, and were accordingly released. Their potential dangerousness was not of overriding significance as it was in the maximum security setting. The older patients, however, were kept in confinement in the civil hospitals, not because of their potential danger but because of their perceived inability to cope with community living as a result of their age, mental and physical disease, and the difficulty of placing them in the community. Hence, at the civil hospitals, age is inversely related to the probability of being released.

One result of this discrepancy in policy between Farview and the civil hospitals is that a sizable minority of Dixon patients were ineligible for release under both regimes. While at Farview they were too young and dangerous, but once transferred to a civil hospital they were too old and frail.

This discrepancy in discharging policies was also uncovered in the Baxstrom research: "The psychiatrists in the correctional hospital system were evaluating older, less violent patients as no longer in need of special security and as more likely to succeed in the civil hospitals." But in the civil hospitals Steadman and Cocozza "found other factors to be related to whether civil hospital psychiatrists saw patients as no longer in need of care and likely to succeed in the community. One of the main characteristics of these patients was that they had been institutionalized in the criminally insane hospitals for fewer years" (Steadman and Cocozza 1974, p. 134).

Thus, the first major finding of this chapter concerns the differing impact of age and institutionalization on release patterns in maximum security and civil mental hospitals. This difference is consistent with orientations of the two types of hospitals—one being primarily concerned with security and social control and the other with providing treatment and care for those who need it.

The second major finding concerns one of the central themes of this study—the accuracy of the political prediction made by the Farview staff that the Dixon patients required maximum security care. In the preceding chapter the data presented did not support this contention since the Dixon patients were not inordinately disruptive at the transfer hospitals. The data analyzed here tend to confirm that conclusion. The psychiatrists at the various transfer hospitals released the majority of the Dixon class—65 percent of them—to the community. They did not agree with the Farview staff that the majority of the Dixon patients required institutionalized care and certainly not maximum security care. Moreover, they released the very patients the Farview staff was most likely to confine—the younger, less institutionalized subjects. If the psychiatrists at the civil hospitals are viewed as a validating sample, their decisions clearly do not support the decisions made at Farview.

8   The Dixon Patients in the Community

      The preceding chapters have been primarily concerned with the validity of the political predictions made by the Farview staff. We have examined the rate of assaultive behavior at Farview and the transfer hospitals and the frequency of release to the community and in each case found little or no support for the contention that the Dixon patients were dangerous. The next chapter will complete our examination of these political predictions by examining postrelease violence. In the present chapter, however, our attention will shift to the other major research question of this project, the success of the court's decision in protecting and enhancing the social rights of the Dixon patients.

      In the Dixon decision the court ordered the Commonwealth of Pennsylvania to transfer the Dixon patients to civil mental hospitals and then, unless the state could show cause for not doing so, to the community. This order was based on the fact that the Dixon patients had been unconstitutionally committed to Farview and therefore the state had no legal right to continue their confinement. While this is a rather clear-cut and logical decision from a legal perspective, and one that does protect and expand the civil rights of mental patients, it raises a number of questions when viewed from other perspectives.

One of these perspectives is the extent to which the court's order was consistent with social needs and rights of the Dixon patients. By social rights we are referring to an individual's ability to secure the basic necessities of life, such as food, shelter, financial stability, and, for the mentally ill, adequate medical treatment and the opportunity to live in an environment to which they can psychologically adjust. While the court order guaranteed the legal rights of the Dixon patients, it may not have been the best vehicle for securing social rights such as those just mentioned.

The Dixon patients had spent an average of fourteen years in maximum security confinement, additional time at the transfer hospital, and, in most cases, periods in institutions before the Dixon commitment. Given this history of institutionalization, it is quite possible that they had become so dependent on the regimented life at Farview that they were unable to cope with more open environments, especially the openness and freedom attached to community living. Nevertheless, the members of the class were to be transferred to more open civil hospitals and then, through the procedures stated in the court order,[1] were to be released to the community. If the end result of this order was to release to the community hundreds of men who could neither socially nor psychologically cope with the strains of living in noninstitutional settings, the constitutional victory of the Dixon patients would be Pyrrhic indeed.

The present chapter will analyze data which bear on the issue of the ability of the Dixon patients to adjust to community living. Their attitudes toward living in the community, their residential, occupational, and medical histories after release, their psychological adjustments and other variables will be analyzed to see if these long-term, criminally insane patients could in fact cope with the strains of living outside of institutions. Such an analysis should not only contribute to our knowledge about the community adjustment of long-term patients, it should also suggest guidelines for dealing with similar groups of mental patients released in the future.

THE PREFERENCES OF THE DIXON PATIENTS
We can begin by examining the opinions of the Dixon patients concerning the desirability of living in the community. The data presented in chapter 6 indicated that these patients preferred the

greater freedom of the transfer hospitals to the regimentation they experienced at Farview. We are now concerned with the location of community living along this continuum of desirability and with the advantages and disadvantages that the Dixon patients attach to noninstitutional living.

The data in table 8.1 make it quite clear that if the Dixon patients had a choice about where they would live, they would choose the community over either of the hospitals. Only 6.8 percent of all the patients interviewed stated they would rather live at Farview than in the community, while a slightly larger percentage, 12.4 percent, preferred the transfer hospital to the community. In both cases the overwhelming majority—92.3 percent in the Farview comparison and 87.2 percent in the transfer hospital comparison—preferred living at home. There were very

TABLE 8.1   Preference for Hospital vs. Community Living by Location of Subject

Preference	All Subjects Interviewed	Subjects Who Lived in Community
Farview vs. Community		
Farview	6.8%	2.8%
	(16)	(5)
Community	92.3	96.6
	(217)	(168)
Neither	0.9	0.6
	(2)	(1)
Total	100.0	100.0
	(235)	(174)
Civil Hospital vs. Community		
Transfer hospital	12.4	7.7
	(28)	(13)
Community	87.2	92.3
	(198)	(155)
Neither	0.4	. . .
	(1)	. . .
Total	100.0	100.0
	(227)	(168)

NOTE: This presentation is based on subject interview schedule questions 80 and 81 where the subjects were asked, "If you could choose to live at Farview or in the community, which would you choose?" Next, the hospital to which they were transferred was substituted for Farview in the question.

few Dixon patients who disagreed with the thrust of the court order, which was to release them to the community.

When the responses of only those patients who had been released to the community are examined, the preferences for community living are even more pronounced. Ninety-seven percent of these patients preferred the community to Farview and 92.3 percent preferred the community to the transfer hospital.

When asked what they liked most about living in the community, the most frequent response concerned the feeling of independence that came with noninstitutional living (table 8.2). Four percent of the subjects who responded to this open-ended question liked "everything" about community living and 74 percent indicated that freedom and independence were the most positive aspects of living at home. Their responses incorporated elements of both physical and mental freedom, that is, the ability to go where they wanted and to engage in the activities and hobbies of their choice, as well as the feeling of being free, of making their own decisions, and of being their "own boss." Related to this concern with freedom is the category of living conditions. Twenty-four percent of the respondents indicated that the ability to select their own life style—in such areas as food, clothing, privacy, and living arrangements—was what they liked most about community living. The other factors mentioned concerned better relationships with their families (13.3 percent) and others (16.9 percent) and their ability to work and have an income (9.7 percent). Only ten subjects (5.1 percent) indicated that there was nothing to like about living at home. The data for those subjects who actually resided in the community parallel the overall data quite closely. A slightly higher percentage (80.6 percent) of these subjects mentioned independence as the factor they liked most about the community.

The paramount issue in the minds of the Dixon patients in comparing Farview, the transfer hospital, and the communty was the amount of freedom and independence they had. They liked Farview, the most regimented milieu, the least, and they liked community living, the least regimented environment, the most. It is worth noting again that these questions were open-ended and the subjects were able to respond in whatever way they wished. Even with this flexibility, the responses to questions about the three environments were quite uniform. After spending long peri-

TABLE 8.2   Reasons Subjects Stated for Liking Community Living

Reason	All Subjects Interviewed			Subjects Who Lived in Community		
	Responses	% of Responses	% of Subjects[a]	Responses	% of Responses	% of Subjects[b]
Everything	8	2.8	4.1	7	2.8	4.2
Being independent	145	50.0	74.4	133	53.8	80.6
Living conditions	46	15.9	23.6	36	14.7	21.8
Better relations with family	26	9.0	13.3	20	8.1	12.1
Better relations with others	33	11.4	16.9	27	10.9	16.4
Work	19	6.6	9.7	13	5.3	7.9
Other	3	1.0	1.5	3	1.2	1.8
Nothing	0	3.3	5.1	8	3.2	4.8
Total	290	100.0		247	100.0	

[a]Number of subjects responding, 195. Percentages do not sum to 100 because subjects could give more than one response.
[b]Number of subjects responding, 165. Percentages do not sum to 100 because subjects could give more than one response.

ods in a maximum security environment, the Dixon patients preferred and valued their independence above all other factors. The court order, which facilitated their release to the community, was quite consistent with the interests of Dixon patients in this respect.

The overall enthusiasm of the Dixon patients for community living is also reflected in the data in table 8.3. In response to the question "What do you dislike most about living at home rather than at a hospital?" the majority of the subjects (68.5 percent) said there was nothing they disliked about living at home. Even with interviewer probing, two-thirds of the Dixon patients would not respond further to this question.[2]

This does not mean, however, that living at home was entirely without problems. Twelve percent disliked the added responsibilities, in such areas as self-care, household chores, and finances, that community living entailed, 9 percent complained of loneliness and boredom, 6 percent of poor relationships with others, and 5 percent of inadequate living conditions. The thrust of their negative comments seems to center on a feeling of isolation. The major disadvantages of living in the community were experienced when the protection of the hospital was withdrawn and the patients suffered the burdens of day-to-day responsibilities and loneliness.

TABLE 8.3   Reasons Subjects Stated for Disliking Community Living

Reason	All Subjects Interviewed			Subjects Who Lived in Community		
	Responses	% of Responses	% of Subjects[a]	Responses	% of Responses	% of Subjects[b]
Nothing	126	65.3	68.5	113	67.7	71.1
Too many responsibilities	22	11.4	11.6	18	10.7	11.3
Loneliness	17	8.8	9.2	12	7.2	7.5
Poor relations with others	12	6.2	6.5	11	6.6	6.9
Poor living conditions	9	4.7	4.9	7	4.2	4.4
Other	7	3.6	3.8	6	3.6	3.8
Total	193	100.0		167	100.0	

[a]Number of subjects responding, 184. Percentages do not sum to 100 because subjects could give more than one response.
[b]Number of subjects responding, 159. Percentages do not sum to 100 because subjects could give more than one response.

Again there are few differences between all subjects and those who had been released. If anything, those who had actually lived in the community reported fewer problems than the larger group.

Although these disadvantages do exist, the major conclusion is still that the Dixon patients preferred community living. The majority of the Dixon patients could find no disadvantages to living at home, and only a minority voiced any negative attitudes. Another indication of the subject's enthusiasm for living at home is the low level of multiple responses to the question of why they disliked living at home. The 184 subjects who responded to the question produced only 193 responses. Comparatively, the 195 subjects who responded to the question of why they liked living at home produced 290 responses. Thus, a minority of the Dixon patients disliked community living, and even for this minority, the problems tended to be specific and limited to one area of adjustment.

In addition to these general questions about community living, the Dixon patients were asked to indicate their preference for Farview, the transfer hospital, or the community in relation to a number of specific factors. The data are presented in table 8.4. In questions that concern physical living conditions it is clear that the Dixon patients preferred the community. Approximately 80

TABLE 8.4   Preference Ranking of Hospital and Community Living on Living Conditions and Treatment

Question	Community Preferred	Equal Preference	Community Not Preferred	Total
Is the food you eat better at Farview, the transfer hospital or home?	75.7% (162)	7.5% (16)	16.8% (36)	100.0% (214)
Are the living conditions better ...?	83.4 (176)	2.8 (6)	13.8 (29)	100.0 (211)
Is the psychiatric treatment better ...?	48.2 (69)	5.6 (8)	46.2 (66)	100.0 (143)
Is the medical treatment better ...?	67.5 (110)	8.6 (14)	23.9 (39)	100.0 (163)
Where do you see your family more often?	85.5 (159)	0.5 (1)	14.0 (26)	100.0 (186)

percent of the respondents preferred home to either of the hospitals in relation to the quality of food and general living conditions, as well as in relation to the frequency with which they saw their families. When asked about medical treatment, 67 percent thought they received better care in the community and another 9 percent thought the medical care received at home and the hospitals was about equal. In relation to psychiatric treatment, the Dixon patients are evenly split between the community and the hospitals. Forty-eight percent thought the psychiatric care better at home, 46 percent thought it better in the hospitals, and 6 percent viewed it as approximately equal.

Again we see an overall preference for living at home on the part of the Dixon patients. In terms of physical living conditions the members of the Dixon class clearly preferred the community, and in terms of the quality of medical treatment a majority of the subjects thought that the care they received at home was better than the care received in the hospital. Only when psychiatric treatment was discussed did a minority of the Dixon patients prefer the community, and in this instance their preferences were evenly divided. There is no evidence in these attitudinal data to suggest that the Dixon patients preferred to live in hospitals, nor did the data uncover any distinct advantages associated with hospital living.

ADJUSTING TO THE COMMUNITY: RESIDENTIAL STABILITY

It is clear from the preceding section that the Dixon patients preferred to live in the community, yet the central issue of this chapter—the *ability* of the Dixon patients to adjust to community living—remains unanswered. If the Dixon class members who were released exhibited poor social and psychological adjustment, regardless of their preference for community living, one could not conclude that the federal court protected and enhanced the social rights of the Dixon patients. The remainder of this chapter will focus on the issue of adjustment, beginning with an examination of the residential histories of the Dixon patients after release. The central issue here concerns the stability of their living arrangements. In light of their poor family backgrounds, low marriage rate, and the length of their confinement, we are especially concerned with the possibility that the Dixon patients became "homeless" transients, either with no family to return to or else rejected by existing families.

The data presented in tables 8.5 and 8.6 do not offer strong support for a finding of rootlessness, however. Between their release from the transfer hospital and the interview, the Dixon patients had spent an average of 28.6 months in the community, during which they had an average of 2.4 residences. Forty-three percent had only one residence after release and approximately two-thirds had 1 or 2 residences. The data in table 8.5 indicate that there was a small group of Dixon subjects who moved often— 8.2 percent had 6 or more residences—but by and large the number of different homes was small.

TABLE 8.5   Number of Residential Moves of the Dixon Patients

No. of Residences	Frequency	Subjects	Cumulative %
1	78	42.9%	42.9
2	40	22.0	64.9
3–5	49	26.9	91.8
6+	15	8.2	100.0
Total	182	100.0	
Mean	2.4		
SD	1.8		

Three-quarters of the Dixon patients who were interviewed indicated that they had relatives with whom they could live (table 8.6), a surprisingly high figure given their low marriage rate (29 percent ever married) and the length of their confinement at

TABLE 8.6 Frequency with Which Dixon Patients Lived with Relatives

Question	N	%
Did you have relatives to live with?		
No	41	24.8
Yes	124	75.2
If yes, did they ask you to live with them?		
No	30	24.2
Yes	94	75.8
If yes, did you live with them?		
No	14	14.9
Yes	80	85.1

Farview. Moreover, their families, by and large, did not abandon them. For those patients with families, 76 percent of the families asked the released patients to live with them, and virtually all of Dixon patients who received offers (85 percent), accepted them. The image of the Dixon patients as homeless men with no families to return to is simply not borne out by these data. Indeed, when all the released patients, not just those with a family are considered, half of the Dixon patients (51.9 percent) lived with a family member after their release from the transfer hospital (see table 8.7).

TABLE 8.7 Living Arrangements of Dixon Patients for First Three Residences after Release

Patient Lived With	First Residence	Second Residence	Third Residence
Parents	29.0%	5.9%	12.3%
	(52)	(6)	(7)
Other family	22.9	12.8	17.5
	(41)	(13)	(10)
Friends	2.8	8.9	3.5
	(5)	(9)	(2)
Self	26.8	33.7	31.6
	(48)	(34)	(18)
Institution	12.3	32.8	29.8
	(22)	(33)	(17)
Other	6.1	5.9	5.3
	(11)	(6)	(3)
Total	100.0	100.0	100.0
	(179)	(101)	(57)

The data in tables 8.7 to 8.9 display the residential histories of the Dixon patients through their first three homes after release from the transfer hospital. Immediately after release the patients were most likely to have lived with their parents, other family members, or by themselves, but for the second and third homes this pattern changed considerably. The proportion living with their families decreased, the likelihood of their living alone increased slightly, and the likelihood of living in an institution increased sharply—from 12.3 percent for the first residence to approximately 30 percent for the next two. The latter increase was due both to rearrest and rehospitalization.

TABLE 8.8   Type of Residence for First Three Residences

Residence	First Residence	Second Residence	Third Residence
House or Apartment	60.1%	42.0%	50.0%
	(107)	(42)	(29)
Boarding house	21.9	13.0	12.1
	(39)	(13)	(7)
Institution	6.6	29.0	29.3
	(12)	(29)	(17)
Other	11.2	16.0	8.6
	(20)	(16)	(5)
Total	100.0	100.0	100.0
	(178)	(100)	(58)

At all three periods the Dixon patients were most likely to live in a house or apartment (table 8.8), and the fear that the Dixon patients would be forced to live in dingy boarding houses was not realized. Only a fifth of the Dixon subjects resided in a boarding house for their first residence, and this rate declined to 12.1 percent by the third residence. As would be expected, the rate of institutional living increased from the first to the third period.

The reasons the Dixon patients gave for moving from one residence to another are presented in table 8.9. As an indication of their residential stability, we note that the proportion of patients who did not move remains consistently high for each of the three residences—43.5 percent for the first, 38.2 percent for the second, and 40.7 percent for the third. Nonproblematic reasons for moving, for example, finding a nicer apartment, decreased, as did the problematic reasons of having difficulty relating to others, while

TABLE 8.9   Reasons Patients Left Residence

Reasons for Leaving	First Residence	Second Residence	Third Residence
Never left	43.5% (73)	38.2% (34)	40.7% (22)
Nonproblematic	16.7 (28)	12.4 (11)	13.0 (7)
Difficulty with others	13.1 (22)	9.0 (8)	9.3 (5)
Arrest/rehospitaliza- tion	12.5 (21)	12.4 (11)	13.0 (7)
Other	14.3 (24)	28.0 (25)	24.1 (13)
Total	100.0 (168)	100.0 (89)	100.0 (54)

being rearrested or rehospitalized remained constant across the three periods. The only category that did increase is the one labeled "other," and this was primarily due to the inclusion of institutional transfers in this category.

Finally, we can examine the interaction of the two most important variables in this triumvirate—living arrangements and reasons for leaving the residence—to see if some living arrangements were more likely than others to lead to problematic reasons for leaving. The appropriate data are presented in tables 8.10 and 8.11.[3] Because low frequencies occur in some of the categories,

TABLE 8.10   Living Arrangements by Reason for Leaving First Residence

	Patient Lived With		
Reason for Leaving	Family	Self	Other
Nonproblematic[a]	59.3% (54)	61.7% (29)	58.6% (17)
Arrest/rehospitalization	17.6 (16)	8.5 (4)	3.4 (1)
Other problematic	23.1 (21)	29.8 (14)	37.9 (11)
Total	100.0 (91)	100.0 (47)	100.0 (29)

NOTE: $\chi^2 = 6.27$; $df = 4$; $p < .17$.

[a]Includes those patients who did not leave.

several categories had to be collapsed for this analysis. For the variable of living arrangements, the categories of living with parents and other family members have been combined; for the reason for leaving, those who never left and those who left for nonproblematic reasons are combined on the premise that neither indicates unfavorable social adjustment.

TABLE 8.11   Living Arrangements by Reason for Leaving Second Residence

Reason for Leaving	Patient Lived With		
	Family	Self	Other
Nonproblematic[a]	44.4%	52.9%	52.8%
	(8)	(18)	(19)
Arrest/rehospitalization	22.2	11.8	5.6
	(4)	(4)	(2)
Other problematic	33.3	35.3	41.7
	(6)	(12)	(15)
Total	100.0	100.0	100.0
	(18)	(34)	(36)

NOTE: $\chi^2 = 3.43$; $df = 4$; $p < .48$.

[a]Includes those patients who did not leave.

Overall there is no significant relationship between type of residence and reason for leaving, as the chi-square statistics indicate, for either the first or second residence of the patients. Whether the Dixon subjects lived with their families, by themselves, or in other settings had little impact on whether they left their homes for problematic or nonproblematic reasons. Examining the first residence we see that 59.3 percent of those who lived with their families either did not leave or left for nonproblematic reasons, as did 61.7 percent of those who lived alone and 58.6 percent of those who had other living arrangements. Although there were few differences between problematic and nonproblematic reasons, differences did emerge between the two problematic factors. Patients who lived with their families were more likely to leave because of rearrest or rehospitalization (17.6 percent), while patients who lived alone or in other situations were more likely to leave for other problematic reasons (29.8 percent and 37.9 percent respectively). Since the latter category includes such factors as "difficulty in relating to others," "financial problems," and the like, it should be considered indicative of less serious social maladjustment than rearrest or rehospitalization. Thus, the most serious difficulties occurred in cases in which the patient lived with his family.

The same pattern exists when the second residence is examined (table 8.11). The overall relationship is not significant and for each of the three types of living arrangements nonproblematic reasons for leaving are the most frequent. Again we see that those who lived with their families had higher rearrest and rehospitalization rates than those who lived alone or in other situations.

These data are consistent with the others concerning the general stability of the residential histories of the Dixon patients following release. Although these patients lived in a variety of circumstances, no one circumstance was exceptionally likely to lead to social maladjustment as measured by the reasons for leaving a residence. The general relationship between these two variables was found to be statistically nonsignificant. Nevertheless, those who lived with their families were somewhat more likely to be rearrested or rehospitalized. This finding suggests that one focus for the aftercare of the released criminally insane should be on the pressures that are placed on a patient when he returns to his family. [4]

EMPLOYMENT AND UNEMPLOYMENT

The next issue to be discussed concerns the occupational careers of the Dixon patients following their release from the transfer hospitals. As the data in table 8.12 indicate, these careers were not very extensive. Slightly more than half of the subjects who had been released to the community (56.6 percent) [5] never looked for work, and a similar percentage, 55.6 percent, never held a job after their release. Of those subjects who were in the community at the time of the interview, only 28.2 percent were actually working, which means that the unemployment rate of the released Dixon patients was 71.8 percent.

TABLE 8.12   Employment History of Released Dixon Patients

Question	Yes	No	Total
Did subject look for work?	43.4%	56.6%	100.0%
	(76)	(99)	(175)
Did subject ever work?	44.4	55.6	100.0
	(80)	(100)	(180)
Was subject employed at time of interview?	28.2	71.8	100.0
	(37)	(94)	(131)

One explanation for this exceptionally high rate of unemployment is the fact that Dixon patients were quite old at the time of their release. It is possible that the high rate of unemployment is attributable to the oldest patients, with the younger patients having employment careers that are closer to those of the general population. Table 8.13 presents data on employment patterns for those patients who were above and below the median age at the time of the interview. Although the older patients had lower rates of employment than did the younger ones, it is clear that age does not account for the poor employment histories of the Dixon patients. Among the younger patients, 48.3 percent never looked for work, 47.8 percent never worked, and 67.7 percent were not working at the time of the interview. These rates represent only a slight improvement over the general rates presented in table 8.12. Regardless of age, the Dixon patients who were released to the community had an exceptionally high rate of unemployment.

TABLE 8.13   Employment History of Released Dixon Patients by Age at Interview

	Interview Age			
	≤46		47+	
Question	Yes	No	Yes	No
Did subject look for work?	51.7% (45)	48.3% (42)	35.2% (31)	64.8% (57)
Did subject ever work?	52.2 (47)	47.8 (43)	36.7 (33)	63.3 (57)
Was subject employed at time of interview?	33.3 (21)	67.7 (42)	23.5 (16)	76.5 (52)

Moreover, the data available for those who did work indicate that the types of jobs they held were rather menial (see table 8.14). Subjects employed at the time of the interview worked an average of thirty-six hours a week, receiving a weekly take-home pay of $68.79, which indicates that on the average, the Dixon patients worked for $1.90 per hour. For those subjects who were unemployed at the time of the interview, data on the last job they held were collected. These patients worked an average of thirty-three hours, received $51.00 per week in take-home pay, for an hourly wage of $1.55. Combining the two income figures in table 8.14, the average weekly income is $63.76 and the average annual salary is $3,315.64.

In addition to employment and income data, information on why subjects did not look for work and, for those who did, the

TABLE 8.14   Occupational Data for Patients Who Worked after Release

	Mean	SD	N
Currently employed			
Hours worked per week	35.91	12.97	34
Weekly take-home salary	$68.79	$39.42	33
Last job of those currently unemployed			
Hours worked per week	32.83	16.90	12
Weekly take-home pay	$51.00	$37.73	13

problems encountered was also collected. For the 56 percent of the Dixon patients who never looked for work after their release from the hospital, the reasons why they did not are presented in table 8.15. One-fifth of the subjects already had a job arranged before their release and did not have to search for one. Among the other subjects, the most common reason given was that of illness—39.8 percent of the reasons and 45.7 percent of the subjects. Within this category, only two patients specified that the problem was related to mental illness, twenty specified physical illness, while the remaining twenty-one only indicated that they did not look for work because of a "disability." In addition to illness, 17 percent of the patients did not look for work because they thought they were too old or too poorly educated or because there were too few jobs. Twelve percent said they had other incomes, 7.4 percent did not want to work, 5.3 percent received no help in searching for a job, and 7.4 percent mentioned other reasons.

Those subjects who had looked for work were presented with a

TABLE 8.15   Reasons for not Looking for Job after Release

Reason	No. of Responses	% of Responses	% of Respondents[b]
Had a job	19	17.6	20.2
Illness	43	39.8	45.7
Negative beliefs[a]	16	14.8	17.0
Had other income	11	10.2	11.7
Did not want to work	7	6.5	7.4
No help in looking	5	4.6	5.3
Other	7	6.5	7.4
Total[c]	108	100.0	

[a]Includes beliefs on the part of the subjects that they were too old, too poorly educated, and that there were no jobs available.

[b]Percentages do not sum to 100 because the subjects could give more than one response.

[c]Number of subjects responding, 94.

list of employment problems and asked if they encountered any in looking for or in keeping a job. These problems are presented in table 8.16, arranged according to the frequency with which they occurred. The most common problem was that they did not receive any help in looking for a job (76.3 percent) and, relatedly, 43.7 percent indicated that employment offices did not provide enough help. Other frequently mentioned problems were that employers did not like their previous record (59.1 percent), the subject had not yet found the right job (58.9 percent), the belief that there were not many jobs available (47.2 percent), and the belief that the subject lacked the training necessary to get a job (41.9 percent). On the other hand, problems relating to illness were not so commonly mentioned. Twenty-three percent said they were too nervous, 18.9 percent said they had not felt well, and 10.7 percent said that jobs were too tiring.

When the data in tables 8.15 and 8.16 are examined in combination, one sees that many of the problems mentioned by the Dixon subjects are ones that could be dealt with by professional employment counselors. In addition to not receiving help in looking for a job in the first place, these problems include feeling too old or too poorly educated, believing that there are too few jobs available, that one has not found the right job, or that employers will not even consider ex-mental patients. All of these problems are of a type that could be ameliorated, and in some cases solved, by professional intervention, through counseling, job training, and intervention with potential employers. Yet 76.3 percent of the Dixon patients indicated they did not receive help in looking for a job and only 11.6 percent received employment services from a public agency. It seems clear that the aftercare services provided to the Dixon patients with respect to employment were woefully inadequate. They did not receive the help they should have in searching for and keeping jobs, yet they encountered many problems in this area that are amenable to professional intervention.

The postrelease employment histories of the Dixon patients indicate rather poor social adjustment. There is an exceptionally high unemployment rate, many subjects never looked for work, and those who were employed received minimum wages. For these reasons, as well as the problems the subjects encountered in seeking employment, it would seem that employment counseling

TABLE 8.16   Problems Subject Encountered on Looking for or in Keeping a Job

Problem	Yes	No
No one to help	76.3%	23.7%
	(58)	(18)
Employers didn't like subject's record	59.1	40.9
	(39)	(27)
Didn't find right job	58.9	41.1
	(43)	(30)
There aren't many jobs	47.2	52.7
	(35)	(39)
Employment offices didn't help	43.7	56.3
	(31)	(40)
Didn't have training	41.9	58.1
	(31)	(43)
Trouble getting transportation to and from work	30.0	70.0
	(21)	(49)
Didn't look very hard	24.3	75.7
	(18)	(56)
Too nervous	22.7	77.3
	(17)	(58)
Didn't feel well	18.9	81.1
	(14)	(60)
People at work gave subject a hard time	18.5	81.5
	(12)	(53)
Too tiring	10.7	89.4
	(7)	(59)
Didn't need money	8.1	91.9
	(6)	(68)
Went back to school	7.9	92.1
	(6)	(70)
Welfare paid too well	6.8	93.2
	(5)	(69)

for the released Dixon patients should have been provided. It also seems clear that such counseling should be provided as a routine part of aftercare services for criminally insane patients released in the future.

TREATMENT AND REHOSPITALIZATION

In addition to being interviewed about residential and occupational histories, the Dixon patients were asked about the post-release psychological counseling they had received. As an additional measure of adjustment the frequency with which they were rehospitalized and the factors that led to readmission were collected from hospital records.

Forty-nine, or 28.5 percent of the Dixon patients indicated that they had received no treatment in the community, while 71.5 percent indicated that they had (table 8.17). Of those who had received counseling, approximately half (52.0 percent) received only one type, 30.4 percent received two types, and 17.6 percent received three or four types. The data in table 8.18 indicated the four types of counselors that the Dixon patients could have seen and the frequency with which each was seen. Almost half of the patients (49.4 percent) saw social workers at one time or another while 38.8 percent saw psychiatrists. These two types of counselors account for the bulk of the treatment services provided to the Dixon patients. The other two—psychologists and other counselors (including ministers, psychiatric nurses, and so forth)—were infrequently utilized by these patients. Only 16.6 percent of the released patients saw a psychologist and 14.4 percent saw other counselors.

TABLE 8.17   Frequency of Treatment in the Community

	N	%
Received treatment		
No	49	28.5
Yes	125	71.5
Total	174	100.0
If yes, number of types of treatment received[a]		
1	65	52.0
2	38	30.4
3	20	16.0
4	2	1.6
Total	125	100.0

[a]The types of treatment included individual therapy, group therapy, electroshock, and drugs. The number receiving each is indicated in table 8.20.

The preceding data on types of counselors seen include all the released Dixon patients in the base. Table 8.19 presents the same information for those Dixon patients who had received some form of treatment at the time of the interview. The pattern of results for these groups is identical to that in table 8.18, although the absolute values of the percentages change, as would be expected. The most frequently used counselor was still the social worker, with 70.1 percent of those ever in treatment and 37.9 percent of those currently in treatment indicating that they received social work assistance. Psychiatrists were the next most frequently

TABLE 8.18   Types of Counselors Who Furnished Treatment

Type of Counselors Seen	Released Subjects		Total
	Yes	No	
Psychiatrist	38.8%	61.2%	100.0%
	(64)	(101)	(165)
Psychologist	16.6	83.4	100.0
	(26)	(131)	(157)
Social worker	49.4	50.6	100.0
	(82)	(84)	(166)
Other	14.4	85.6	100.0
	(20)	(119)	(139)

utilized type, 55.2 percent and 33.3 percent of the respective groups responding in the affirmative to this question. Again we see that psychologists and other counselors were infrequently used by the Dixon patients as sources for treatment.

TABLE 8.19   Types of Counselors Seen by Dixon Subjects Ever in Treatment and Currently in Treatment

Type of Counselors Seen	Subjects Who Had Ever Received Treatment		Subjects Currently Receiving Treatment[a]	
	Yes	No	Yes	No
Psychiatrist	55.2%	44.8%	33.3%	66.7%
	(52)	(64)	(29)	(58)
Psychologist	24.1	75.9	12.6	87.4
	(26)	(82)	(11)	(76)
Social worker	70.1	29.9	37.9	62.1
	(82)	(35)	(33)	(54)
Other	21.7	78.3	19.5	80.5
	(20)	(72)	(17)	(70)

[a]This question was only asked if the subject was in the community at the time of the interview.

The setting in which the treatment was administered was most likely to be in the public sector, as we would expect given the economic situation of the released patients. Approximately one-fifth of the patients saw counselors in private practice, while 68 percent of the patients saw counselors in community mental health centers and 40 percent saw counselors in hospital clinics.

The types of treatment that the Dixon patients received in the community are displayed in table 8.20. As during their stay at

TABLE 8.20   Types of Treatment Received in Community

Types of Treatment	Treatment Received	
	Yes	No
Individual therapy	23.5%	76.5%
	(28)	(91)
Group therapy	16.8	83.2
	(20)	(99)
Electroshock	1.7	98.3
	(2)	(117)
Drugs	79.8	20.2
	(95)	(24)

Farview, the Dixon patients were most likely to be treated psycho-pharmacologically. Eighty percent of the subjects indicated that they had used prescribed drugs since their release. The more social-psychological forms of treatment were used less frequently —23.5 percent had individual therapy and 16.8 percent had group therapy. As would be expected given the time of the study— the early 1970s—very few patients, two in fact, report having received electroshock therapy.

In general, the picture that emerges about the quality of the aftercare treatment received by the Dixon patients is somewhat uneven. Although the majority of released Dixon patients received some form of treatment in the community, a sizable minority, 28.5 percent, received no treatment at all. Moreover, the Dixon patients were more likely to see social workers than psychiatrists or psychologists, the treatment was more likely to occur in the public than private sector, and the type of treatment was more likely to involve the use of drugs than either individual or group therapy.

The rehospitalization data that were collected indicated that, 58, or 15.7 percent of the 368 patients who were discharged from the civil hospitals, were rehospitalized during the follow-up period. The average number of rehospitalizations per patient was only slightly more than one, since the 58 patients accounted for a total of 72 readmissions. This rehospitalization rate compares quite favorably to the rate for "typical" mental patients during a one-year follow-up, where 37.4 percent of the patients were rehospitalized at least once (Michaux et al. 1969, p. 68).[6]

The reasons for readmission that were recorded in the hospital files are as follows: 24 percent were rehospitalized for violent behavior, 43 percent for exhibiting psychopathological symptoms, and 33 percent for unknown reasons. This rather large unknown category is primarily due to rehospitalizations that were based on the continuation or reoccurence of prior symptoms and, as such, most of these cases involve psychopathological symptoms.

Thus the rate of rehospitalization was relatively low when compared to noncriminal mental patients and the reasons for readmission indicate that mental illness, not violent behavior, was the primary factor leading to further periods of institutionalization. If the avoidance of rehospitalization is an indication of the ability to adjust to community living, it is clear that the majority of the Dixon patients were capable of such adjustment.

SOCIAL SERVICES IN THE COMMUNITY

In addition to psychological treatment, a complete aftercare program would also provide social services for these patients in basic day-to-day activities. After spending fourteen years in confinement, the Dixon patients might have been expected to need assistance in such areas as seeking housing, employment, and medical care. To see how much assistance the Dixon patients actually received they were asked if anyone helped them to find a place to live; find a job; apply for welfare, social security, or veteran's benefits; receive psychiatric treatment; receive medical treatment; or receive any other kind of help. Their responses are reflected in table 8.21.

By and large the amount of assistance the Dixon patients received, especially from public agencies, was quite low. This is especially true in the areas of finding employment and receiving psychiatric treatment and medical care. Three-quarters of the Dixon patients did not receive help in the employment and psychiatric treatment areas, and 60.7 percent did not receive assistance in finding medical care. In these areas the majority of the released Dixon patients were left to fend for themselves. Only in the areas of finding a home and receiving welfare, social security, or veteran's benefits did a majority of the Dixon patients receive assistance. And even in these areas the proportion of Dixon subjects not receiving assistance is sizable—36.0 percent for home and 46.7 percent for welfare.

TABLE 8.21   Assistance Received in Various Areas After Release to the Community

| Assistance in Gaining | No | Yes | | | Total |
		Private	Public	Unspecified	
Home	36.0%	34.3%	29.7%	...	100.0%
	(62)	(59)	(51)	...	(172)
Job	76.2	11.0	11.6	1.2	100.0
	(131)	(19)	(20)	(2)	(172)
Welfare	46.7	21.9	29.0	2.4	100.0
	(79)	(37)	(49)	(4)	(169)
Psychiatric treatment	73.8	4.9	20.1	1.2	100.0
	(121)	(8)	(33)	(2)	(164)
Medical care	60.7	11.9	25.6	1.8	100.0
	(102)	(20)	(43)	(3)	(168)
Other	88.2	5.9	5.2	0.7	100.0
	(135)	(9)	(8)	(1)	(153)

When the column labeled "Yes, public" is examined, it is evident that the public agencies have not been providing social services to sizable numbers of the Dixon patients. In none of these areas did the public agencies provide support for as many as 30 percent of the Dixon subjects. Even in the area of finding a home, the area in which the Dixon patients received the most help, the majority of the help came from private sources, mainly friends and relatives. The area in which the Dixon patients received the least assistance is that of employment. Only 11.6 percent of the Dixon patients received help from a public agency in this area, and, as we have already seen, this is the area in which the social adjustment of the Dixon patients was weakest.

Overall, one cannot be satisfied with the social service assistance that the Dixon patients received after they left the transfer hospitals. The finding that fewer than 30 percent of the patients report receiving assistance from public agencies in securing such basic necessities as a home, job, and medical treatment indicates that a firm policy of providing extensive aftercare to these patients was not implemented. Since the Dixon patients were mentally ill recidivists who had spent many years in confinement and who had been released from confinement by court order, the court could have anticipated their special needs by providing aftercare services in order to maximize the likelihood of a successful outcome. No stipulation about aftercare was made in the court order and, as the above data indicate, the regular social service procedures of the mental health system provided services for only a minority of the Dixon patients.

Similarly, court actions like the Dixon decision ought to make psychological treatment readily available for patients after release. Although the majority of the Dixon patients received some counseling after release, a sizable minority, 28.5 percent did not. Moreover, the patients were more likely to be counseled by social workers than psychiatrists and clinical psychologists, and the most common type of treatment was the administration of drugs.

We contend that a court which releases patients to protect their constitutional rights should also protect their social rights. One method of doing this would be by affirmatively providing for aftercare services of both treatment and social service varieties. Better aftercare would help to ease the difficulties that are associated with moving from institutional living to the freedom of the community. It should also help to reduce the probability that the securing of the constitutional rights of the criminally insane would exacerbate their problems in other areas which in turn might lead to behavioral problems and future confinement. Releasing patients from unconstitutional confinement is not enough. Providing services that will insure their continued freedom is also necessary.

SOCIAL AND PSYCHOLOGICAL ADJUSTMENT

The last issue to be discussed in this chapter concerns adjustment of the Dixon patients as measured by the Katz Adjustment Scale (Katz and Lyerly 1963). This scale, the KAS, measures behavioral and attitudinal adjustment in relation to psychological variables, such as psychopathological symptoms, as well as social variables, such as the ability to interact with others. The KAS is composed of twenty-two subscales measuring adjustment in the following areas: *clinical adjustment*, that is, freedom from symptoms of psychopathology; *the level of functioning* in the behavioral areas of day-to-day social activities and free-time activities; and, *attitudes* toward the level of expectation about and satisfaction with both social and free-time activities. The actual content of the KAS subscales will be discussed in more detail in the data analysis which follows.

In the chapter on methodology a number of advantages associated with the use of the KAS were enumerated. In brief they suggest that the measure of adjustment being employed contains a number of subscales measuring different aspects of adjustment, collects data from both the subject and a respondent, has demonstrated validity and reliability, and is geared to a population with a low educational level. For these reasons it seemed quite suited to our purposes and was therefore included in the interview schedule.[7]

Although the interviews with the Dixon patients provided data on their adjustment, we are left with an interpretative problem; do the scores exhibited by the Dixon subjects indicate adequate or inadequate social adjustment? To facilitate the interpretation of these data, we will compare the scores of the Dixon patients with the scores of subjects from three other studies.

In the first of these studies Hogarty and Katz (1971) collected data on the social and psychological adjustment of a "normal population," through the use of the KAS informant scales. "The non-patient or 'normal' population of 450 subjects was drawn from a 3% systematic sample of households in Carroll County, Md." one of the counties in the metropolitan Baltimore area (Hogarty and Katz 1971, p. 471). The subjects were adults, fifteen years of age or older, who had no history of psychiatric illness. Once a subject was selected for the sample, a relative completed the KAS respondent interview, reporting on the subject's behavior during the three weeks prior to the interview. Although we would not expect the adjustment scores of the Dixon patients to be as positive as the scores of a normal population, the existence of these normative data allows us to standardize the comparisons that will be made among the mentally ill samples.

The Dixon patients will be compared to two samples of "typical" mental patients who had been hospitalized in civil mental hospitals for comparatively brief periods of time. In these comparisons there is no need to assume at the outset that the Dixon patients will exhibit poorer adjustment. Indeed, our hypothesis is that the KAS scores will be approximately equal for the various mental patient groups. Failure to reject this null hypothesis would suggest that long-term confinement of criminally insane patients such as the Dixon patients cannot be justified on the basis of their poor community adjustment prospects. If the Dixon patients can adjust to community living with as much facility as civil mental patients confined for short periods of time in regular mental hospitals, the confinement of the criminally insane in special maximum security hospitals for extended periods of time can be viewed as excessive and unnecessary. Whether this hypothesis of no difference is supported or not, the issue of adjustment is only one of many that needs to be considered in suggesting policies for the future treatment of the criminally insane. Because of these other issues, we will only evaluate the evidence bearing on adjustment in the present chapter and return to the more general issue of interpreting the results in terms of future policy decision in the final chapter.

The first group of typical mental patients was analyzed in a study designed to investigate the "in-community clinical and social adjustment manifested by typical ex-patients of a state mental hospital" (Michaux et al. 1969, p.2). The hospital studied by Michaux and his colleagues was Spring Grove State Hospital in Maryland, which "is a large, long-established, moderately progressive public mental institution. . . . It continually admits all kinds of adult psychiatric patients except mental defectives and convicted criminals" (Michaux et al. 1969, p. 4). The sample of patients who were studied had all left Spring Grove "with medical sanction, were considered to have a reasonable chance of remaining out for at least a year, and were free to resume ordinary home and community living without major clinical or legal restrictions" (Michaux et al. 1969, p. 7). Moreover, for their last hospitalization, the one that led to their inclusion in the Michaux study, the median duration of their confinement had been 2.4 months.

Clearly this was quite a different situation from the one in which the Dixon patients found themselves. Farview could not be typified as even a moderately progressive hospital. It did not admit "all kinds of adult psychiatric patients," but was specifically designed to handle disruptive patients, especially the criminally insane. Moreover, the Dixon patients did not leave with medical sanction, the outlook for their success was dim, and they had been confined for fourteen years, not two months.

Although vast differences exist between the two settings, the subjects in the two studies are not markedly different on a number of personal characteristics. Table 8.22 presents data on the background variables that are found in both studies. Both groups are middle-aged, the mean age being forty-one for Spring Grove and

TABLE 8.22   Characteristics of Spring Grove and Dixon Patients

Variable	Spring Grove[a]	Dixon[b]
Mean age, yr	41.1	47.1
Average highest grade of school completed	10.4	6.7
% ever married	82.7	29.0
Mean number of previous hospitalizations	1.4	0.9
% diagnosed as schizophrenic	54.7	64.5

[a]These data are taken from Michaux et al. (1969), pp. 34–35, table 11.1. The number of subjects for all these statistics is 139.

[b]The number of subjects for these statistics are 524 for highest school grade, 573 for diagnosis, and 586 for the other variables.

forty-seven for Dixon, and neither was well educated, the average Dixon subject did not quite finish grade school while the typical Spring Grove subject had started but did not complete high school. Both groups had previous histories of hospitalization, albeit not extensive ones since the average patient had one previous hospitalization, and the majority of both groups were diagnosed as schizophrenic, 55 percent of the Spring Grove group and 64 percent of the Dixon group being so classified. Thus far the two groups are quite comparable.

The major difference between the two samples concerns the variables of marital status, sex, and race. The vast majority of the Spring Grove sample (83 percent) had been married while only 29 percent of Dixon patients had ever married. In relation to sex 68 percent of the patients in the Michaux study were female, while all of the Dixon patients were male, because Farview does not admit women. While this latter difference might invalidate the comparisons, since Michaux et al. do not present data divided by sex, we can report that Michaux and his colleagues found that in their own data "as well as in considerable earlier work which was known to [them], sex differences on the KAS are negligible" (1969, p. 31).[8] For the variable of race, Michaux et al. only studied white subjects, while 40 percent of the Dixon sample were black. To control for the effect of this racial difference, we will compare the KAS scores of all Spring Grove subjects with those of the white Dixon patients.

In addition, we should note that the Spring Grove interviews were conducted one month after release from the hospital, while for the Dixon patients the time interval between release and interview varied considerably—from one to sixty months. Although adjustment scores for the Spring Grove patients taken a year after release could have been used, we decided to use the first month's scores for three reasons. First, although there was a trend toward improvement in the Spring Grove scores during the first year after release, the absolute values of the scores were not greatly different and the results of our comparisons would be substantially the same using the first month's or the twelfth month's scores. Second, given that similarity, we opted for the first month's scores because they were based on a larger sample, 139 versus 51 subjects, which was more representative of the Spring Grove population. Finally, the Spring Grove subjects interviewed at month 12 had already responded to the KAS items eleven times—once each month—and there was no way of estimating the effect of this test/retest situation in comparison with the Dixon patients, who only responded once to the KAS items.

Thus the major difference between the Spring Grove and Dixon samples concern marital status, sex, race, and length of time in the community. When possible we will statistically control for these differences. In addition, we can note that most of these differences do not exist for comparisons between the Dixon patients and the second comparison group, which serves to reduce further the overall problem of assessing the effect of these differences on the comparisons between the Dixon patients and other mental patients.

The second group of mental patients was studied by the National Institute of Mental Health Psychopharmacology Service Center Collaborative Study Group (NIMH 1964). This was a nine-hospital collaborative study of the effectiveness of phenothiazine drugs in the treatment of acute schizophrenia. The hospitals were located in eight states and the 344 subjects were all newly admitted schizophrenic patients between the ages of sixteen and forty-five, who had no significant hospitalization during the twelve months prior to admission and who met certain clinical criteria (see NIMH 1964, pp. 247–48). Although both males and females were studied, only data relating to the males will be presented here since the Dixon class was composed solely of males.

Table 8.23 presents a comparison of the schizophrenics and Dixon patients for background variables that were measured in both studies. In general the two groups are similar in terms of marital history, previous hospitalizations, and race. The major

TABLE 8.23   Characteristics of Schizophrenics and Dixon Patients

Variable	Schizophrenics[a]	Dixon Patients
Mean age, yr	26.8	47.1
% ever married	32.1	29.0
% schizophrenic	100.0	64.5
% of patients with first hospital admissions	58.1	56.7
% white	77.0	60.0

[a]These data are taken from NIMH (1964), p. 249, table 4, with the exception of the data for race, which were calculated from material presented in the text (NIMH 1964, p. 247).

differences occur for age—the schizophrenics being younger—and, of course, for diagnosis. These differences can be controlled, however, by looking at appropriate subsets of the Dixon patients and should not, therefore, seriously affect the results.

The KAS data for the schizophrenic subjects were collected for those patients who had been discharged from the hospital and were residing in the community twelve months after the discharge (Schooler et al. 1967, p. 987). Thus, patients who were discharged, rehospitalized, and not discharged again were excluded from the analysis. In all, 299 patients were discharged and 254, or 85 percent, were in the community at the time of the data collection. KAS data are available for ninety-two males, and this is the group that will be analyzed here.[9]

In sum, the comparative situation that exists is one in which we can compare the psychological and social adjustment of the Dixon patients to two other groups of mental patients, and in all three cases standardize the results on the basis of data collected from a normal population. The three mental patient groups exhibit a fair degree of similarity on most background variables, and in cases in which the groups do differ, the effect of the difference can be controlled by looking at relevant subgroups of the Dixon patients.[10] Although the groups of patients are relatively similar in terms of background variables, the major difference among them is that the Dixon patients were confined for long periods of time in a maximum security hospital, while the other groups were hospitalized for brief periods in civil mental hospitals. This is precisely the type of comparison that is required since we are interested in seeing if the Dixon patients can adjust to community living as well as "typical mental patients."

GENERAL KAS COMPARISONS

We can begin the analysis of the KAS data by comparing the mean scores of all the Dixon subjects who were interviewed with the mean scores of the subjects from the other three samples for each of the twenty-two scales of the KAS. It should be noted at the outset that the inclusion of all the Dixon subjects in the data base biases the comparisons in a direction that favors rejection of the null hypothesis. The schizophrenic and Spring Grove samples only included patients who were well enough to be discharged and remain in the community while the total Dixon group included subjects who were never discharged or who were discharged and then rehospitalized. Logically one would expect these Dixon patients to be less well adjusted than the more selective samples in the comparison groups. Nevertheless, all the Dixon subjects are included in this first analysis so that an overall picture of their adjustment can be presented.

The basic data are displayed in table 8.24 and figure 8.1. In both cases *lower scores* are indicative of *more favorable adjustment*. A number of general statements can be made about these data. First, in terms of absolute values the mean scores for the four samples are rather tightly clustered. Overall, no substantial differences exist among the groups and the pattern of change from one scale to the next is quite uniform for the four samples, as figure 8.1 indicates. Nevertheless, within the rather tight clustering of the data, a number of rather consistent differences are evident.

In line with the previous literature, the normal, nonpatient sample had the lowest, that is, the most favorable scores, of the four groups. In only two of the fifty-one possible comparisons did a patient population have lower average score than the normal group—the schizophrenics having a lower average score for the scales dealing with the level of free-time activity and satisfaction with free-time activity. Otherwise the normal subjects exhibited better adjustment than the patient subjects.

Although all three patient groups exhibited poorer adjustment than the normal population, a major distinction appears within the patient grouping. The mean scores for the schizophrenic and Spring Grove samples are lower than the means for the Dixon patients and, when compared with one another, are remarkably

TABLE 8.24 Mean KAS Scores for Various Samples

KAS Scales	Symbol	Range[a] (Best–Worst)	Normal Population[b] (Mean)	Schizo-phrenics[c] (Mean)	Spring Grove[d] (Mean)	All Dixon Subjects (Mean)	N[e]
Patient scales							
Symptom discomfort	Sym	0–165	...[f]	20.4	20.1	20.3	242
Level of performance of socially expected behavior	SEA-P	16–48	...	32.2	29.0	31.8	102
Level of expectations of socially expected behavior	LOE-P	16–48	...	30.2	27.7	30.7	99
Level of free-time activities	FTA-P	22–66	...	41.6	48.0	51.5	101
Satisfaction with free-time activities	SFA-P	22–66	...	27.3	30.1	28.2	84
Informant scales: symptoms							
Belligerence	Bel	4–16	4.6	4.7	4.6	5.3	209
Verbal expansiveness	Exp	5–20	5.9	6.4	6.3	6.9	206
Negativism	Neg	9–36	11.5	14.3	12.9	14.8	203
Helplessness	Hel	4–16	4.5	5.7	6.0	6.5	205
Suspiciousness	Sus	4–16	4.3	5.5	5.5	5.7	204
Anxiety	Anx	6–24	6.2	7.1	7.7	7.4	199
Withdrawal and retardation	Wdl	6–24	8.9	10.7	10.0	12.6	207
General psychopathology	Psy	24–96	30.7	36.4	36.1	39.7	207
Nervousness	Ner	4–16	6.1	7.6	7.9	7.5	209
Confusion	Con	3–12	3.1	3.3	3.5	4.8	203
Bizarreness	Biz	5–20	5.2	6.1	5.8	6.6	200
Hyperactivity	Hyp	3–12	4.3	4.8	4.9	5.9	201
Emotional stability	Sta	9–36	13.7	18.3	16.2	24.1	202

Informant scales: social behavior

Level of performance of socially expected activities	SEA-I	16–48	25.2	32.0	29.5	35.3	77
Level of expectations of socially expected activities	LOE-I	16–48	25.2	31.1	29.9	33.1	53
Level of free-time activities	FTA-I	22–66	46.5	40.7	49.2	54.5	61
Level of satisfaction with free-time activities	SFA-I	22–66	27.0	25.6	30.5	29.3	53

[a]Five scales—SEA-P, LOE-P, Sta, SEA-I, and LOE-I—have been reverse-scored for all the data sets so that lower scores always indicate better adjustment and higher scores indicate poorer adjustment.

[b]These data were taken from Hogarty and Katz (1971), pp. 474–75. The number of subjects is 221.

[c]These data were supplied by Alice Lowery of the National Institute of Mental Health. The number of subjects is 92.

[d]These data were taken from Michaux et al. (1969) p. 36, table 11.3. The number of subjects is 139.

[e]Since the number of subjects vary for the various subscales, they are presented for the Dixon patients.

[f]These data are not available for the normal group since that study only collected data using the KAS informant scales.

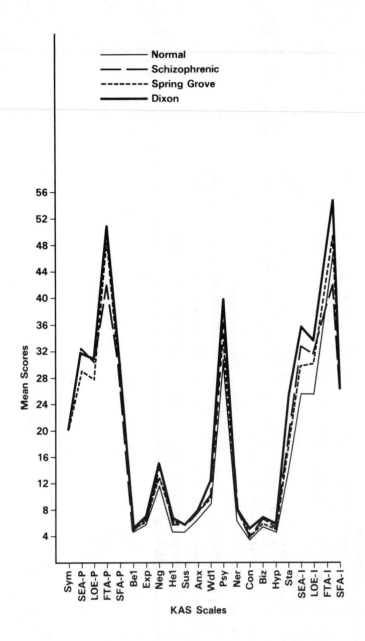

Fig. 8.1. Mean KAS scores for four experimental groups.

close. Neither group seems better adjusted than the other. Examining the twenty-two scales of the KAS we see that the schizophrenics have higher means for twelve of the scales, the Spring Grove sample has higher scores for nine, and for one scale the two groups are equal. The adjustment of these two groups of patients is quite comparable.

Finally, the scores for the Dixon patients are consistently the poorest scores presented. For sixteen of the twenty-two scales the Dixon patients exhibited the poorest adjustment, and for all of the respondent scales the Dixon patients exhibited poorer adjustment than the normal subjects. In comparison with the other two patient populations, the Dixon subjects have the most favorable score for only one scale—nervousness.

One cannot conclude on the basis of these data that the social and psychological adjustment of the Dixon patients is equal to that of the other three groups. Indeed, a rather clear gradient is evident. The best adjusted group is the normal population, followed by the schizophrenics and Spring Grove patients, who are approximately equal, followed by the Dixon subjects, who exhibited the poorest adjustment. The question now is how much poorer is the adjustment of the Dixon subjects, compared to the adjustment of the other two patient populations.

To answer this question the scores for the normal population will be used as baseline data and the scores for the other three groups will be standardized in relation to this baseline. The means contained in table 8.24 can be expressed as the percentage difference between the mean for the normal population and the mean for the particular patient group, allowing statements such as "On scale A the schizophrenics are X% worse or better." If the percentages for the three groups are rather close, one could conclude that the mean differences found in table 8.24 between the Dixon patients and the other two patient samples are not substantial. On the other hand, large negative percentage differences would indicate that the particular patient group was substantially worse than the normal population in terms of adjustment. The relevant data are presented in table 8.25 and figure 8.2.[11]

Relative to the normal population, the adjustment of the Dixon patients is substantially worse than the adjustment of the other

TABLE 8.25 Percentage Difference between Normal Population and Schizophrenic, Spring Grove, and Dixon Samples

| Scale[a] | % Difference between Normal Population and | | |
	Schizophrenic	Spring Grove	Dixon
Bel	− 2.2	0	−15.2
Exp	− 8.5	− 6.8	−16.9
Neg	−24.4	−12.2	−28.7
Hel	−26.7	−33.3	−44.4
Sus	−27.9	−27.9	−32.6
Anx	−14.5	−24.2	−19.4
Wdl	−20.2	−12.4	−41.6
Psy	−18.6	−17.6	−29.3
Ner	−24.6	−29.5	−23.0
Con	− 6.4	−12.9	−54.8
Biz	−17.3	−11.5	−26.9
Hyp	−14.3	−16.7	−37.2
Sta	−33.6	−18.2	−75.9
SEA-I	−27.0	−17.1	−40.1
LOE-I	−23.4	−18.6	−31.3
FTA-I	12.5	− 5.8	−17.2
SFA-I	5.2	−13.0	− 8.5

[a]These comparisons can only be made for the informant scales since only these scales were used in the study of the normal population.

two patient groups. The percentages associated with the schizophrenic and Spring Grove samples are of approximately the same magnitude and neither group is consistently better adjusted than the other. The percentages for the Dixon subjects, however, are consistently worse than the percentages for the other two groups and are, in general, of a much greater magnitude. For example, the data for the first scale—belligerence (Bel)—indicate that the schizophrenics are 2.2 percent worse than the normals, the Spring Grove subjects are equal to the normals, but the Dixon patients are 15.2 percent worse than the normal, nonpatient sample. The other percentages in table 8.25 can be interpreted in the same manner.

Doing so indicates that the Dixon subjects exhibit substantially poorer adjustment than the other two groups for five scales: belligerence, withdrawal, confusion, hyperactivity, and emotional stability. Of these, the greatest differences occur for confusion—scale scores of the Dixon patients are 54.8 percent worse than the normals while the scores of the schizophrenics are

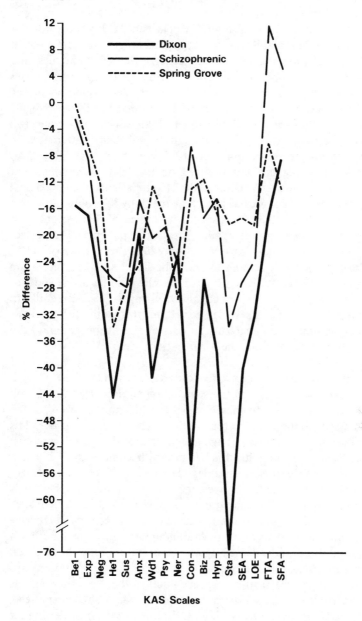

Fig. 8.2. Percent difference between normal patients and three patient samples.

6.4 percent and the Spring Grove patients 12.9 percent worse—and emotional stability—where the percentages are -75.9 percent for the Dixon patients, -33.6 percent for the schizophrenics, and -18.2 percent for Spring Grove patients. Although these scales stand out from the others in terms of the magnitude of the differences, the major conclusion is still that the Dixon patients exhibited poorer overall adjustment than either of the other two patient populations. Even though the absolute differences in the mean scores are not great (see table 8.24 and figure 8.1), when the data are standardized on the basis of a nonpatient population, the KAS scores of the Dixon patients are a good deal worse than the scores of two other mentally ill groups.

At the beginning of this section we indicated that the data just presented were biased against the Dixon patients. The schizophrenic and Spring Grove scores were based on subjects who had been judged well enough to leave the hospital, while the Dixon scores included subjects who were, in the opinion of the staffs of the transfer hospitals, not capable of living in the community. In the following analysis we will correct for this major difference, as well as others, by analyzing subsets of the Dixon patients who more closely resemble the other patient groups.

COMPARISON OF DIXON AND SCHIZOPHRENIC GROUPS
In the comparison with the schizophrenic patients, those Dixon patients who were diagnosed as being schizophrenic, who resided in the community at the time of the interview, and who were less than forty-seven years of age at the time of the interview will be analyzed. By doing this, the two groups become comparable on a number of significant variables. The reason for choosing schizophrenic Dixon patients is evident. The community criterion is necessary since the study on schizophrenics only collected KAS data on those patients who resided in the community twelve months after discharge, including patients who had been rehospitalized and released again. By selecting only those Dixon patients who were interviewed in the community, the two groups are comparable in this respect. Finally, the age criterion was selected since the schizophrenic sample was limited to patients fifteen to forty-five years of age at time of admission. Allowing for the period of hospitalization and the year between discharge and interview in the community for the schizophrenics led us to select

Dixon patients who were less than forty-seven. The appropriate data are presented in table 8.26 and figures 8.3 and 8.4.

Examining the mean scores first, we do not see the consistent differences between the two groups that were evident when all the Dixon patients were included in the analysis. Indeed, the two samples are quite similar. For ten of the twenty-two scales the Dixon patients have lower means, indicating more favorable adjustment; the schizophrenics have lower scores for ten scales; and for two scales the scores are identical. The two scales in which the Dixon patients exhibit substantially poorer adjustment concern the level of free-time activities. For both the patient and respondent free-time activity scales the Dixon patients have means that are considerably higher than the schizophrenics. Nevertheless, the major finding is that the two groups are quite similar in terms of overall adjustment.

TABLE 8.26   Comparison between Schizophrenic Sample and Comparable Dixon Patients

| | Mean KAS Scores | | % Difference between Normal Population and | |
Scale	Schizophrenics	Dixon Patients	Schizophrenics	Dixon Patients
Sym	20.4	16.9	...	...
SEA-P	32.2	31.9	...	...
LOE-P	30.2	34.5	...	...
FTA-P	41.6	50.3	...	...
SFA-P	27.3	28.7	...	...
Bel	4.7	5.0	− 2.2	− 8.7
Exp	6.4	6.3	− 8.5	− 6.8
Neg	14.3	13.3	−24.4	−15.6
Hel	5.7	5.7	−26.7	−26.7
Sus	5.5	4.7	−27.9	− 9.3
Anx	7.1	6.6	−14.5	− 6.5
Wdl	10.7	10.1	−20.2	−13.5
Psy	36.4	35.8	−18.6	−16.6
Ner	7.6	7.1	−24.6	−16.4
Con	3.3	3.8	− 6.4	−22.6
Biz	6.1	6.2	−17.3	−19.2
Hyp	4.8	4.8	−14.3	−11.6
Sta	18.3	21.6	−33.6	−57.7
SFA-I	32.0	30.0	−27.0	−19.0
LOE-I	31.1	31.8	−23.4	−26.2
FTA-I	40.7	54.0	12.5	−16.1
SFA-I	25.6	29.0	5.2	− 7.4

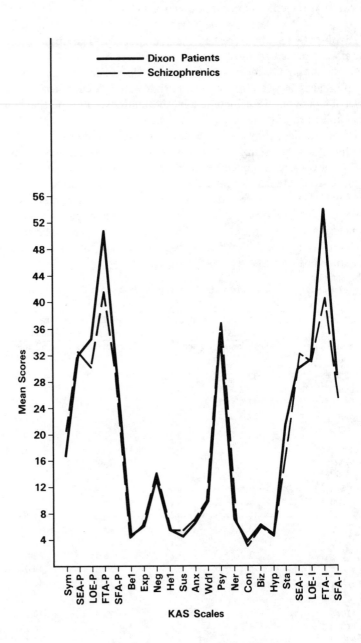

Fig. 8.3. Mean KAS score for Dixon patients and schizophrenics.

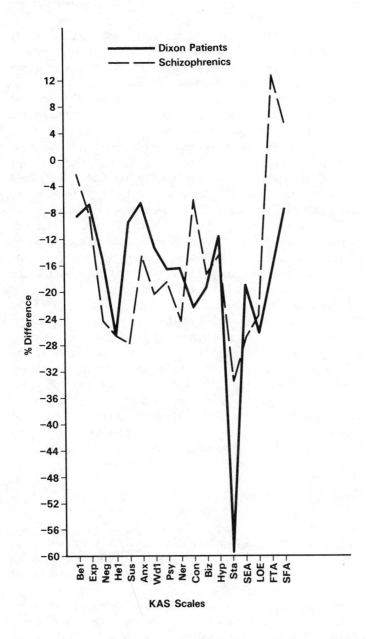

Fig. 8.4. Percentage difference between normal patients and Dixon and schizophrenic patients.

The same result is evident when the data are standardized by expressing them as the percentage of difference between the mean scores of the normal population[12] and the means presented in table 8.26. For the seventeen scales on which data are available, the Dixon patients are closer to the normal population on nine, the schizophrenics are on seven, and the percentages are equal on one. Again we see very comparable data for the two groups. Moreover, the percentages are in general of the same magnitude and the Dixon patients are substantially worse on only three scales—emotional stability, level of free-time activity, and satisfaction with free-time activity. For the free-time activity scales, however, the major difference occurs primarily because the schizophrenics exhibit better adjustment than the normals rather than the Dixon patients exhibiting substantially poorer adjustment. Thus only for the scale of emotional stability do the Dixon patients exhibit substantially poorer adjustment than the schizophrenics, relative to the normal subjects.

In general, the social and psychological adjustment of the Dixon patients is comparable to the adjustment of the schizophrenics. When a comparable group of Dixon subjects is studied, the mean scores of the two groups are of the same magnitude, the relative distances between these groups and a normal, nonpatient group are the same, and, from scale to scale, one group is about as likely as the other to exhibit better adjustment. The psychological adjustment of the schizophrenic, Dixon patients who had been released to the community was no worse than the adjustment of a group of schizophrenic patients treated in a civil mental hospital for comparatively short periods of time.

Comparison of Dixon and Spring Grove Groups

Finally, the adjustment of the Spring Grove sample is compared with that of a similar group of Dixon subjects. The Spring Grove study included only white subjects and the KAS first month data, which are being used here, were based on interviews with all patients released, regardless of whether or not they were rehospitalized. Hence the Dixon subjects used in this analysis will be white patients who were released from the transfer hospitals, including those who were rehospitalized at the time of the interview. We should again point out that the Spring Grove group contains a large proportion of female subjects, while the Dixon class is composed only of males. With this qualification in mind, the appropriate data are presented in table 8.27 and figures 8.5 and 8.6.

As with the comparisons with the schizophrenics, there are very few differences between the Spring Grove subjects and a comparable set of Dixon patients. In fact, the mean scores for these two groups are exceptionally close, as can be seen in figure 8.5. For nine of the twenty-two scales the Dixon subjects exhibit better adjustment while on thirteen of the scales the Spring Grove sample exhibit better scores. In no case are the means for the Dixon group substantially lower than the means for the Spring Grove sample.

Examining these scores relative to the scores for the normal

TABLE 8.27   Comparison between Spring Grove Sample and Comparable Dixon Patients

	Mean KAS Scores		% Difference between Normal Population and	
Scale	Spring Grove	Dixon Patients	Spring Grove	Dixon Patients
Sym	20.1	16.2 (105)[a]	...	...
SEA-P	29.0	33.9 (62)	...	...
LOE-P	27.7	35.1 (58)	...	...
FTA-P	48.0	51.7 (70)	...	...
SFA-P	30.1	28.0 (61)	...	...
Bel	4.6	4.8 (69)	0	− 4.3
Exp	6.3	6.4 (69)	− 6.8	− 8.5
Neg	12.9	13.9 (69)	−12.2	−20.9
Hel	6.0	5.8 (68)	−33.3	−28.9
Sus	5.5	5.3 (68)	−27.9	−23.2
Anx	7.7	6.8 (67)	−24.2	− 9.7
Wdl	10.0	11.2 (69)	−12.4	−25.8
Psy	36.1	35.4 (69)	−17.6	−15.3
Ner	7.9	7.3 (71)	−29.5	−16.4
Con	3.5	3.7 (68)	−12.9	−19.3
Biz	5.8	6.1 (66)	−11.5	−17.3
Hyp	4.9	5.1 (68)	−16.7	−18.6
Sta	16.2	22.2 (67)	−18.2	−62.0
SEA-I	29.5	29.2 (43)	−17.1	−15.9
LOE-I	29.9	31.8 (26)	−18.6	−26.2
FTA-I	49.2	54.3 (43)	− 5.8	−16.8
SFA-I	30.5	28.7 (38)	−13.0	− 6.3

[a]The numbers in parentheses are the number of cases included in the analysis. The number of subjects for the Spring Grove group is 139.

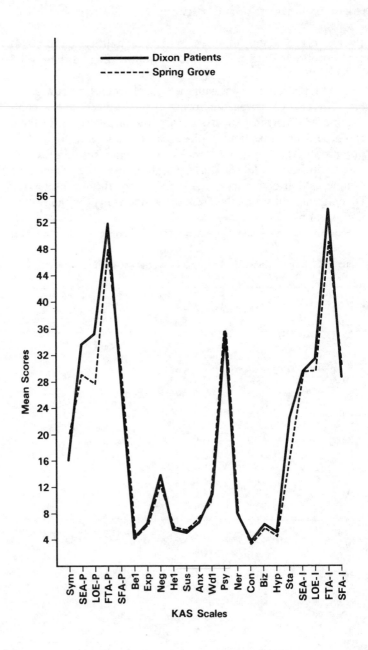

Fig. 8.5. Mean KAS scores for Dixon and Spring Grove patients.

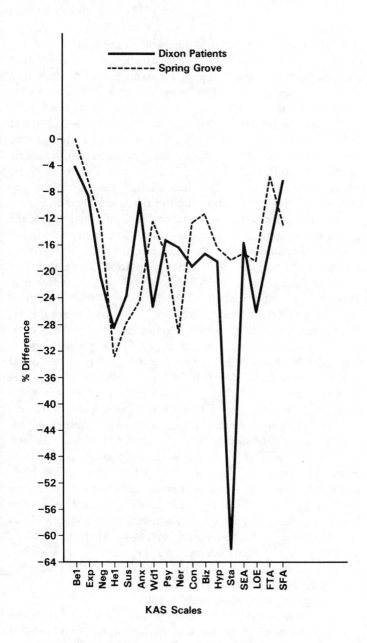

Fig. 8.6. Percentage difference between normal patients and Dixon and Spring Grove patients.

population replicates this finding. The percentages are of the same relative magnitude, with one exception, and the Dixon group is closer to the normal population on seven of the seventeen scales available for comparison, while the Spring Grove scores are closer to the normal group on ten. The two groups are quite similar on the informant free-time activity scales—FTA-I and SFA-I—even though the Dixon patients were substantially worse than the schizophrenic patients on these two scales. This supports our contention that the earlier differences were due more to the exceptionally favorable adjustment of the schizophrenic group than it was to the poor adjustment of the Dixon patients.

The only major exception to the overall similarity between the Spring Grove group and the comparable Dixon patients concerns the scale of emotional stability. The score for the Dixon patients is 62 percent worse than the normal population's score, while the score for the Spring Grove subjects is only 18.2 percent worse. This finding is quite consistent for all the comparisons that have been made. Whether the data are based on all the Dixon subjects, those comparable to the schizophrenic group, or those comparable to the Spring Grove group, the Dixon patients exhibit substantially poorer adjustment scores in relation to emotional stability. Since this is the only scale that consistently differentiates the Dixon patients from the other two patient groups it is worth presenting the items contained in this scale. The traits are generous, friendly, pleasant, dependable, responsible, independent, not envious of other people, gets along well with people, and shows good judgment. Although the Dixon patients exhibit these traits less often than the other two patient groups, the traits themselves do not seem to be of great theoretical importance for a study of the criminally insane. That is, the one area in which the Dixon patients show poorer adjustment is not, on its face, related to assaultiveness, dangerousness, or sexual aberration—which are the areas of primary concern in studies and policy decisions about the criminally insane. Thus we are left with the descriptive statement that the Dixon patients have poorer scores in relation to the single scale of emotional stability.

There are four scales of the KAS that are concerned with issues that are related, albeit not directly, to the question of dangerousness. They are belligerance, negativism, suspiciousness, and bizarreness. (The items for these scales can be found in appendix 8.) The scores of the three patient groups on these scales (presented in tables 8.26 and 8.27) are of approximately the same magnitude and one cannot conclude that the Dixon patients exhibit poorer adjustment for these scales than either the schizophrenic patients or the Spring Grove patients.

Community Adjustment

The hypothesis that the social and psychological adjustment of the Dixon patients was comparable to the adjustment of "typical" mental patients receives considerable support from the foregoing analysis of responses to the KAS. When all the Dixon patients, including those who were judged not well enough to be released from the transfer hospitals, were used in the analysis, the Dixon patients exhibited poorer adjustment scores on some subscales. When the subsets of the Dixon patients that most closely resemble the comparison groups were analyzed, the mean scores of the Dixon, schizophrenic, and Spring Grove patients were quite comparable. Moreover, when the KAS scores were standardized in terms of the scores of a normal, nonpatient sample, the data indicated that the Dixon patients exhibited the same level of adjustment as the schizophrenic group and the Spring Grove sample. Substantial differences emerged for only one scale, that of emotional stability, and for scales more closely related to dangerousness—belligerence, negativism, suspiciousness, and bizarreness—the adjustment of the three groups was approximately equal.

On the basis of these data we conclude that a large number of the criminally insane can adjust to the freedom of community living with the same degree of success as noncriminal mental patients who had been confined in civil mental hospitals for relatively short periods of time. This statement needs to be qualified by noting the necessity of having prerelease, clinical screening, since it is clear that the adjustment scores of the Dixon patients never released to the community are considerably worse than the scores of those who were. Although not all criminally insane patients are equally capable of adjusting to the community, these data do support a conclusion that criminally insane patients who are judged at civil mental hospitals as being able to live in the community are capable of adjusting to the community with the same facility as typical mental patients who are also judged able to live in the community.

We stated in the introduction to this section that confirmation of this hypothesis would support the policy implication that criminally insane patients similar to the Dixon patients could be treated in the same manner as "typical mental patients." That is, since the Dixon patients can adjust to the community as well as typical mental patients, they should be hospitalized for considerably briefer periods of time in civil mental hosptials that stress rehabilitation rather than maximum security. This implication of course assumes that the Dixon patients who had been confined for comparatively short periods of time under the Dixon commitment exhibit the same social and psychological adjustment as their counterparts who had been confined for longer periods of time. The following analysis is designed to test the assumption that length of stay is not related to postrelease psychological adjustment.

The KAS scores of the Dixon patients who had been confined at Farview for less than six years and those who had been confined at Farview six years or more are presented in tables 8.28 and 8.29 and figures 8.7 to 8.10. We will refer to the subjects who had been at Farview less than six years as the "short-term" group and those who had been at Farview six or more years as the "long-term" group.[13] The data are presented separately for those who had ever been released to the community and those who resided in the community at the time of the interview. Examining the former group first we see that the results are rather mixed. For the eight scales that deal with social behavior (SEA-P to SFA-P and SEA-I to SFA-I) the two groups are rather similar since the mean scores and the percentage differences for the informant scales are of the same relative magnitude. The short-term subjects exhibit the same level of social adjustment as the long-term subjects.

The same conclusion does not hold for the scales dealing with psychological symptoms, however. For the patient scale of Sym and the respondent scales of Bel to Sta, the short-term group had KAS scores that are substantially higher, that is, worse, than the long-term patients. These differences are quite evident in the two figures, especially figure 8.8, which depicts the differences between the scores for the normal group and the two Dixon patient subgroups.

TABLE 8.28   KAS Scores for Dixon Patients Interviewed in the Community by
Length of Stay at Farview

Scale	Mean KAS Scores		% Difference between Normal and Dixon Patients	
	Short-Term	Long-Term	Short-Term	Long-Term
Sym	24.3 (47)	17.5 (126)	...	...
SEA-P	32.7 (23)	32.1 (78)	...	...
LOE-P	32.4 (21)	33.6 (77)	...	...
FTA-P	53.0 (20)	51.2 (81)	...	...
SFA-P	29.7 (16)	27.9 (68)	...	...
Bel	5.9 (30)	4.6 (78)	−28.3	0
Exp	7.6 (31)	6.2 (77)	−28.8	− 5.1
Neg	15.2 (30)	13.6 (78)	−32.2	−18.3
Hel	6.6 (31)	5.7 (76)	−46.7	−26.7
Sus	6.6 (29)	5.1 (77)	−53.5	−18.6
Anx	7.9 (28)	6.6 (77)	−27.4	− 6.4
Wdl	10.9 (31)	11.7 (77)	−22.5	−31.5
Psy	41.7 (31)	34.4 (77)	−35.8	−12.1
Ner	8.1 (31)	7.0 (79)	−32.8	−14.8
Con	3.9 (30)	4.2 (76)	−25.8	−35.8
Biz	7.0 (29)	6.0 (76)	−34.6	−15.4
Hyp	6.3 (30)	4.7 (76)	−46.5	− 9.3
Sta	22.0 (29)	21.5 (77)	−60.6	−56.9
SEA-I	30.9 (13)	28.5 (56)	−22.6	−13.1
LOE-I	31.6 (11)	30.8 (36)	−25.4	−22.2
FTA-I	53.7 (9)	54.6 (47)	−15.5	−17.4
SFA-I	29.4 (8)	28.8 (42)	− 8.9	− 6.7

Turning to the data that are based on those Dixon patients who
resided in the community at the time of the interview, however
(table 8.29 and figs. 8.9 and 8.10), the differences between the
groups on the psychological scales are no longer evident. Indeed,
the mean scores for all the scales are remarkably close and of the
same relative magnitude. This conclusion is also supported when
the data are standardized in terms of the scores of the normal
population. The percentage differences between the normal
group and the short-term Dixon patients and between the normal
group and the long-term Dixon patients are quite comparable.
For nine of the seventeen scales the long-term group exhibits
more favorable adjustment, for five scales the short-term group
does, and for three scales the two groups are identical. Thus, for
patients who were interviewed in the community, the length of
time spent at Farview did not affect their social and psychological
adjustment.

TABLE 8.29 KAS Scores for Dixon Patients Interviewed in the Community by Length of Stay at Farview

	Mean KAS Scores		% Difference between Normal and Dixon Patients	
Scale	Short-Term	Long-Term	Short-Term	Long-Term
Sym	16.0 (25)	16.4 (99)	...	...
SEA-P	33.0 (22)	32.2 (77)	...	...
LOE-P	32.5 (20)	33.7 (76)	...	...
FTA-P	52.6 (19)	51.2 (81)	...	...
SFA-P	29.7 (16)	27.9 (68)	...	...
Bel	5.2 (16)	4.5 (57)	−13.0	+ 2.2
Exp	6.2 (16)	6.0 (56)	− 5.1	− 1.7
Neg	13.7 (16)	13.1 (57)	−19.1	−13.9
Hel	5.6 (16)	5.7 (55)	−24.4	−26.7
Sus	4.7 (15)	4.7 (56)	− 9.3	− 9.3
Anx	6.5 (15)	6.5 (56)	− 4.8	− 4.8
Wdl	9.6 (16)	11.6 (56)	− 7.9	−30.3
Psy	35.3 (16)	32.8 (56)	−15.0	− 6.8
Ner	6.6 (16)	6.8 (56)	− 8.2	−11.5
Con	3.6 (15)	3.8 (57)	−16.1	−22.6
Biz	5.8 (16)	5.8 (55)	−11.5	−11.5
Hyp	4.8 (16)	4.5 (56)	−11.6	− 4.7
Sta	21.6 (16)	21.2 (56)	−57.7	−54.7
SEA-I	31.0 (12)	28.5 (55)	−23.0	−13.1
LOE-I	31.5 (10)	30.7 (35)	−25.0	−21.8
FTA-I	53.7 (9)	54.6 (47)	−15.5	−17.4
SFA-I	29.4 (8)	28.8 (42)	− 8.9	− 6.7

In general, the KAS data support the notion that the favorable adjustment of the Dixon patients is not a function of their having been confined at Farview for extremely long periods of time. When data based on those patients ever released to the community and those interviewed in the community were examined, the social adjustment of the Dixon patients confined for shorter and longer pariods of time at Farview was indentical. In terms of psychological adjustment, however, the scores are the same only for those patients interviewed in the community. For the group who had been released to the community, which includes those released and rehospitalized, the patients confined at Farview for longer periods of time exhibited substantially better adjustment than those confined for shorter periods of time. Given the available data it is difficult to explain this difference. Nevertheless,

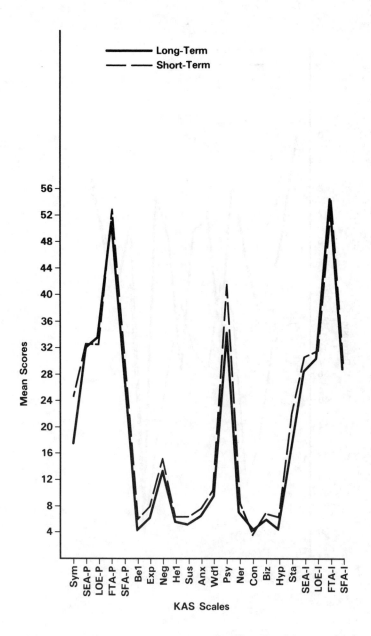

Fig. 8.7. Mean KAS scores for Dixon patients ever released to the community, by length of stay at Farview.

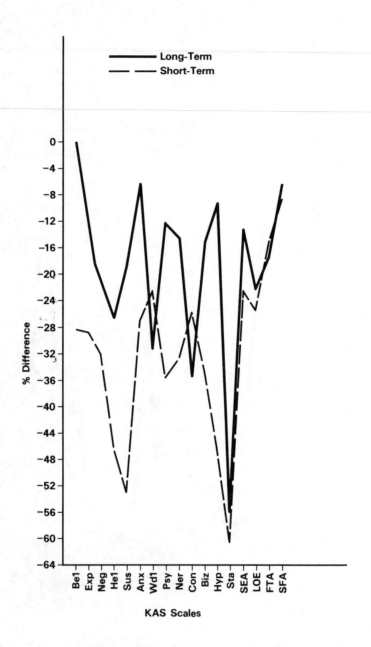

Fig. 8.8. Percentage difference between normal patients and Dixon patients ever released to the community, by length of stay at Farview.

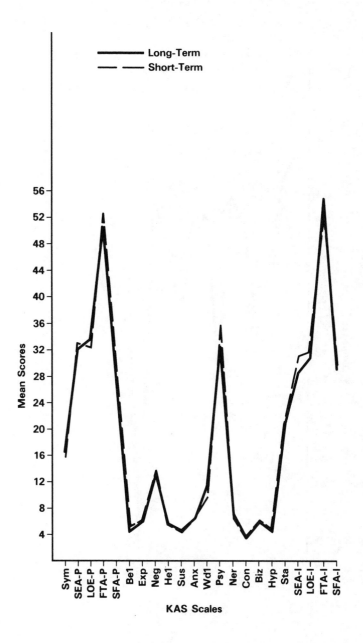

Fig. 8.9. Mean KAS scores for Dixon patients interviewed in the community, by length of stay at Farview.

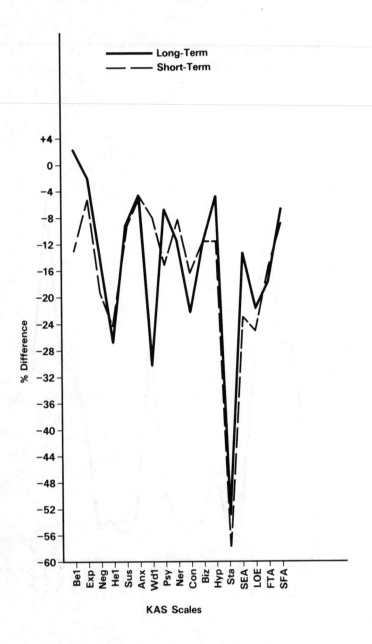

Fig. 8.10. Percentage difference between normal patients and Dixon patients interviewed in the community, by length of stay at Farview.

the weight of the evidence indicates that there is not a substantial association between the adjustment of the Dixon patients and length of stay at Farview. In all cases the social adjustment of those confined for longer and shorter periods of time is comparable and the psychological adjustment of those who were interviewed in the community is the same for these two groups. We will return to the policy implication of this finding in the concluding chapter, after we have dealt with the final issue of this work—the postrelease dangerousness of the Dixon patients.

One of the most important questions being addressed in this research is the extent to which the Dixon patients engaged in violent behavior after their release to the community. This question is intimately linked to the validity of political prediction and, through that, to the more general policy question of how the criminally insane should be treated in an enlightened society. If the prediction that a majority of the Dixon patients would be violent offenders after release is substantiated, the policy issue in many respects would be resolved. There would be strong empirical support for the policy of longterm confinement of the criminally insane, even though such patients are not disruptive while hospitalized and are able to adjust to community living. The increased danger posed to the community by released mentally ill offenders who are predominantly violent would simply outweigh these other considerations. If, on the other hand, the rate of violence exhibited by the Dixon patients was relatively low, the inaccuracy of the political prediction would be demonstrated. In conjunction with the previous conclusions, such a finding would suggest that long-term confinement of the criminally insane is not required for the protection of either the community or the criminally insane themselves.

To examine this issue the recidivism of the Dixon patients will be compared with the recidivism of three other groups. The first, the Baxstrom patients, represents the only existing data on the recidivism of released criminally insane offenders. The other two groups represent institutional populations who suffer from one of the two stigmata associated with the criminally insane—released prisoners and released mental patients. Our hypothesis is that there will be little difference in the postrelease recidivism of the criminally insane in comparison with nonmentally ill prisoners and noncriminal mental patients.

The data used to test this hypothesis cannot be considered a complete accounting of the postrelease dangerousness of the Dixon patients because of the underreporting of criminal activity. Nevertheless, the most important offenses from our perspective, serious violent offenses, should be more fully enumerated because of the higher police clearance rates that exist for these offenses. Thus these official data are most appropriate for our needs—the evaluation of the frequency of serious, violent offenses. Furthermore, the underreporting of offenses does not invalidate the comparison of recidivism rates among various offender populations since no reason exists to assume that underreporting will affect these different populations at different rates.

THE FREQUENCY OF ARREST

The Dixon subjects studied at this stage of the analysis are those 414 men who obtained release from hospitalization and imprisonment for some period between the time of their transfer from Farview and the date of our search through the files of the Pennsylvania State Police.[1] Subjects were considered to be "at risk" whether they had obtained their freedom through discharge, escape, or long-term leave.[2]

We can begin by presenting what can be called the crude recidivism rate for the Dixon patients—that is, the percentage of subjects ever released to the community who were rearrested. Of the 414 subjects at risk during the follow-up period, 23.7 percent (N=98) were arrested at least once, 10.4 percent were arrested only once, 7.0 percent twice, and 6.3 percent three or more times (table 9.1). Based on this crude rate of 23.7 percent, the political prediction made by the Farview staff that the Dixon patients were as a group dominated by likely recidivists is not confirmed. Over

TABLE 9.1 Distribution of Arrests after Release from the Transfer Hospital

New Arrests	Subjects		Cumulative %
	N	%	
None	316	76.3	76.3
1	43	10.4	86.7
2	29	7.0	93.7
3	8	2.0	95.7
4	7	1.7	97.4
5	4	1.0	98.4
6	2	0.5	98.9
7	1	0.2	99.1
8	1	0.2	99.3
9	2	0.5	99.8
10	1	0.2	100.0
One or more	98	23.7	
Total	414	100.0	

three-fourths of the subjects ever at risk were not arrested after their release.

Although the above rate describes the likelihood of rearrest for the Dixon patients, it is an inadequate descriptor for our purposes. In the first place, it ignores the distribution of rearrests across time. We do not know, for example, if all the Dixon patients who committed a subsequent offense did so within a few months of their release, or if the rearrests were evenly spaced across the four-year follow-up. If all the rearrests actually occurred within weeks of release, the social costs of releasing the Dixon patients to the community could be considerably greater than the crude rate of 24 percent suggests. Moreover, such a finding would indicate that future decisions concerning the release of the criminally insane would have to consider the rather immediate threat to which the community is exposed by the release of such patients. A complete examination of the recidivism of these patients, therefore, should include an analysis of the distribution of arrests across time so that issues such as these can be addressed.

The second difficulty with relying on a crude rate to measure recidivism is that it does not provide an accurate estimate of the proportion of subjects who will recidivate after being exposed to risk for a certain period of time. In a crude rate, all subjects ever at risk are given equal weight in the composition of the population base, even though some subjects were exposed to risk for a very brief period while others were exposed for a rather longer period. For the Dixon patients time at risk varied from less than a month to over four and a half years, with a median of thirty months. With such a data base the crude rate of the proportion of subjects who have recidivated by the end of the four-year follow-up period tends to underestimate the proportion who would recidivate after being at risk for four continuous years, precisely because the crude rate includes all subjects, even those exposed only for brief periods. Once the data are adjusted to account for the fact that all subjects do not contribute a full first year, a full second year, and so forth, the estimate of the proportion of subjects failing after certain exposure periods becomes more accurate.

One appropriate method of adjusting the data in this manner can be found in an adaptation of demographic life table methodology.[3] In essence, one uses life table techniques to estimate the proportion of subjects who will recidivate after a certain period of time instead of the traditional concern with the proportion of subjects who will die. Such an approach has been used to measure contraceptive failure (Potter 1966), intermarital fertility (Rindfuss and Bumpass 1977), failure in cancer treatments (Peto et al. 1976), and other social phenomena that are analogous to recidivism. For example, the measurement of the failure to avoid conception is directly analogous to the measurement of the failure to avoid rearrest.

The use of a life table technique provides a number of advantages for our purposes: it estimates the proportion of subjects who will recidivate in each of a series of successive time intervals; the population used at each interval includes only those who are still at risk, that is, those who have not already recidivated and who still reside in the community; it estimates the cumulative proportion who will recidivate after an exposure time of K intervals, as well as the standard error of this estimate; and finally, an examination of these cumulative failure rates indicates the shape of the distribution of recidivism over time.

The calculation of the cumulative failure rate is rather straightforward and, as described by Potter (1966, pp. 299–300), has three basic steps. In the first the subjects are classified according to their total exposure time and their terminal status. In the present analysis, the exposure time is equal to the interval between their release to the community and the date on which they died; they returned to an institution without subsequent release;

their criminal history was secured from the Pennsylvania state police; or, they were rearrested.[4] The terminal status of the subjects was dichotomized into successful exit from exposure, the first three states just mentioned, and failure, that is, rearrest.

In the second step these basic data are reordered so that for each time interval, i, the number of subjects exposed to risk, n_i, and the number of subjects who were rearrested, r_i, can be calculated. From these data the proportion of subjects rearrested during each interval is given by $p_i = r_i / n_i$, and its complement, $q_i = 1 - p_i$, equals the proportion who survived. The cumulative product of these survival proportions, $q_1 \times q_2 \ldots \times q_k$, is equal to the cumulative proportion surviving at the kth interval, $Q(K)$, and its complement, $1 - Q(K)$, produces the cumulative failure rate, which is the statistic of interest. Moreover, this statistic has a specific interpretation. Paraphrasing Potter, it represents "the proportion of [subjects] who would be expected to [recidivate] within k months if a large population of [subjects] were exposed to the monthly [recidivism] rates observed in the sample and if none of these hypothetical [subjects] interrupted [exposure] except for [rearrest] until after the kth month" (1966, pp. 299–300). Finally, in the third step, the standard error of $P(K)$ can be calculated (see Potter 1966).

With these methodological notes as background, the results of the life table approach for measuring recidivism are presented in table 9.2 and figure 9.1 for three-month intervals following release to the community. The effective number exposed to the risk of rearrest starts with 406 subjects, 8 fewer than the total of 414 released to the community. Information was missing for four subjects who have been excluded entirely from this analysis. The remaining reduction is due to adjustments in the population base for subjects who did not remain at risk during the entire first interval. The effective number for the second interval is further reduced by those who were rearrested during the first interval as well as those who did not remain at risk during the entire second interval, and so forth. It is this successive reduction in the number of subjects at risk that renders the life table approach superior to the crude rate.

Substantively, the most important data are the cumulative proportion recidivating which are arrayed in column 4 and

TABLE 9.2 Cumulative Proportion Recidivating for Three-Month Intervals following
          Release

Months since Release	Effective No. Exposed to Risk of Rearrest	Proportion Rearrested	Cumulative Proportion Rearrested	SE
3	406	0.06	0.06	0.01
6	374	0.05	0.10	0.01
9	345	0.05	0.14	0.02
12	318	0.03	0.17	0.02
15	301	0.03	0.19	0.02
18	287	0.02	0.21	0.02
21	271	0.01	0.22	0.02
24	256	0.01	0.22	0.02
27	244	0.01	0.23	0.02
30	230	0.01	0.24	0.02
33	208	0.00	0.24	0.02
36	176	0.01	0.25	0.02
39	141	0.01	0.26	0.02
42	115	0.00	0.26	0.02
45	86	0.02	0.27	0.03
48	51	0.00	0.27	0.03

depicted in figure 9.1. Twenty-seven percent of the subjects were
rearrested, at least once, during the first forty-eight months after
release. As expected, this figure is somewhat higher than the
crude rate of 23.7 percent. Nevertheless, the two figures are quite
close and lead to the same substantive conclusions. Namely, the
political prediction grossly overestimated the proportion of Dixon
subjects who would be rearrested.

Examining Figure 9.1, we see that the rate of recidivism is
rather high during the first year, begins to level off during the
second year, and increases only slightly during the last two years.
By the end of the first year, 17 percent of the subjects had been
arrested, which constitutes more than half of those arrested during the entire four-year follow-up. Thus, recidivism, if it is to
occur, is likely to occur relatively soon after release.

Although it is difficult to estimate the proportion of subjects who
would be arrested after the fourth year, the data are at least suggestive in this respect. During the last two years the cumulative
proportion of subjects recidivating only increases from .23 to .27.

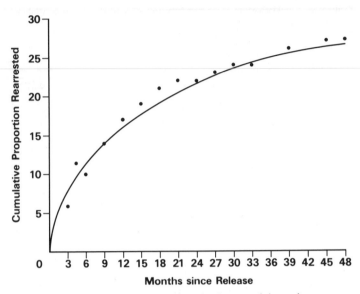

Fig. 9.1. Cumulative proportion recidivating, by three-month intervals.

Unless an extremely odd distribution occurs after the fourth year, these data suggest that the proportion recidivating is not likely to increase substantially after the four-year follow-up.

In general the data indicate that the majority of the Dixon patients did not recidivate after their release to the community. The crude recidivism rate is 23.7 percent and the cumulative proportion recidivating after forty-eight months of exposure is 27 percent. Morover, the relationship of recidivism to time suggests that the cumulative proportion of failures is not likely to increase substantially in the future. These data lend very little support to the validity of the political prediction that the majority of the Dixon patients would be dangerous after release. Nevertheless, it remains to be seen whether, in comparison with released prisoners and released mental patients, the criminally insane were sufficiently greater risks to deserve the preventive detention to which they alone were subject.

COMPARISONS WITH OTHER GROUPS
Comparison data for released prison inmates come from a national study of 104,182 prisoners paroled between 1965 and 1970

(Gottfredson et al. 1973). This study (1) included only paroled offenders, excluding prisoners who were released unconditionally after serving maximum sentences (approximately 30 percent); (2) included technical parole violations in the definition of failure; (3) covered a one-year follow-up period; and (4) examined subjects who were considerably younger than the Dixon subjects. While these differences make comparisons with the Dixon patients less than ideal, the effects of these differences are probably offsetting. The younger subjects and the inclusion of technical violations in the recidivism rate most likely increased the proportion of failure among the parolees, while the exclusions of time-expired inmates (predicated to be poor risks) and the shorter follow-up period probably decreased the proportion of failures.

Gottfredson et al. found an overall recidivism rate, including rearrest and parole violation, of 25 percent in the first year after release. The comparable general figure for the Dixon patients, after an average three-year follow-up, was 23.7 percent, and the cumulative proportion recidivating after twelve months was found to be 17 percent (see table 9.2). Given the methodological differences between the two studies, however, it is difficult to draw very specific conclusions from these data. Perhaps the most robust statement that should be made is that there is no evidence that the Dixon patients were more likely to recidivate than were the parolees.

The general recidivism rate of the Dixon patients, 23.7 percent, is also quite similar to the rate for the Baxstrom patients. Among this sample of ninety-eight criminally insane patients released from civil mental hospitals in New York State, 20.4 percent were rearrested after a follow-up period that extended for a maximum of four years (Steadman and Cocozza 1974, p. 139). Thus neither the Dixon nor Baxstrom patients, mentally ill offenders who had experienced long-term hospitalization and who were predicted at security hospitals to be dangerous after release, were more likely to be arrested than comparable members of a national sample of paroled, nonmentally ill offenders. On the basis of these data it is no more justifiable to place the mentally ill offender in preventive detention than it is the nonmentally ill offender.

For a variety of reasons, comparing the recidivism of the Dixon patients with the number of offenses of civil mental patients after

hospitalization is somewhat more difficult. The primary factor
that distorts these comparisons is the changing character of the
clientele at civil mental hospitals over time. Steadman et al. (n.d.)
present convincing evidence that the proportion of patients at
these hospitals with criminal records has increased considerably
in the past decade and, concomitantly, the recidivism rates of
released patients has increased as well. As a result, comparisons
between the criminally insane and older studies of released
mental patients are rather meaningless. Thus, we will only consider the three most recent studies of former mental patients
(table 9.3).

TABLE 9.3   Published Arrest Rates of Former Mental Patients

Year of Study	% Arrested	Sample Definition	Follow-up Period	Reference
1967	13.7	1,142 male veterans	4 yr	Giovannoni and Gurel (1967), p. 147f.
1968	6.9	1,920	19 mo	Steadman et al. (n.d.)
1975	9.4	1,938	19 mo	Steadman et al. (n.d.)
1975	23.3	867 males and females	4 yr	Zitrin et al. (1975)

Four years after release, 23.7 percent of the Dixon patients
were rearrested while all of the studies listed in table 9.3 indicate lower rates. For the two studies with four-year follow-up
periods, however, the recidivism rates of 13.7 percent and 23.3
percent are similar to the crude recidivism rate exhibited by the
Dixon patients. The data collected by Steadman et al. cover a
nineteen-month follow-up period and produce recidivism rates of
6.9 percent for patients released in 1968 and 9.4 percent for
patients released in 1975. Both of these rates are considerably
lower than the cumulative proportion of Dixon patients recidivating after eighteen months, which is 21 percent (See table 9.2).
    In general, when the recidivism rates of released Dixon patients
are compared to those of former prisoners, former mental patients, and another group of released criminally insane patients,
the recidivism rates are of the same general magnitude and
indicate that approximately one in every five will commit another

offense. Moreover, the evidence suggests that the subjects of our research more closely resemble released prisoners than released mental patients in their subsequent arrest history. That finding is not surprising, considering that the Dixon patients prior to admission to Farview had long and serious offense histories, more characteristic of the careers of prison inmates than of mental patients. Nevertheless, the point remains that only a minority of the Dixon patients were arrested following their release to the community.

We can now turn to an analysis of the type of offenses that were committed by the released Dixon subjects as a prelude to our discussion of dangerousness.

OFFENSE TYPES

During the four years after their transfer from Farview the Dixon patients accumulated a total of 228 arrests, among which arrests for property offenses were the most common, 34.6 percent (table 9.4). Violent offenses accounted for one-fourth of all arrests, with 11.1 percent of the subjects being arrested for this type of offense. Only two sex offenses were committed, both by the same subject. A fairly large proportion of the arrests, 25.4 percent, were for victimless and public order offenses and 11.0 percent were for "other" offenses. The specific offenses included in these latter two categories, listed in table 9.4, are not among the most serious violations of the criminal code and tend toward being "nuisance" offenses. Contrary to expectations generated by the clinical literature, the offenses committed by Dixon patients are neither predominantly violent nor are they sex oriented. Property offenses are, however, quite frequent and, as in most distributions of criminal acts, relatively minor offenses are frequently committed.

A third of the offenses were property offenses not involving violence, but if the seventeen arrests for robbery, which involves violence and theft, were added to this category, the proportion of arrests for property-related offenses would increase to 42.1 percent or slightly more than two in every five. Acquisitive crimes play a major role in the nature of recidivism among the Dixon patients, which could well be related to the subjects' high unemployment rate and difficulty in finding work. Although the data do not demonstrate a causal relationship in this area, the logical consistency is worth noting and provides further impetus

TABLE 9.4   Offenses Resulting in Rearrest

Offense Category[a]	Offenses	Subjects Arrested for One or More Offenses
Violent	25.0%	11.1%
	(57)	(46)
Sex	0.9	0.2
	(2)	(1)
Property	34.6	9.9
	(79)	(41)
Victimless offenses and offenses against public order	25.4	7.5
	(58)	(31)
Other	11.0	4.3
	(25)	(18)
Unknown	3.1	1.7
	(7)	(7)[b]
Total	100.0	
	(228)	

[a]Violent offenses included homicide (3), forcible rape (1), robbery (17), aggravated assault and battery (17), assault with intent to rape (1), indecent assault (4), simple assaults (11), threats (3). Sex offenses included corrupting morals of a minor and an unspecified sex offense. Property offenses included burglary (36), larceny (23), auto theft (11), forgery (4), stolen property (3), possession of burglary tools (1), and vandalism (1). Victimless offenses and offenses against public order included drunken driving (1), traffic (4), trespassing (6), sending false alarms (3), prostitution and commercialized vice (2), narcotics (12), gambling (2), liquor laws (1), drunkenness (6), disorderly conduct (11), vagrancy (4), suspicious person (1), corner lounging (1), other minor statutes (4). Other offenses included weapons (4), offenses against family (1), probation/parole violation (5), contempt of court (12), prison breach (3).

[b]These numbers add to more than 98, the number of subjects rearrested, since the same subject can be counted in more than one category.

for policy considerations concerning the improvement of aftercare services for the released mentally ill offender.

The rate of violent offenses—25 percent of all arrests—is somewhat higher than found in general crime distributions. For example, the *1970 Uniform Crime Reports* indicate that 13 percent of the Index offenses were for violent crimes. Although violent offenses are proportionately large in this study, one should not assume that the Dixon offenders committed many heinous offenses. Indeed eighteen of the fifty-seven violent arrests were, from the perspective of the amount of injury involved, relatively minor—four were for indecent assault, eleven for simple assaults, and three for threats. Nevertheless the released Dixon patients were arrested for three homicides, one rape, seventeen robberies, and seventeen aggravated assaults.

DISPOSITION AFTER ARREST

The fact that the Dixon patients suffer from the double stigma of being both mad and bad complicates the issue of how their cases are handled after arrest. The knowledge that a suspect or defendant had previously been hospitalized for mental illness may affect disposition decisions within the criminal justice system. Hospitalization may be more readily considered for suspects whose previous history of hospitalization is known, than for suspects, evidencing similar behavior, who are not known to be ex-patients. Some data to support this notion exist (Levine 1970), although the extent of the impact is not well documented.

If the histories of the Dixon patients are typical of other mentally ill offenders, however, prior hospitalization has a strong bearing on the dispositon of new offenses (table 9.5). Although the disposition for eighty-eight arrests is unknown, the data for the remaining 140 cases are quite informative. In 19.3 percent of the cases, the subject was found to be not guilty, while in 16.4 percent, a fine or sentence of probation was imposed. The modal disposition was a prison or jail sentence, given to 35 percent of the cases, while 29.3 percent of the cases were disposed of through rehospitalization. In terms of the number of subjects receiving the various dispositions, more (8.3 percent) were rehospitalized following an arrest than were imprisoned following a conviction (7.9 percent). This disparity supports Steadman and Braff's (1974) contention that diversion to the mental health system is "the easy way in" for many mentally ill offenders. The fact that a subject was committed to a mental hospital after arrest does not imply that he was convicted for any offense, since rehospitalization orders can occur at pretrial hearings.

DANGEROUSNESS AFTER RELEASE

The knowledge that a mentally ill suspect has a high probability of being hospitalized after being arrested, possibly without formal charges being entered, suggests the advisability of adopting a broader definition of dangerousness than arrest for a violent offense. The records of all civil mental hospitals in Pennsylvania were examined for readmissions of Dixon patients and the be-

TABLE 9.5   Court Disposition of New Arrests

Disposition	Cases[a]	Subjects with One or More Dispositions[b]
Jail or prison sentence	35.0%	8.2%
	(49)	(34)
Hospital commitments	29.3	8.7
	(41)	(36)
Fine or probation	16.4	4.6
	(23)	(19)
Not guilty, discharged	19.3	4.3
	(27)	(18)
Unknown[c]	. . .	14.7
	(88)	(61)
Total	100.0	. . .
	(228)	. . .

[a]Percentage of dispositions based on 140 known dispositions.

[b]Percentages of subjects based on 414 at risk.

[c]It appears that a large proportion of cases in which the police did not record dispositions, reported here as "unknown," were actually disposed of by release without
judicial action. It is unlikely that these cases resulted in jail or prison sentences or
rehospitalization. The additional processing by various agencies would have been reflected in the state police records. Had an arrest resulted in rehospitalization our review
of hospital records would have revealed that disposition.

havior or circumstances precipitating admission were noted,
including readmission for violent behavior in which there was no
court action. As we saw in the last chapter, fourteen subjects,
which represents 24 percent of the episodes of rehospitalization,
were rehospitalized for such behavior. Thus the definition of
dangerous behavior that will be used in this analysis is any arrest
for a violent offense or any rehospitalization for a violent act for
which the subject could have been arrested.

Using this definition, 14.5 percent of the Dixon patients can be
classified as being dangerous after their release to the community.
Of the sixty subjects so classified, forty-six, or 80 percent of those
who were dangerous, were arrested for a violent offense and 14, or
20 percent, were rehospitalized after committing a violent act.
The percentage of Dixon subjects who were dangerous, 14.5
percent, is remarkably close to the rate of 14.3 percent observed
for the Baxstrom patients (Steadman and Cocozza 1974, p. 151).

Following the model developed for the analysis of rearrests, we can now examine the cumulative proportion of subjects who will be dangerous after various periods of exposure to risk (table 9.6). For the entire forty-eight month period the proportion failing is 18 percent, an increase of 3.5 percent when compared to the crude rate of 14.5 percent. As with the rearrest data, the life table approach leads to a slightly higher estimate of failure than does the crude rate.

TABLE 9.6   Cumulative Proportion Exhibiting Dangerous Behavior for Three-Month Intervals following Release

Months since Release	Effective No. Exposed to Risk of Being Dangerous	Proportion Dangerous	Cumulative Proportion Dangerous	SE
3	405	0.03	0.03	0.01
6	382	0.02	0.03	0.01
9	364	0.03	0.07	0.01
12	344	0.02	0.09	0.01
15	328	0.02	0.11	0.02
18	317	0.01	0.12	0.02
21	304	0.01	0.13	0.02
24	288	0.01	0.13	0.02
27	275	0.01	0.14	0.02
30	259	0.01	0.15	0.02
33	231	0.00	0.15	0.02
36	194	0.00	0.15	0.02
39	160	0.01	0.15	0.02
42	133	0.01	0.16	0.02
45	101	0.03	0.18	0.02
48	62	0.00	0.18	0.02

Violent behavior, if it is to be exhibited, is likely to occur relatively quickly after release (fig. 9.2). After twelve months of exposure, 9 percent of the subjects had engaged in such behavior, a figure which represents half of the forty-eight month rate of 18 percent. As with rearrest, the proportions increase sharply during the first year, tend to level off during the third year, and increase somewhat more slowly after that. Given the shape of the distribution in figure 9.2, it seems unlikely that the cumulative proportion of Dixon patients engaging in violent behavior will increase dramatically after the forty-eighth month of exposure.

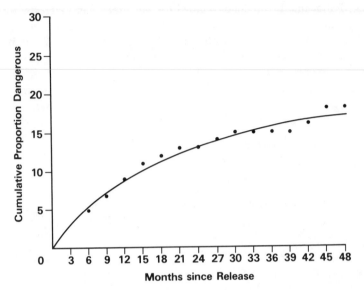

Fig. 9.2. Cumulative proportion exhibiting dangerous behavior, by three-month
intervals following release.

We should point out that our definition of dangerous behavior
is quite broad. It includes all arrests and rehospitalizations for
violent acts regardless of the seriousness of the act and, as we saw,
many of these acts were relatively minor, such as the four arrests
for threats. This definition of dangerous behavior cannot be
considered overly restrictive. Yet even within this rather inclusive
definition, only 14.5 percent of the subjects were classified as
dangerous, and after forty-eight months of exposure to risk, we
estimate that only 18 percent of the Dixon patients would exhibit
such behavior.

The results of this empirical investigation are quite discrepant
with what would be expected based on the political prediction of
the Farview staff. If these political predictions had been accurate,
the majority of the Dixon patients would have been dangerous
after their release to the community.

ESCAPES FROM THE TRANSFER HOSPITALS
Of the 414 Dixon patients who resided in the community during
our follow-up, 6 percent (N = 25), entered the community by

escaping from the transfer hospitals. Given the negligible rate of escapes from Farview, this higher escape rate can be attributed to the lower emphasis that is placed on security by civil mental hospitals. Our concern now is in examining the extent to which the transfer of the Dixon patients to these less secure facilities posed a substantial threat to the community by increasing the likelihood of escape by serious, violent offenders.

A comparison of those who escaped and those who entered the community with the sanction of the clinical staffs at the transfer hospitals does not indicate any substantial differences between the two groups. The two groups did not differ in terms of age ($\chi^2 = 3.9$, $df = 3$, $p < .25$)[5], the variable that was found to be most highly related to the decision to discharge (see chapter 7). Moreover, the two groups did not differ in terms of their prior criminal behavior. For example, the Dixon offense type is not related to type of release—escape vs. all other types ($\chi^2 = .09$, $df = 3$, $p < .8$). Forty-five percent of those who escaped had been committed to Farview for a violent offense, while 54 percent of those who did not escape had been committed for a violent act.

In terms of their postrelease behavior, those who escaped are no different from those who secured their release via discharge (tables 9.7 and 9.8). Although 28 percent of the escapees were rearrested, while 23.4 percent of the discharged group were, the chi-square for this association is not significant. For the variable of dangerousness the two groups are almost identical. Of those who escaped, 16 percent were classified as dangerous while of those who were discharged, 14.4 percent were so classified. Again the chi-square statistic was not significant.

TABLE 9.7 Rearrest by Escape Status

Rearrest Status	Escape Status	
	Escaped	Discharged
Rearrested	28.0%	23.4%
	(7)	(91)
Not rearrested	72.0	76.6
	(18)	(298)
Total	100.0	100.0
	(25)	(389)

NOTE: $\chi^2 = .282$; df=1, NS.

TABLE 9.8   Dangerousness by Escape Status

Dangerousness status	Escape Status	
	Escaped	Discharged
Dangerous	16.0%	14.4%
	(4)	(56)
Not dangerous	84.0	85.6
	(21)	(333)
Total	100.0	100.0
	(25)	(389)

NOTE: $\chi^2 = .055$; df = 1, NS.

While the transfer of the Dixon patients to civil mental hospitals increased the frequency of escapes, those subjects who secured their release via escape were no different from their counterparts who left with medical sanction. The groups do not differ in terms of key background variables and they do not differ in their postrelease behavior.

PREDICTION OF REARREST AND DANGEROUSNESS

One of the most important theoretical and policy-oriented questions that can be addressed with these data is the ability to predict membership in the 23.7 percent of the subjects who were rearrested and, more important, in the 14.5 percent who were dangerous. Those variables that could potentially differentiate between subjects who were and were not arrested and between subjects who were and were not dangerous are presented in table 9.9.

The groups were not significantly different from one another on any of the following variables: previous sex offenses, race, type of commitment to Farview, type or seriousness of the Dixon offense, and age on admission to Farview. Subjects who were arrested had more formal schooling, were hospitalized more often, and had longer and more serious offense careers, which began at an earlier age, than their counterparts who were not arrested. They also spent a briefer period at Farview and were younger at the time of their transfer. With few exceptions the dangerous subjects differed from the nondangerous subjects in the same ways. When compared to the nondangerous subjects, the dangerous subjects were hospitalized more often, were younger at the time of their first hospitalization, committed more offenses and more violent

TABLE 9.9   Rearrest and Dangerousness by Background Variables

Variable	Rearrest		Dangerousness	
	Not Arrested	Arrested	Not Dangerous	Dangerous
Highest school year completed	6.9 *	7.7	7.0	7.5
No. of previous hospitals	0.9 *	1.6	0.9 *	1.6
Age at first hospitalization, yr	29.6	27.8	29.9 *	26.1
Total seriousness score	879 *	1,430	966 *	1,346
No. of prior arrests	4.8 *	7.8	5.7	6.6
No. of arrests for violent offenses	0.8	1.1	0.1 *	1.3
No. of arrests for sex offenses	0.2	0.4	0.3	0.4
Seriousness of Dixon offense	504	415	484	489
Age at first arrest, yr	22.5 *	19.2	22.2 *	19.1
Race				
% of blacks	75.3	24.7	84.8	15.2
% of whites	78.4	21.6	87.1	12.9
Commitment to Farview				
% criminally committed	78.6	21.4	87.0	13.0
% civilly committed	67.7	32.3	80.6	19.4
Dixon offense type, %				
Violent offenses	79.5	20.5	88.4	11.6
Sex offenses	81.4	17.6	88.2	11.8
Property offenses	80.7	19.3	89.5	10.5
Other offenses	69.4	30.6	75.5	24.5
Age on admission to Farview, yr	32.5	32.2	32.7	30.7
Length of stay at Farview, yr	14.0 *	6.9	13.2 *	7.2
Age on transfer from Farview, yr	46.4 *	38.9	45.8 *	38.3

*Indicates difference significant at .05 level (t tests were used, except for the variables of race, commitment to Farview and Dixon offense type, where chi-square tests were employed).

offenses, and were younger at the time of their first arrest. They were also younger at the time of their transfer from Farview and had spent a shorter period at Farview.

In general the arrested and the dangerous subjects are similar, and both differ from their counterparts in the same manner. These subjects are younger and have had more extensive contact with both the criminal justice and mental health systems. Although statistically significant differences do exist, they do not, even in combination, provide the basis for accurate statistical predictions.

In an extensive attempt to predict both rearrest and dangerousness among the Dixon patients, Jacoby (1976) found the rate of false positives to be so high as to prohibit accurate prediction. A multivariate analysis employing the starred variables listed in table 9.9, as well as other variables, failed to achieve a high level of predictive accuracy. The arrested/not arrested analysis resulted in the correct classificaton of 69 percent of the subjects. However, the high rate of false positives, 60 percent, resulted in the prediction that 105 men would be arrested when in fact they were not.

Jacoby's results for the prediction of dangerousness resulted in quite similar findings. Seventy-two percent of all subjects were correctly classified and 77 percent of those who became dangerous were correctly "predicted." Again, however, a high false positive rate (70 percent) contaminated the prediction and resulted in 107 men being predicted dangerous when they were not.

In the attempt to predict both dangerousness and rearrest, Jacoby found that the variable that accounted for the most explained variation was an age-related one. Because of this, the relationships between age on release from Farview and the likelihood of being rearrested and being dangerous are presented in table 9.10. As expected, the younger subjects exhibit higher rates of rearrest and dangerous behavior and both chi-square values are significant. Nevertheless, for the youngest age group, the majority of the subjects were not rearrested, nor were they dangerous. Of the subjects under thirty-five years of age, 39.6 percent were rearrested and 23.8 percent were dangerous. Although the younger subjects are more likely to exhibit violent or criminal behavior, the variable of age, both singularly and in combination with other variables, does not produce an accurage prediction of postrelease failure. Nevertheless, the data in table 9.10, especially those concerning rearrest, support the existing evidence that younger persons are more likely to recidivate, and indicate that releasing young mentally ill offenders will be fraught with greater risks.

Using a combination of age and a summary score of past criminal history, Steadman and Cocozza (1974, p. 148) attempted to predict rearrest and dangerousness among the Baxstrom patients. In predicting rearrest they correctly predicated 77 percent of the cases but obtained a false positive rate of 52 percent. In predicting dangerousness, 70 percent of the cases were correctly classified but there was a false positive rate of 70 percent. Steadman and Cocozza's method proved even less accurate when applied to the Dixon patients. Using their criteria (subjects under

TABLE 9.10   Rearrest and Dangerousness by Age

Age at Transfer from Farview	Rearrest		Dangerousness	
	Subjects Not Rearrested	Subjects Rearrested	Subjects Not Dangerous	Subjects Dangerous
<35	60.4%	39.6%	76.2%	23.8%
	(61)	(40)	(77)	(24)
35–49	79.5	20.6	85.8	14.2
	(140)	(36)	(151)	(25)
50–64	79.0	21.0	89.5	10.5
	(83)	(22)	(94)	(11)
65+	100.0	0	100.0	0
	(32)	(0)	(32)	(0)
	$\chi^2 = 25.63$; $df = 3$; $p = .001$		$\chi^2 = 13.8$; $df = 3$; $p = .004$	

fifty years of age with a legal dangerousness score of 5 or more), 60 percent of the Dixon patients were correctly predicted to be arrested or not arrested, with a false positive rate of 70 percent. In predicting dangerousness, 61 percent were correctly predicted, with a false positive rate of 80 percent.

The ability to predict dangerousness among the released Dixon patients is severely hampered by the high rate of false positives. While the statement that 72 percent of the subjects could be accurately classified may seem relatively high, it should be kept in mind that the simplistic prediction that none of the patients would be dangerous is correct in 86 percent of the cases. In fact, we arrive at the same conclusion reached by Steadman and Cocozza:

> If we were to attempt to use this information for statistically predicting dangerousness, our best strategy would be to assume that none of the patients were dangerous. In this case, we would be wrong in 14 of the 98 cases. *Any other method would increase our error* (1974, p. 151, emphasis in original).

The situation is not substantially different for the Dixon patients.

The findings presented in this chapter regarding the recidivism and dangerousness of released mentally ill offenders are quite consistent with those in previous research. Unlike the popular image of these patients as violent offenders, the empirical evidence indicates that only a distinct minority of these offenders are recidivists (23 percent), and an even smaller minority (14 percent) are dangerous. Although the dangerous patients differ from the nondangerous ones in a number of respects, the differences reported here do not provide the basis for accurate predictions of violence or recidivism.

The political prediction that the Dixon patients would be dangerous after release is largely inaccurate and should not be used in future policy decisions. Nevertheless, there is some degree of violence after release and therefore society does incur some social costs by releasing the criminally insane. In the next chapter we will summarize the evidence bearing on this theme and attempt to draw appropriate theoretical and empirical conclusions.

Much has been written about mentally ill offenders from legal, psychological, and sociological perspectives. Yet surprisingly little is known about the behavior of these offenders after their release from confinement. Indeed, only one study has examined the behavior of these patients after release (Steadman and Cocozza 1974), and none has interviewed these subjects in the community to measure their attitudes and adjustment. This research project has attempted to fill this lacuna.

It was generated by a federal court suit, *Donald Dixon et al.* v. *Attorney General of the Commonwealth of Pennsylvania*, which alleged that 586 mentally ill offenders had been unconstitutionally committed to Farview State Hospital. In ruling for the plaintiffs the court ordered the state to transfer these patients to civil mental hospitals and then, following clinical evaluation, to the community. This book has examined the aftermath of the Dixon decision, concentrating on two general theoretical concerns.

The first involved an examination of the political prediction of dangerousness. Such predictions are based, not on characteristics of the individual, but on characteristics of a group to which the individual belongs. Since all members of the group share characteristics which are *assumed* to be accurate predicators of danger-

ousness, the group prediction is applied to each member. Moreover, since the predictions are made in a highly charged political
atmosphere, the predictions tend to be conservative, that is, to
overestimate the rate of dangerousness.

In the case of the Dixon patients, the political prediction that
most of the subjects would be dangerous if released was based on
the undemonstrated assumption that mentally ill offenders, as a
group, contain a high proportion of people likely to be violent if
not restrained. This prediction led to decisions by the Farview
staff to retain the Dixon patients in confinement. By so doing, the
staff minimized their exposure to the adverse political consequences that could occur should violent acts be committed by
released patients.[1] These predictions notwithstanding, the Dixon
decision released most of these patients, thereby creating a
natural experiment which has allowed us to assess the accuracy of
this type of prediction.

The second question posed by this project centered on the
impact of the decision on the lives of the Dixon patients and
stemmed from our concern with the appropriateness of the
court's remedy. The accumulative disadvantage of the social histories of the Dixon patients and the fact that they had averaged
fourteen years in confinement at Farview suggest that they may
have been unable to achieve an adequate level of adjustment in
the community. If these patients preferred institutional living and
were unable to adjust to the freedom and independence of the
community, the conclusion that the decision fostered the needs of
the class members would be unjustifiable. This research concern
led to an examination of the attitudes of the Dixon patients as
well as their social and psychological adjustment in the
community.

The empirical evidence that relates to each of these questions
will be summarized below. Following that, the theoretical and
policy implicaitons that flow from these findings will be presented.

The Accuracy of the Political Prediction

Was the political prediction that the Dixon patients would be
dangerous after their release from Farview accurate? Based on
the evidence presented above the answer is quite simple—no, it
was not. Information on the assaultiveness of the Dixon patients,
both during and after hospitalization, was analyzed and in every

instance the rates of assaultive behavior were relatively low. At no point in the analysis was evidence uncovered that would substantiate the claim that a majority of the Dixon subjects were dangerous.

While at Farview the Dixon patients exhibited low rates of assaultive behavior as measured by both incident reports and ward notes. Over half of the patients had no incident reports in their records and those that did were as likely to be victims as they were to be offenders. The typical incident was a scuffle among patients and the level of injury that resulted indicates that the assaults were not exceptionally serious. The behavior of these patients as reflected in the ward notes was similar in that it did not indicate frequent assaultive behavior, the most common notations indicating negative attitudes and psychotic symptoms. For both measures there was a strong inverse relation with temporal variables. The highest rates (0.36 incidents per patient per year) were associated with the youngest patients and patients' first years of hospitalization, but at no time could the rates be considered high.

This low level of assaultive behavior was not a function of the strict security at Farview. Data collected at the transfer hospitals where security was not a central concern substantiate the above findings. Although disruptive behavior did not decrease with time at the transfer hospitals, possibly because of the relatively short lengths of stay, both incident reports and ward notes indicate low levels of such behavior. Incident rates never exceeded 0.04 incidents per month per patient. As was the case at Farview, the data indicate that the assaults that did occur were relatively minor in that there were very few serious injuries. These conclusions, based on hospital records, were reinforced by informal interviews conducted with administrators at the transfer hospitals. Almost invariably they reported little disruptive behavior on the part of the Dixon patients, and they did not feel compelled to take special security precautions when the Dixon patients arrived at their hospitals. By and large, the Dixon patients were assimilated, with little difficulty, into the general population at each of the civil mental hospitals.

Their confinement at these hospitals was rather brief however, and over two-thirds were eventually released to the community. Once in the community the Dixon subjects did not exhibit high rates of violent behavior. After forty-eight months of continuous exposure, 27 percent were rearrested, and the offenses they committed ran the gamut of seriousness. They were most frequently arrested for property crimes and crimes that can be classified as victimless or against the public order. Contrary to the popular image of the criminally insane, sex offenses were quite rare and violent offenses accounted for a small proportion of their criminal activity. Only 11 percent were arrested for a violent offense.

Dangerousness was defined as an arrest or rehospitalization for a violent act, and 14.5 percent of the subjects who had been released to the community were classified as dangerous, with an expected failure rate of 18 percent after forty-eight months of exposure. Our definition of dangerousness, is, by design, quite broad and includes rearrest or rehospitalization for *any* violent offense, even relatively minor ones. Even so, fewer than one in every seven of the Dixon patients could be classified as dangerous after an average four-year follow-up.

In sum, the Dixon patients were not frequently disruptive at Farview, in the civil mental hospitals, or in the community. An image of the Dixon patients that is based on the premise that the majority of these patients are and will be dangerous is erroneous. Assaultive behavior is typical of only a minority of these patients, and serious assaultive behavior is typical of even fewer.

The Adjustment of the Dixon Patients

Even though the Dixon patients did not pose a substantial threat to others, the question of whether they should have been released from Farview must also address the issue of their ability to adjust to community living. If their mental illness and long-term institutionalization at Farview rendered them incapable of achieving an adequate life style in the community, the transfer of these patients to the community may not have been the most effective way of securing their constitutional rights. The data collected in this study, however, suggest that this concern is unfounded.

In the first place, the Dixon patients clearly preferred to be discharged from Farview. Their attitudes about that institution were extremely negative and they viewed life at Farview as brutal and nontherapeutic. Although they preferred living at the civil mental hospitals to living at Farview, their strongest preference was for life in the community. Despite, or perhaps because of, their long periods of institutionalization, very few of the Dixon patients evidenced a preference for institutional life. The members of the class agreed with the result of the Dixon decision which released them from Farview.

The day-to-day living arrangements of the released Dixon patients also indicate their ability to adjust to community living. The residential histories of the Dixon patients demonstrated a high degree of stability. Many patients lived with their families, the number of residential moves was not large, and few patients were forced to live lonely degrading lives in boarding houses.

Although their residential patterns were stable, the adjustment of the Dixon patients in relation to employment was quite poor. There was an exceptionally high unemployment rate, 71.8 percent at the time of the interviews, and over half of released Dixon patients never held a job after release. Moreover, for those who did work the types of jobs they held were rather menial and the weekly salaries were quite low. The interviewed subjects indicated that they had a good deal of difficulty in finding work and reported that they had received little help from employment services.

In general, the released Dixon subjects did not receive many aftercare services. A sizable minority, 28 percent, received no psychological treatment in the community and more than 70 percent received no assistance from public agencies in obtaining such necessities as a home, job, and medical treatment. Nevertheless, this lack of aftercare did not seem to provide a serious obstacle to their adjustment, as indicated by the low rate of rehospitalization. After an average four-year follow-up, only 16 percent had been rehospitalized and very few were rehospitalized more than once.

The final data on adjustment came from the Katz Adjustment Scale (KAS), which provides an overall assessment of social and psychological adjustment. The Dixon patients were compared to two groups of mental patients who had been confined for comparatively brief periods of time in civil mental hospitals, and the scores of all three groups were standardized in terms of the scores of a normal, nonhospitalized group. When the entire Dixon class, including, those who were never released from the transfer hospitals, was analyzed, the Dixon patients exhibited poorer adjustment than the civil patients. However, when comparable subsets of the Dixon patients were compared to the two groups of civil mental patients, there were virtually no discernible differences among the groups. On only one of twenty-two scales of the KAS, emotional stability, did the Dixon patients exhibit substantially poorer adjustment. Moreover, the favorable scores of the Dixon patients are not explained by the fact that they were relatively old at the time of their release, as length of stay at Farview was not related to the adjustment scores of the Dixon patients.

Given the attitudes of the Dixon patients, their residential stability, the low rate of rehospitalization, and their favorable social and psychological adjustment on the KAS, one can conclude that the Dixon patients were able to adjust to the freedom of living in the community. The only area in which they consistently demonstrated poor adjustment was that of employment. This generally favorable adjustment was achieved in the absence of strong and frequent contact with social service agencies. Nevertheless, the Dixon patients adjusted to the community as well as "typical" patients released from civil mental hospitals.

THE IMPLICATIONS OF THE DIXON RESEARCH

The general issue of how the criminally insane should be treated in a democratic society is quite complex and involves the consideration of clinical, constitutional, and political factors, as the work of Kittrie (1971) and Wexler (1976) has shown. It is also an issue that quite possibly cannot be resolved through the analysis of quantifiable data alone, since some of the most important issues resist quantification. For example, it is extremely difficult to place a value on the amount of crime that is tolerable or on the pain and suffering experienced by the victims of crime or by offenders incarcerated because they might commit offenses if released. Nevertheless, the resolution of the issue can be advanced, albeit not completed, by the empirical examination of those variables that can be quantified. Indeed, in many respects, this has been the major purpose of the present research project. Our final task, therefore, is to discuss the implications that the empirical findings just summarized have on the general issue of how the criminally insane should be treated in the future.

These implications flow from the data collected in the Dixon research project and, as such, are most directly applicable to the handling of the criminally insane in Pennsylvania. As we have already noted, however, the situation in Pennsylvania is not unique (see Kittrie 1971; Steadman and Cocozza 1974; Wexler 1976) and virtually all of these implications can be generalized to other jurisdictions. Specifically, we believe they can be generalized to jurisdictions in which the criminally insane are institutionalized on indeterminate commitments, in specialized maximum security hospitals that emphasize custodial rather than rehabilitative care, and in which release from the institution is at the discretion of the staff. Whenever the paradigm for treating the criminally insane differs from this model, however, the applicability of the discussion which follows will need to be tempered.

The Necessity of Maximum Security Hospitals

Perhaps the most basic question in this area is whether the criminally insane should continue to be institutionalized in special, maximum security hospitals like Farview. The weight of the evidence collected in this project suggests that they should not. This conclusion is quite consistent with recent legal changes which place stringent limitations on the extent to which incarceration can be used as a primary treatment modality for the mentally ill.

> Lawyers are arguing, and courts are increasingly accepting, the principle of the "least restrictive alternative"—i.e., that full-scale hospitalization, particularly of civil patients, is not constitutionally warranted where alternatives less restrictive of liberty are preferred by proposed patients and at the same time are deemed medically feasible (Wexler 1976, p. 4).

Given the principle of the least restrictive alternative and the data analyzed in this monograph, it is difficult to conclude that institutions like Farview are necessary.

The first legal criterion mentioned in the above passage is quite clearly not met. The Dixon patients overwhelmingly preferred not to be incarcerated at Farview and were much more favorably disposed to the less restrictive environment of civil mental hospitals. More importantly, however, the data collected in this project suggest that the criminally insane can be managed in civil mental hospitals without posing a substantial threat to themselves, other patients, or the staff. The Dixon patients who were transferred to civil hospitals were not assaultive, did not require lengthy periods of treatment, and were quickly integrated into the general populations at these hospitals. In brief, the Dixon data indicate that the criminally insane can be successfully treated with alternatives less restrictive than maximum security confinement.

In addition to this legal issue, the doctrine of the right to treatment also suggests that large-scale maximum security hospitals may be an outmoded method of treating the criminally insane.

The outlines may not be clear yet, but a new right has been born under the therapeutic state . . . . Its implication is that effective treatment must be the *quid pro quo* for society's right to exercise its *parens patriae* controls (Kittrie 1971, p. 398).

Wexler has more recently suggested that the principle of the right to treatment has been, and will continue to be, expanded to include not only *parens patriae* cases, usually civil commitments, but also "security status" patients, which includes most criminally insane commitments (Wexler 1976, pp. 9–12). The key question in this area is, Can maximum security hospitals fulfill the patient's right to treatment?

The existing evidence suggests that, up to the present, they have not. The material in the first chapter indicates that Farview has never provided an adequate clinical program for its charges and the NIMH Medicare evaluation of 1976 indicates that even the Dixon decision has not altered that situation. Moreover, the literature on the treatment of the criminally insane (see, for example, Kittrie 1971, chapter 6; Prettyman 1972; Steadman and Cocozza 1974; Wexler 1976) suggests that the situation at Farview is typical for this country. The paradoxical policy of committing the criminally insane until cured, in institutions that do not provide treatment, is unfortunately "par for the course."

The extent to which this situation can be ameliorated in the future is also problematic. Whenever an institution is designated as a special facility to handle "dangerous" patients, it seems that the potential of that institution to deliver effective therapy is severely limited. Such facilities are usually constructed in remote geographical areas, have difficulty in securing adequate funding and adequate staffs, and often, whether by design or practice, become institutions of the last resort to which difficult patients are transferred and forgotten. This is the sad history of such institutions and the prospects for significant improvement in the forseeable future must be viewed with some skepticism.

In combination, the legal doctrines of the least restrictive alternative and the right to treatment, and the data collected in this project lead to the conclusion that large-scale maximum security hospitals should not be used to treat the criminally insane. These hospitals have not provided adequate treatment and, as we have seen with the Dixon patients, they are not the least restrictive setting under which such patients can be handled without adverse consequences. We agree with Wexler's recommendations in this respect:

> . . . *it ought to be possible to convert some of the space* [in civil hospitals] *into security units.* In economic terms, groups and commentators who have studied the problem of conversion have concluded that the venture need not be very difficult or very costly. Moreover . . . there are numerous administrative and therapeutic advantages that flow from having a security unit as part of a general state or regional mental hospital rather than as a wholly separate institution (1976, p. 6, emphasis in original).

In fact, the necessity of having specialized security wards may even be overestimated if the experiences of the Dixon patients are replicated, since virtually all of these patients were integrated into the general population of Pennsylvania's civil hospitals following their transfer from Farview. If required at all, security wards may be most useful for younger, newly admitted patients since the only time at which the assaultive behavior of the Dixon patients was even moderately high was immediately after their admission to Farview.

LENGTH OF COMMITMENTS

If the treatment of the criminally insane is transferred from special facilities to civil mental hospitals, a number of other issues emerge. Among the most important are those which concern the duration of confinement. The implications of the Dixon research for these issues can only be stated in rather general terms for a variety of ancillary issues, for example, criminal sentences, would have to be considered in a complete assessment.

In general, the length of confinement for criminally insane

patients can be relatively short. The Dixon patients were confined for an average of 14.1 years and, in New York State, the Baxstrom patients had been confined for an average of 14.7 years before they were transferred by court decisions (Steadman and Cocozza 1974, p. 78). In both cases the empirical evidence suggests that confinement for this length of time is excessive and is not required for the benefit of either the patients or the community.

For the Dixon patients two sets of data lead to this conclusion. The first concerns the postrelease adjustment of the patients which, as we have seen, indicates that the Dixon patients exhibit social and psychological adjustment scores that are comparable to "typical" mental patients. Yet these typical patients were hospitalized for much shorter periods of time, on the average for a year. If the Dixon patients can adjust to the community as well as these patients, why should they not be treated in a manner similar to these patients? We have already suggested that these two groups can be treated in the same facilities; we are now suggesting that they can also be treated in the same programs which emphasize short-term confinement, supplemented by postrelease community treatment.[2] The inclusion of aftercare services in our recommendation is based on the use of these techniques in the studies that examined the successful adjustment of the "typical" mental patients (Michaux et al. 1969; NIMH 1964) as well as the overall effectiveness of treating the mentally ill in the community (Pasamanick et al. 1967). Regardless of the exact form of the treatment program, the available data suggest that extremely long periods of confinement are not necessary for enhancing the social and psychological adjustment of the Dixon patients.

Although the data on adjustment suggest that short-term confinement is appropriate, the issue ultimately turns on the postrelease dangerousness of these patients. If released criminally insane offenders prey on society, the protection of the commonweal would demand their continued confinement, regardless of their psychological adjustment. The present findings on dangerousness also suggest, however, that long-term confinement is excessive. After a forty-eight-month exposure period, 18 percent of the Dixon patients were dangerous, which is quite similar to the crude rate of 14.3 percent found in the Baxstrom research (Steadman and Coccozza 1974, p. 151). Thus a policy of long-term confinement which is based on the premise of preventing violent behavior is grossly inefficient. It results in the confinement of 100 patients of whom 82 will not be dangerous during the first four years following release. Moreover, the definition of dangerousness used here is based on all violent offenses, including a number of relatively minor ones. If only the more serious violent offenses were included in the definition, for example, homicide, rape, robbery, and aggravated assault, the rate of dangerousness would be reduced to approximately 7 percent, and the policy of long-term confinement would be even less efficient.

Even though the rate of dangerous behavior is inversely related to age and length of confinement, the incidence of such behavior among the youngest patients still involves a minority (24 percent) of the Dixon patients. Thus the overall crude rate of 14 percent cannot be attributed to the success of the policy which retains younger, extremely violent patients and releases older nonviolent patients. At all ages the rate of dangerousness is quite low.

Given these data on community adjustment and dangerousness, we conclude that the long-term confinement of the criminally insane is excessive and inefficient. These data, along with those collected by Steadman and Cocozza (1974), strongly suggest that a policy which emphasized shorter periods of confinement in civil mental hospitals where treatment programs are available will be at least as efficient as the present policy of long-term confinement in maximum security institutions. Such a policy would also be far more consistent with the legal doctrines of the least restrictive alternative and the right to treatment.

This recommendation is based on the aggregated data analysis conducted in this project. As such it is a suggestion for a general policy of how the criminally insane should be treated and needs to be tempered in the individual case and by other considerations. It does not imply that all mentally ill offenders should be confined only briefly. Indeed, it may be quite appropriate to confine some subgroups of the criminally insane for considerable periods of time because they committed heinous acts.

Offenders who committed mass murders or particularly bizarre, brutal, and wanton acts are candidates for such subgroups. It is important to note, however, that the long-term confinement of such subgroups is based on the nature of their past acts and not on the assumption that they will repeat these acts. It is also predicated on models of punishment, such as the "just deserts" model or the reaffirmation of community standards that have been seriously violated, that are not concerned with preventive detention. Regardless of their expected future behavior and regardless of their mental state, justice and society may be served by confining some offenders for long periods of time in response to their behavior.

Proportionately, however, such offenders are relatively rare. In any population of the criminally insane, the proportion who would repetitively commit serious violent acts is quite small and the overall policy concerning the treatment of the criminally insane should not be based on the behavior of this small subgroup. Hence our general recommendation, based on our data and the legal doctrines of least restrictive alternatives and the right to treatment remains the same—overall, the criminally insane should be confined for relatively brief periods of time.

We realize that the suggestion that periods of confinement should be relatively short is rather vague, but defining appropriate lengths of commitment goes well beyond the boundaries of our research. To do so would involve a consideration of clinical and psychiatric treatment modalities as well as legal factors, such as the impact of criminal sentences on commitment times and appropriate methods for handling offenders found incompetent to stand trial (see Burt and Morris 1972, for a discussion of the complexity of this last factor). Nevertheless there is one aspect of this issue which can be discussed here and which will indicate how the objective of shorter commitment periods can be achieved. This issue concerns procedures for releasing the criminally insane from confinement.

PROCEDURES FOR RELEASE

As long as the power to release involuntarily committed patients is vested in the clinicians who are responsible for providing treatment, the likelihood of conservative decisions and concomitantly long commitments is ensured. This relationship has been noted by a number of authors. Steadman has discussed the "psychiatrist as a conservative agent of social control" (1972), Prettyman has noted that in such a setting "the psychiatrist becomes more of a jailer than a healer" (1972, p. 19), and Morris has said that

The rehabilitative ideal is seen to impart unfettered discretion. Whereas the treaters seem convinced of the benevolence of their treatment methods, those being treated take a different view, and we, the observers, share their doubts. The jailer in a white coat and with a doctorate remains a jailer—but with larger powers over his fellows (1966, p. 637).

This same issue has also been discussed in depth in this work. It is our view that the political environment in which maximum security hospitals operate increases the likelihood that the criminally insane will be denied release, when even a slight risk of recidivism exists. Because negative consequences attend erroneous decisions, clinicians at security hospitals make the political prediction that most of these patients will be dangerous after release, and, as a result, opt for long periods of confinement. As we have seen, however, these predictions are grossly inaccurate.

Because these predictions are inaccurate, their impact on decisions to release the criminally insane must be minimized. The most important step in achieving this objective is to remove the authority for releasing the patient from the hands of those who are responsible for treating the patient. For only by doing this can we separate the roles of healer and jailer and reduce the political pressures that contaminate both the treatment and the decision to release the patient. This does not mean that the views of the treating clinician should be ignored in the decision-making process. On the contrary, if the decision to release is withdrawn from the clinician's role, the clinician would hopefully focus more attention on the progress the patient has made, and not, to the same extent as he currently does, on the consequences of the decision. In such a setting, the import of the clinician's professional opinion may well be enhanced.

In lieu of decisions made at the discretion of the hospital staff, a number of alternatives are available. The most direct approach to limiting both discretion and the amount of time served by the criminally insane would be to set durational limits on their commitments. This option has been discussed by Wexler, who cites a number of recent court cases in which such limits based on the notions of "just deserts" and "proportionality" have been suggested (1976, p. 26 ff.). Legislative and judicial decisions may well lead to this path and the criminally insane may not be subjected to indeterminate sentences in the future.

Even within the framework of indeterminate sentences, however, a number of procedural changes could occur which would drastically reduce the likelihood that the criminally insane would spend many years in confinement because some of them will be dangerous. Among these changes the following, which could be used in combination, can be mentioned.

1. The decision to release offenders could be diffused so that the final decision is made by a group rather than an individual. "Psychological studies suggest that if a legal decision-making structure could be designed in which ... release responsibility is shared or diffused, the decision to release might be made with fewer inhibitions" (Wexler 1976, p. 54). The model of parole boards that are used in determining the length of criminal sentences could be explored in this context.

2. The periodic review of cases, perhaps every six months, could be mandated so that patients could not be "lost" in hospitals for years at a time. At each of these reviews, the decision to continue the confinement would have to be reaffirmed.

3. Specific criteria for retaining a patient would have to be created. The state would be obliged to demonstrate that these criteria have been met rather than forcing the patient to demonstrate, through *habeas corpus* proceedings or independent psychiatric review, that they are not met.

4. Wexler has suggested that "statutes could—and should—be enacted immunizing institutions and therapeutic staff from liability for release decisions made in good faith exercise of professional discretion" (1976, p. 54). The same type of immunization could also be extended to decision-making bodies that exist independently of the hospital staffs.

No doubt there are other alternatives that could be suggested and experimented with in an attempt to improve the rationality of decisions concerning the release of the criminally insane. The foregoing have been presented as illustrations of the type of changes that are needed. Although these suggestions are not exhaustive, the data collected about the Dixon patients are conclusive in suggesting that the present situation is inefficient and results in excessively long periods of confinement.

Moreover these recommendations conform quite closely to judicial and legislative changes that have occurred in the last twenty years. Courts have become increasingly willing to hear cases challenging the casual and indetermine commitment of mentally ill offenders. In 1966, *Baxstrom* v. *Herold* (383 U.S. 107) established for the first time that an original criminal commitment to a mental institution could not be extended by perfunctory administrative procedures, but that a criminally committed patient, at the expiration of his sentence, had a right to due process protections available to other persons whom the state attempted to commit under civil commitment proceedings. In *Jackson* v. *Indiana* (406 U.S. 715 [1972]) the U.S. Supreme Court declared that the state could not hold for an unlimited period a defendant judged not competent to stand trial. Either a defendant must be brought to trial, or the state must determine that he is not likely to attain competency in a reasonable period and release him from criminal confinement.

Subsequent to the Dixon case, a federal court declared unconstitutional, as a violation of due process, Section 411 of the Pennsylvania Mental Health Act of 1966 under which prison inmates were transferred to Farview without a formal hearing.[3] With several sections of the Mental Health Act of 1966 voided or under attack, the 1976 session of the Pennsylvania Legislature passed a new Mental Health Procedures Act repealing most of the old law and containing many of the changes we have recommended above. It states as a matter of policy that treatment will be under "the least restrictions consistent with adequate treatment," requires that individualized treatment plans be formulated and reviewed at least once a month, and places the burden of proof that treatment is being conducted under the least restrictive alternative on the treatment team. The new law grants immunity from civil and criminal liability, except for gross negligence or willful misconduct, to any person who makes decisions about the treatment, hospitalization, or discharge of patients.

The law provides limits on the maximum duration of every type of commitment. Persons under sentence or awaiting trial receive credit toward their sentences, including sentences not yet imposed, for time spent in a hospital. Defendants committed as incompetent to stand trial may not be held for longer than the maximum sentence they could have received, or five years, whichever is less.

The procedures surrounding commitment and release of mentally ill offenders are being made more just by the legislative and judicial actions described above. The results of this project suggest that additional significant changes in the handling of the criminally insane in our society could and should be implemented. Our findings suggest that the criminally insane can be treated in civil mental hospitals rather than special maximum security institutions, that they need not be kept for excessively long periods of time, and that releasing procedures which reduce the likelihood of political predictions should be implemented. The criminally insane are not exceptionally dangerous, and they are as capable as typical mental patients of adjusting to community living. We hope that the future treatment of these patients will conform to this reality rather than to the myth of the sexually deranged violent offender who continually preys on society. We also hope that the evidence collected in this project will facilitate this change.

Prior to 1 January 1967	Patients at Farview whose criminal commitments had expired were retained without judical action under section 308 of the Mental Health Act of 1923, later section 348 (*b*) of the Mental Health Act of 1951.
1 January 1967	The Mental Health Act of 1967 became effective. All Farview patients currently hospitalized and subsequently admitted were recommitted on sentence expiration under Section 404 of this act.
25 July 1969	Complaint (civil action no. 69-293) filed in U.S. District Court for the Middle District of Pennsylvania by attorneys Richard L. Bazelon, James F. McClure, Jr., and Curtis R. Reitz. Full title of the complaint was as follows:

Donald Dixon, Blair Finkenbinder, John Nichols, Dominic Rizzelli, Albert Singletary, Richard Tyciak, and Harold Vanderpool on behalf of themselves and others similarly situated Plaintiffs,

v.

The Attorney General of the Commonwealth of Pennsylvania, the Secretary of Public Welfare, the Commissioner of Mental Health of the Commonwealth of Pennsylvania and the Superintendent of Farview State Hospital, Defendants.

The complaint requested a permanent injunction restraining the commonwealth from using section 404 to commit inmates to Farview after the original authority for commitment expired and the convening of a three-judge court.

At the end of July 1969 Farview had a total of 1,170 inmates.

August 1969	The state conducted a mass review of all section 404 commitments at Farview.

26 August 1969

Superintendent of Farview submitted a report on section 404 commitments to the deputy secretary for mental health and mental retardation:

Total considered for transfer	199
Total recommended for retention	101
Alternative placements planned	74
Day-night patients working in community	6
On leave of absence	21
Left the hospital since complaint was filed	84
Died since complaint was filed	12
Total	497

October 1969

Farview transfers increased dramatically, from twenty-nine in September to ninety-five in October.

9 February 1970

Court appointed one guardian *ad litem*.

13 March 1970

First hearing.

2 June 1970

First decision, 313 F. Supp. 653 (1970), denying summary judgment and interim relief and authorizing a hearing before a three-judge panel.

22–23 July 1970

Second hearing.

8 January 1971

Posttrial hearing. Only 15 percent of the class remained at Farview. The court appointed two more guardians *ad litem*, one for each judicial district in Pennsylvania.

30 March 1971

Second decision filed, 325 F. Supp. 966 (1971).

22 April 1971

Date of consent decree and closing date of admission to Dixon class. At the end of April 1971 Farview had 734 inmates, a reduction of 436 since the filing of the complaint.

May 1971

Farview transfers again increased sharply, from eighteen in April to sixty-nine in May.

September 1971	Farview transfers returned to pre-Dixon levels, about twenty per month.
13 January 1972	Stipulation filed excluding four Dixon class patients from being transferred because they required full-time nursing care, had little or no comprehension, had spent many years at Farview, and would probably be upset by a move.
10 August 1972	Farview population reached a low of 477.

APPENDIX 2
Dixon Case Record Summary

1. Code No.
2. Did subject return to Farview *after* transfer under Dixon? If yes, give date of return.
3. Date subject was admitted to Farview.
4. Date subject was transferred from Farview.
5. Provisional mental diagnosis.
6. Revised mental diagnosis. Date.
7. Offense subject was arrested for immediately before admission to Farview.
8. If subject was convicted immediately prior to hospitalization or imprisonment leading to hospitalization, what was the length of the sentence? If determinate, number of years. If minimum-maximum, minimum and maximum years.
9. Date of court sentence.
10. Minimum expiration date of court sentence.
11. Maximum expiration date of court sentence.
12. Bad time accumulated in prison.
13. New maximum expiration date resulting from accumulated bad time in prison.
14. County of court subject was commited by.
15. Was subject transferred to Farview from a prison? If yes, specify prison. If no, specify transferring institution.
16. Race.
17. Date of birth.

Items in this and the following appendix represent, in abbreviated form, the information that was collected from the hospital files. The actual data collection forms that were used are available from the authors.

18. Martial status at time of admission to Farview.
19. Last known occupation before admission to Farview.
20. State of nativity.
21. Place of residence.
22. Reading and writing skill.
23. Other "insane hospitals"? If yes, first hospital. Second?
24. Mental hosptial to which subject was transferred from Farview.
25. Are there any independent psychiatric evaluations recorded in the file?
    If yes, give date, diagnosis, diagnostician, and recommended action.
26. Are there any records of incidents (excluding accidents) in the File? If yes,
    give incident number, date of incident, circumstances surrounding incident
    (who brought "charges" or accused subject, location of incident, who started
    it, give brief description of circumstances surrounding incident), number of
    persons injured (including subject), identity of persons injured, number of
    other patients and staff members injured, if subject was injured, who inflicted
    the injury on him? Treatment of injuries of all concerned (transferred, treated
    and sent back to ward, required no treatment, or died from injuries)?
    Description of items damaged, destroyed, or stolen, and disposition or
    punishment of subject?
27. Is there evidence in the file indicating that attempts had been made to transfer
    the subject? If yes, give date of initial transfer attempt letter or memo, form of
    evidence of transfer attempt, who initiated transfer attempt. Was a lawyer
    involved? Was there a court hearing? If the Farview staff did not initiate the
    transfer, did they consider the subject transferable? If another hospital was
    contacted regarding possible transfer, what was the name of that hospital?
    Who made the decision not to transfer? What reason was given for not trans-
    ferring subject?
28. When subject stood trial for the Dixon offense, was the question of com-
    petence to stand trial raised?
29. Who initiated the procedures that resulted in subject's being sent to Farview
    for the Dixon offense?
30. Was there any attempt to keep the committing court or institution appraised
    of the subject's situation or condition. If yes, give number of reports of subject's
    condition.
31. Who investigated subject's competence for initial commitment?
32. Circumstances leading to commitment (copy verbatim).
33. Was subject *convicted* of an offense immediately? If yes, list offenses.
34. Date subject entered prison before transfer to Farview.
35. List all previous criminal offenses before the one resulting in hospitalization
    at Farview, giving arrest date, offense, disposition, and number of years
    served.
36. Highest school grade completed.
37. Length of residence in Pennsylvania.
38. History of mental illness in family members? If yes, specify person and type of
    illness.
39. History of institutionalization or psychiatric treatment of other members of
    subject's family? If yes, specify person.
40. Number of siblings.

41. Number of wives.
42. Physical disabilities of subject. Specify.
43. WAIS score and test date.
44. MMPI score and test date.

APPENDIX 3
Transfer Hospital Record Summary

1. Subject code number.
2. Date of summary.
3. Best current address.
4. Other location information.
5. Date of most recent address information.
6. Diagnosis on admission.
7. Rediagnosis.
8. Date entered transfer hospital from Farview.
9. Transfer hospital name.
10. Has subject ever been out of the transfer hospital (transferred, released, escaped) since his admission from Farview? If yes, give date, type of move, and destination of these subsequent transfers, releases, and admissions to home, hospital, or prison.
11. Evidence of criminal activity since transfer from Farview. Give date, offense, location, circumstances, and disposition.
12. Ward transfers. Give date, ward, and security designation.
13. Dangerous behavior recorded in ward notes (give code and date).
14. Dangerous behavior recorded in incident reports.

221

APPENDIX 4
Violent Behavior Descriptions Derived from Hospital Ward Notes

Overt Violence toward Others
Assaultive
Attack
Fights
Homosexual attack
Sneak (sucker) punch
Toot (bat)
Hits, strikes, kicks, punches, slaps, shoves, pushes, bumps
Violent (episodes of violence, explosive, rampage)

Potential for Violence toward Others
Aggressive
    Potential for aggressive behavior
    Projects aggressive impulses
Dangerous
Says he does harmful things
Says he thinks harmful things
Threatens
Homicidal
Combative
Pugalistic, pugnacious (ready to fight)

Self-injury
Self-injury
    Attempts self-injury
    Threatens self-injury
Attempts suicide
Threatens suicide

Property Destruction
Destroyed property (e.g., punched out windows, "destructive," set fire)

Management Problems
Disturbing
Problem
Management problem
Requires close supervision
Trouble
    Gets into trouble
    Gives trouble
    Makes (causes) trouble

Angry and Anti-authoritarian Attitudes
Antisocial
Angry
Arrogant
Belligerent
Defiant
Hostile
Irritable
Easily takes offense
Oppositional
Quarrelsome
Sullen
Surly
Suspicious

Psychotic
Agitated
Disturbed
Paranoid
Psychotic

APPENDIX 5
Seriousness Scores by Offense Type

Offense Classification	Mean Seriousness Score	SD	No. of Offenses
Homicide	2,734.2	152.1	19
Rape	1,096.4	882.4	58
Robbery	380.6	223.8	230
Aggravated assault	637.3	382.4	249
Burglary	258.7	97.4	682
Larceny-theft	164.5	81.4	1,244
Auto theft	268.4	122.9	469
Other assaults	208.4	171.1	577
Forgery & counterfeiting	274.4	116.4	7
Embezzlement & fraud	174.7	75.4	6
Stolen property (buying, receiving, possession)	103.4	30.5	34
Weapons	197.5	123.2	292
Prostitution & commercial vice	427.3	498.8	4
Sex offenses (not commercial)	242.3	358.8	170
Investigation of persons	193.0	. . .	1
Narcotics violation	402.7	387.6	43
Liquor violations	52.9	25.4	388
Drunkenness	65.9	14.2	219
Disorderly conduct	42.9	177.7	1,806

224

Offense Classification	Mean Seriousness Score	SD	No. of Offenses
Vagrancy	38.0	30.5	24
Gambling	70.1	32.5	138
Hospital cases	1.0	0.0	1
Traffic violations	19.0	0.0	5
Investigations	200.0	0.0	9
Other motor vehicle violations	134.0	49.0	37
All other offenses	32.1	69.7	4,128
Minor disturbances	19.0	0.0	1
Missing persons	1.0	0.0	3
Vandalism (a separate category for post-1964 offenses)	242.5	101.5	6
Total			10,850

APPENDIX 6
Subject Interview Schedule

Hello, my name is _____ and I represent a group at the University of Pennsylvania who are doing a study of people who have been to Farview Hospital.

I would like to hear your opinions about Farview and find out how you have been doing since you left there. You don't have to answer the questions if you don't want to, but by cooperating you can help other people who have experiences similar to yours.

Anything you say will be held in strictest confidence and will be treated as part of the responses of over 600 other men, so no one beyond our research group will ever know your answers. We are an independent research group not connected with any hospital or state agency. May I come in?

Name _____

Address _____   Apartment No. _____

City _____   Telephone _____

RESPONDENT CATEGORIES (CIRCLE CATEGORY NUMBER AND ENTER NUMBER IN LOWER RIGHT HAND CORNER OF LAST PAGE)

1. Respondent lives in the community

2. Respondent lives in a hospital or jail but was in the community since leaving Farview

3. Respondent lives in a hospital and was never in the community since the Dixon transfer

4. Respondent remained at Farview after the Dixon transfer

Interviewer's Signature _____

The first things I am going to ask you deal with your family background, education and things like that.

1. Up to the time you were 16 years old, whom did you live with most of the time?

Both parents	1
Mother	2
Father	3
Grandparent(s)	4
Other relatives	5
Foster parents	6
An institution (specify type)	7
Someone else (specify)	8

2. While you were growing up, what kind of work did your father or the head of your household do for a living?

_____

3. What was the highest grade you completed in school?

| Grade | |

Did you go to any kind of special school?

| Yes | |
| No | |

Next I want to ask you some questions about your marital status. We know that many men have lived with a woman without going through a formal wedding ceremony.

4. First of all, have you ever been married?

| Yes, how many times | |
| No | 0 |

5. Have you ever lived with a woman without being married?

| Yes, how many times | |
| No | 0 |

IF NEVER MARRIED NOR LIVED WITH A WOMAN SKIP TO #9

6. What is your present marital status?

Single	1
Married	2
Divorced	3
Separated	4
Widowed	5
Other (specify)	6

IF 2, 3 OR 4 SKIP TO #8

7.	Are you currently living with a woman to whom you are not formally married?		
		Yes	1
		No	0

8. Marital History-Sample Questions

A. How old were you when you were married or lived with a woman for the first time?

B. How old were you when that marriage ended?

C. How did that marriage end?

D. Was that while you were at Farview?

	Age		How Ended (See Code)	While at Farview
	From	To		
1			1 2 3 4 5	Y N
2			1 2 3 4 5	Y N
3			1 2 3 4 5	Y N
4			1 2 3 4 5	Y N
5			1 2 3 4 5	Y N
6			1 2 3 4 5	Y N
7			1 2 3 4 5	Y N
8			1 2 3 4 5	Y N
9			1 2 3 4 5	Y N
10			1 2 3 4 5	Y N

CODE: 1--Separation
       2--Desertion
       3--Divorced
       4--Widowed
       5--Other (specify)

9.	Have you ever had any children?		
	SKIP TO #12	No	0
		Yes, how many	

10. How many of them are still living?

	Enter number	

IF 2 OR 3 SKIP TO #12. IF 4 SKIP TO #62

11. How many of them are living with you now?

	Enter number	

12. The next group of questions will be about where you have been living since you left Farview.

When you left Farview in ___ ___,
                          Mo. Yr.
you went to _____ Hospital, right?

13. When did you leave _____ ?

    _____ _____
    Month   Year

IF 3, SKIP TO #16

14. When you left _____
    in _____ , did you have
    relatives you could have gone
    to live with if you wanted to?

Yes	1	
No	0	

15. Did any of your relatives ask
    you to live with them?

Yes	1	
No	0	

16. Residence History

    Starting from the time you left
    _____ Hospital in
    _____ , could you
    tell me about all the places
    where you have lived in-
    cluding any time you might
    have been in jail or in a
    hospital?

Sample Questions

A. When you left _____
   Hospital in _____ ,
   with whom did you first live?

B. In what kind of place did you
   live?

C. When did you leave there?

D. Why did you leave? (Or enter
   a hospital, or what did they
   say you did when they put you
   in jail?)

"Lived with" CODE:

1. Wife
2. Parents
3. Siblings
4. Children
5. Other relatives
6. Friend
7. By myself
8. An institution
9. Other (specify)

"Kind of Place" CODE:

1. House
2. Rented room
3. Rented apartment
4. Boarding house
5. Nursing or convalescent home
6. Mental hospital (specify)
7. Jail or prison (specify)
8. Other (specify)

	Date Arr. Mo-Yr	Date Left Mo-Yr	Lived with (CODE)	Kind of Place (CODE)	Reason for Leaving
1					
2					
3					
4					
5					
6					
7					
8					
9					
10					
11					
12					
13					
14					
15					
16					
17					

| IF 3, SKIP TO #62 | | | | 18. | Starting from the time you left _____ Hospital in _____, could you tell me about all the jobs you had and about any period of time you were unemployed, in a hospital, or in jail? |

The next group of questions is about any jobs you have had since you left the hospital

17. Have you worked at all since you left _____ Hospital in _____?

| | Yes | 1 |
| SKIP TO #23 | No | 0 |

"How job found" CODE:

1. Hospital aid
2. Mental health agency
3. Welfare agency
4. Employment agency
5. Relative or friend
6. Ad
7. Found without aid
8. Other (specify)

18. Starting from the time you left _____ Hospital in _____, could you tell me about all the jobs you had and about any period of time you were unemployed, in a hospital, or in jail?

Sample Questions

A. Right after you left _____ Hospital, what did you do?

B. Was that a full or part time job?

C. When did you start in that job?

D. When did you leave it?

E. How did you locate that job?

F. Why did you leave it?

	Job Description	From Mo-Yr	To Mo-Yr	Full or PT	How Found	Reason for Leaving
1				F P		
2				F P		
3				F P		
4				F P		
5				F P		
6				F P		
7				F P		
8				F P		
9				F P		

	Job Description	From Mo-Yr	To Mo-Yr	Full or PT	How Found	Reason for Leaving	
10				F P			
11				F P			
12				F P			
13				F P			
14				F P			
15				F P			
16				F P			
17				F P			
18				F P			
19				F P			
20				F P			

IF CURRENTLY UNEMPLOYED SKIP TO #21. IF 2, SKIP TO #23

19. How many hours do you usually work in a week?

Hours ____

20. How much money do you make each week, on the average, at your current job?

$ ____

SKIP TO #23

21. How many hours did you usually work in a week at your last job?

Hours ____

22. How much money did you make each week, on the average, at your last job?

$ ____

23. Where does the money come from to pay the bills?
(CIRCLE ALL THAT APPLY)

Your job, how much per week	
Wife's job (including woman you live with)	
Welfare and/or social sec.	
Other (family)	
Other (specify)	

24. After you left _____ Hospital in _____, did you go looking for a job?

SKIP TO #26	Yes	1
	No	0

25. Why didn't you look for a job?

_____

_____

SKIP TO #45

26. Now I would like to read you a list of problems people have in finding and keeping jobs. Would you answer true if the item describes a problem you have had in finding or keeping jobs since you left the hospital.

27. There are just not many jobs.

True	1
False	0

28. I haven't felt very well.

True	1
False	0

29. I don't have the training I need.

True	1
False	0

30. I don't need the money.

True	1
False	0

31. I haven't found the right job.

True	1
False	0

32. I went back to school.

True	1
False	0

33. I was too nervous or edgy to work.

True	1
False	0

34. I couldn't get anyone to help me look for work.

True	1
False	0

35. Employers don't like my record.

True	1
False	0

36. I haven't looked very hard for work.

True	1
False	0

37. The jobs I got were too tiring for me.

True	1
False	0

38. The people I worked with gave me a hard time.

True	1
False	0

39. I had trouble getting transportation to and from work.

True	1
False	0

40. Welfare pays too well to bother working.

True	1
False	0

41. Employment offices do not help enough.

True	1
False	0

42. Did anyone refuse you a job because you had been in a mental hospital?

	Yes	1
SKIP TO #45	No	0

43. How many times were you refused a job because you had been in a mental hospital?

Enter number	

44. PROBE. How do you know you were not hired because you were in a hospital? (Did they say that was the reason?)

A. _____

_____

B. _____

_____

C. _____

_____

45. The next group of questions refers to treatment or counseling you may have received since you left the hospital.

Since you left _____ Hospital, have you had any type of treatment or counseling by:

A psychiatrist?

Yes	1
No	0

46. A psychologist?

Yes	1
No	0

47. A social worker?

Yes	1
No	0

48. Any other type of counselor?

Yes (specify)	1
No	0

49. (Yes to any one of #45 - 48, but does not know what type of counselor he saw.)

Yes	1
No	0

IF "NO" TO ALL QUESTIONS #45 - 49, SKIP TO #56

50. Now, you saw a _____ and a _____. Was either in private practice?

Yes	1
No	0

51. At a community health center?

(REPEAT TYPES OF COUNSELORS IF NECESSARY)

Yes	1
No	0

52. At a hospital?

Yes	1
No	0

IF 2, SKIP TO #55

53. Are you currently seeing anyone for treatment or counseling? (CIRCLE ALL THAT APPLY)

	Psychiatrist	1
	Psychologist	2
	Social Worker	3
	Other(specify)	4
SKIP TO #55	None	0

54. How long have you been seeing him/them? (IF MORE THAN ONE RECORD THE LONGEST)

Months	

55. What kinds of treatment have you received outside the hospital? (CIRCLE ALL THAT APPLY)		
	Individual therapy	1
	Group therapy	2
	Electroshock	3
	Drugs	4
	Other (specify)	5

56. When people get out of the hospital they often need some help in a number of areas. After you left _____ Hospital in ____ ____, did anyone help you in:

Finding a place to live?

	Yes,who	
	No	0

57. Finding a job?

	Yes,who	
	No	0

58. Applying for welfare, social security or veteran's benefits?

	Yes,who	
	No	0

59. Getting psychiatric treatment?

	Yes,who	
	No	0

60. Getting medical care?

	Yes,who	
	No	0

61. Getting any other kind of help?

	Yes,who	
	No	0

What kind of help?

_____

_____

62. We want to get your opinion on what it is like at Farview and other hospitals. The next group of questions is about life in the hospital.

What things did you like most about Farview?

A. _____

_____

B. _____

_____

C. _____

_____

63. What things did you dislike most about Farview?

A. _____
_____

B. _____
_____

C. _____
_____

IF 4, SKIP TO #79

64. What things did you like most about _____ Hospital?

A. _____
_____

B. _____
_____

C. _____
_____

65. What things did you dislike most about _____ Hospital?

A. _____
_____

B. _____
_____

C. _____
_____

66. What do you like most about living at home rather than at a hospital?

A. _____
_____

B. _____
_____

C. _____
_____

67. What do you dislike most about living at home rather than at a hospital?

A. _____
_____

B. _____
_____

C. _____
_____

In order from best to worst:

68. Is the food you eat better at Farview, _____ Hospital or at home?

Farview	
_____ Hospital	
Home	

RECORD ORDER: 1 = Best
2 = Next best
3 = Worst

69. Are the living conditions
    better at:

	Farview	
RECORD ORDER	____Hospital	
	At home	

70. Is the psychiatric treatment
    better at:

	Farview	
RECORD ORDER	____Hospital	
	At home	

71. Is the medical treatment
    better at:

	Farview	
RECORD ORDER	____Hospital	
	At home	

72. Where did you see your family
    most often?

	Farview	
RECORD ORDER	____Hospital	
	At home	

73. Why did you see your family
    more often at ____(1 above)
    than at ____(2 above)?

A. _____

_____

B. _____

_____

74. Why did you see your family
    more often at ____(2 above)
    than at ____(3 above)?

A. _____

_____

B. _____

_____

75. In your own words, how would
    you compare the doctors at
    Farview with the doctors at
    _____ Hospital?

_____

_____

_____

76. How would you compare the aides
    at Farview with the aides at
    _____ Hospital?

_____

_____

_____

77. Would you say the programs
    were most helpful to you at:

Farview	1
____Hospital	2
About the same	3

78. Did you have more freedom to move about the hospital and do different things at:

Farview	1
_____ Hospital	2
About the same	3

79. If you could choose to live at Farview or _____ which would you choose?

Farview	1
_____ Hospital	2

80. Between:

Farview or	1
In the community	2

REPEAT "IF YOU COULD CHOOSE BETWEEN . . . WHICH WOULD YOU CHOOSE?" IF NECESSARY

81. Between:

_____ Hospital	1
In the community	2

The next group of questions is about your transfer to Farview and what you think about that.

82. First, why do you think you were transferred to Farview? (BE SURE RESPONDENT UNDERSTANDS THIS IS ABOUT THE DIXON OFFENSE)

_____

_____

_____

_____

83. Before you were transferred to Farview did you attend a court hearing where a judge ordered you sent to Farview?

	Yes	1
SKIP TO #85	No	0

84. Did you have a lawyer representing you at that hearing?

	Yes	1
	No	0

85. What good results came out of your being at Farview?

A. _____

_____

B. _____

_____

C. _____

_____

86. What bad results came out of your being at Farview?

A. _____

_____

B. _____

_____

C. _____

_____

IF 2, 3 OR 4, EXCLUDE WORDS
IN BRACKETS

The next group of questions is designed to give us some idea of how
well you have been feeling from day
to day [and the kinds of things you
have been doing while living here.
In the first part we are interested
in how well you have been feeling
lately.] There are a number of
statements on this list which
describe symptoms that people sometimes have. Please listen to each
of the statements carefully and
decide whether you have had the
complaint today or during the past
few weeks. Then tell me whether
you have not had the complaint,
you have had the complaint but it
only bothered you a little, the
complaint bothered you quite a bit,
or it bothers you almost all the
time.

Today or during the past few weeks

| | 1 | 2 | 3 | 4 |
| | have not had this complaint | bothers me a little | bothers me quite a bit | bothers me almost all the time |

87. Headaches — — — —

88. Pains in the
heart or chest — — — —

89. Heart pounding
or racing — — — —

90. Trouble getting
your breath — — — —

91. Constipation — — — —

92. Nausea, vomiting
or upset stomach — — — —

93. Loose bowel
movements — — — —

94. Twitching of the
face or body — — — —

		1	2	3	4
95.	Faintness or dizziness	—	—	—	—
96.	Hot or cold spells	—	—	—	—
97.	Itching	—	—	—	—
98.	Frequent urination	—	—	—	—
99.	Pains in the lower part of your back	—	—	—	—
100.	Difficulty in swallowing	—	—	—	—
101.	Skin eruptions or rashes	—	—	—	—
102.	Soreness of your muscles	—	—	—	—
103.	Nervousness and shakiness under pressure	—	—	—	—
104.	Difficulty in falling asleep or staying asleep	—	—	—	—
105.	Sudden fright for no apparent reason	—	—	—	—
106.	Bad dreams	—	—	—	—
107.	Blaming yourself for things you did or failed to do	—	—	—	—
108.	Feeling generally worried or fretful	—	—	—	—
109.	Feeling blue	—	—	—	—
110.	Being easily moved to tears	—	—	—	—

	Today or during the past few weeks			
	1	2	3	4
	have not had this complaint	bothers me a little	bothers me quite a bit	bothers me almost all the time

111. A need to do things very slowly in order to be sure you were doing them right __ __ __ __

112. Feeling like you have to do the same thing over and over again, like touching, counting, hand-washing, etc. __ __ __ __

113. Unusual fears, thoughts or impulses which you don't like keep pushing themselves into your mind __ __ __ __

114. Your "feelings" being easily hurt __ __ __ __

115. Feeling that people were watching or talking about you __ __ __ __

116. Preferring to be alone __ __ __ __

117. Feeling lonely __ __ __ __

118. Feeling like you have to ask others what you should do __ __ __ __

119. People being unsympathetic with your need for help __ __ __ __

120. Feeling easily annoyed or irritated __ __ __ __

121. Severe temper outbursts __ __ __ __

	1	2	3	4

122. Feeling critical of others __ __ __ __

123. Frequently took medicine to make you feel better __ __ __ __

124. Difficulty in speaking when you were excited __ __ __ __

125. Feeling you were not functioning as well as you could, feeling blocked or unable to get things done __ __ __ __

126. Having an impulse to commit a violent or destructive act, for example, desire to set a fire, stab, beat, or kill someone, mutilate an animal, etc. __ __ __ __

127. Blurring of vision __ __ __ __

128. Feeling thirsty __ __ __ __

129. Pains in arms or legs __ __ __ __

130. Loss of strength __ __ __ __

131. Dry mouth __ __ __ __

132. Pain in belly __ __ __ __

133. Feeling hungry __ __ __ __

134. Getting tired easily __ __ __ __

	Today or during the past few weeks			
	1	2	3	4
	have not had this complaint	bothers me a little	bothers me quite a bit	bothers me almost all the time

135. Feeling sleepy much of the time ___ ___ ___ ___

136. Keyed up and jittery ___ ___ ___ ___

137. Having no interest in things ___ ___ ___ ___

138. Having trouble keeping your mind on what you were doing ___ ___ ___ ___

139. Loss of appetite ___ ___ ___ ___

140. Having strange sexual ideas ___ ___ ___ ___

IF 2, SKIP TO #219
IF 3 OR 4, SKIP TO #246

People differ in what they are able to do after they come home from the hospital. I want you to listen to each item on this list and decide which of these things you are doing or have done since your return. For each item tell me whether you are not doing it, doing it some, or doing it regularly.

	1	2	3	0
	am not doing	am doing some	am doing regularly	does not apply

141. Help with the household chores ___ ___ ___ ___

142. Visit friends ___ ___ ___ ___

	1	2	3	0
	am not doing	am doing some	am doing regularly	does not apply

143. Visit relatives ___ ___ ___ ___

144. Entertain friends at home ___ ___ ___ ___

145. Dress and take care of myself ___ ___ ___ ___

146. Help with the family budgeting ___ ___ ___ ___

147. Remember to do important things on time ___ ___ ___ ___

148. Get along with family members ___ ___ ___ ___

149. Go to parties and other social activities ___ ___ ___ ___

150. Get along with neighbors ___ ___ ___ ___

151. Help with family shopping ___ ___ ___ ___

152. Help in the care and training of children ___ ___ ___ ___

153. Go to church ___ ___ ___ ___

154. Take up hobbies ___ ___ ___ ___

155. Work ___ ___ ___ ___

156. Support the family ___ ___ ___ ___

People differ in what they expect to be able to do after they have come home from the hospital. Now let's go back over the list we just finished. I would like you to think back to the time just before you left _____ Hospital, and decide which of these things you expected to be doing within a reasonable time following your return. Tell me if you did not expect to be doing it, expected to be doing it some, or expected to be doing it regularly.

	1 did not expect to be doing	2 expected to be doing some	3 expected to be doing regularly	0 does not apply
157. Help with household chores	___	___	___	___
158. Visit friends	___	___	___	___
159. Visit relatives	___	___	___	___
160. Entertain friends at home	___	___	___	___
161. Dress and take care of myself	___	___	___	___
162. Help with the family budgeting	___	___	___	___
163. Remember to do important things	___	___	___	___
164. Get along with family members	___	___	___	___
165. Go to parties and other social activities	___	___	___	___
166. Get along with neighbors	___	___	___	___
167. Help with family shopping	___	___	___	___
168. Help in the care and training of children	___	___	___	___

	1 did not expect to be doing	2 expected to be doing some	3 expected to be doing regularly	0 does not apply
169. Go to church	___	___	___	___
170. Take up hobbies	___	___	___	___
171. Work	___	___	___	___
172. Support the family	___	___	___	___

What do you do with your free time? I would like you to listen to the items on this list and decide which of these things you are now doing. Tell me if you are doing it frequently, sometimes or practically never.

	1 frequently	2 some-times	3 practically never	0 does not apply
173. Work in and around the house	___	___	___	___
174. Work in the garden or yard	___	___	___	___
175. Work on some hobby	___	___	___	___
176. Listen to the radio	___	___	___	___
177. Watch television	___	___	___	___
178. Write letters	___	___	___	___
179. Go to the movies	___	___	___	___
180. Attend lectures or the theater	___	___	___	___
181. Attend club, lodge or other meetings	___	___	___	___

	1 frequently	2 some-times	3 practically never	0 does not apply
182. Shop	—	—	—	—
183. Take part in community or church work	—	—	—	—
184. Bowl or other sports	—	—	—	—
185. Play cards or other table games	—	—	—	—
186. Take rides	—	—	—	—
187. Visit friends	—	—	—	—
188. Entertain friends	—	—	—	—
189. Sew, crochet or knit	—	—	—	—
190. Read	—	—	—	—
191. Go to the library	—	—	—	—
192. Just sit and think	—	—	—	—
193. Take courses at home	—	—	—	—
194. Go to school	—	—	—	—
195. Other (what?)				
_____	—	—	—	—

Are you satisfied with what you do with your free time? Let's go through the list again and this time decide whether you would like to do more or less of these things. Then tell me whether you are satisfied with what you do here, you would like to do more of this, or would like to do less.

	1 satisfied with what I do here	2 would like to do more of this	3 would like to do less	0 does not apply
196. Work in and around the house	—	—	—	—
197. Work in the garden or yard	—	—	—	—
198. Work on some hobby	—	—	—	—
199. Listen to the radio	—	—	—	—
200. Watch television	—	—	—	—
201. Write letters	—	—	—	—
202. Go to the movies	—	—	—	—
203. Attend lectures or the theater	—	—	—	—
204. Attend club, lodge or other meetings	—	—	—	—
205. Shop	—	—	—	—
206. Take part in community or church work	—	—	—	—

	1 satisfied with what I do here	2 would like to do more of this	3 would like to do less	0 does not apply
207. Bowl or other sports	—	—	—	—
208. Play cards or other table games	—	—	—	—
209. Take rides	—	—	—	—
210. Visit friends	—	—	—	—
211. Entertain friends	—	—	—	—
212. Sew, crotchet or knit	—	—	—	—
213. Read	—	—	—	—
214. Go to the library	—	—	—	—
215. Just sit and think	—	—	—	—
216. Take courses at home	—	—	—	—
217. Go to school	—	—	—	—
218. Other (what?)				
_____	—	—	—	—

219. Most people, sometime in their lives, have been the victims of criminal offenses. We would like to know how often you have been the victim of various kinds of offenses since you left _____ Hospital. After I describe each offense, would you tell me how many times since you left _____ Hospital someone has done this to you. Some time has gone by since you left the hospital, so try to remember back as well as you can. Take your time before answering.

How many times since you left _____ Hospital:

220. Did someone break into your home and take something or try to break in?

Enter number	

221. If you have a car, did anyone take it or try to take it?

Enter number	

222. Did anyone actually take or try to take money or property from you by force or threat of force?

Enter number	

223. Did you have anything stolen from you?

Enter number	

224. Were you given counterfeit money, or was your signature forged?

Enter number	

REPEAT "HOW MANY TIMES SINCE YOU LEFT _____ HOSPITAL" AS OFTEN AS NECESSARY

225. Were you given a bad check or cheated out of money or property in any way?

| Enter number | |

226. Were you attacked by another person--including a member of your household?

| Enter number | |

227. Were you threatened with harm for any reason?

| Enter number | |

228. Were you injured or was your property destroyed by a drunk or reckless driver?

| Enter number | |

229. Have you bought anything from someone who cheated you by mis-representing what he was selling or charging a higher price than you were told?

| Enter number | |

230. (IF SUBJECT RENTS THE DWELLING) Has the landlord of this build-ing failed to take care of any-thing that needed repairing or cleaning up after he was told to do so by some public official?

| Enter number | |

231. Have you had to pay money to a public official, such as a policeman or inspector, so he would not make trouble for you even though you had done nothing wrong?

| Enter number | |

From many studies we know that everyone commits delinquent acts that are not discovered by the police. We have found that most people, even those who have never been in trouble with the police, admit to having committed some violations. The kinds of questions we would now like to ask you have been asked of people from all walks of life throughout the United States. How many times since you left _____ Hospital did you do any of the following, alone or with others? Please remember what we said earlier, that everything you say will be kept confidential.

How many times since you left _____ Hospital have you:

232. Made an obscene phone call

233. Hurt somebody badly enough to require medical treatment

234. Used heroin

235. Threatened to hurt someone if he didn't give you money or something else	

236. Taken some money from someone without his knowing it	

237. Smoked pot	

238. Stolen something from a store	

239. Forced a female to have sexual intercourse with you	

240. Broken into a residence, store, school or other enclosed area	

241. Used a weapon to threaten another person	

242. Purposely damaged or destroyed property	

243. Carried a gun without a permit	

244. Hurt someone in a minor way like knocking him down	

245. Bought or accepted property which you knew was stolen	

246. The main part of the interview is over. Now we want to ask you a few questions about the interview itself.

247. First, are you glad you were interviewed, or do you wish you hadn't taken time for it?

Glad	1
Wish I hadn't	2
Not sure	3

248. During the interview, about how often did you hold back and not answer the questions completely even though you had the full information?

A great deal	1
Some of the time	2
A little bit	3
Not at all	4

249. Do you have any comments about anything in the interview you would like to make?

_____

_____

_____

_____

_____

_____

250. We would also like to interview
     someone you spend a lot of time
     with, to ask him how you are
     getting along. Your relative
     or friend whom you see every-
     day and who shares in your
     experiences is the person who
     knows most about how you are
     getting along. You yourself
     have told us a great deal, but
     someone close to you will often
     notice things that you may have
     overlooked. Could you tell me
     which person--a relative or a
     friend--you spend most of your
     time with and whom we could
     interview? Of course we won't
     tell him or her any of the
     answers you gave us.

     Name_____

     Address_____

     _____

     Relationship to subject

     _____

If this person does not know you
have been to Farview and you don't
want him to know, we will not tell
him (her).

251. Does he (she) know that
     you have been to Farview?

Yes	1
No	0

252. Thank you for your time and
     cooperation.

INTERVIEWER''S RATING OF RESPONDENT

253. How cooperative was the respondent during most of the interview?

Very cooperative	1
Somewhat uncooperative	2
Uncooperative	3
Very uncooperative	4

254. What topics or sections of the interview was the respondent reluctant to answer or sensitive about?

Family background?	Yes	1
	No	0
OMIT IF 4 Residence?	Yes	1
	No	0
OMIT IF 3 OR 4 Occupational history?	Yes	1
	No	0
OMIT IF 3 OR 4 After-care?	Yes	1
	No	0
Opinions of Farview?	Yes	1
	No	0
KAS?	Yes	1
	No	0
OMIT IF 3 OR 4 Victimization?	Yes	1
	No	0
OMIT IF 3 OR 4 Self-reported delinquency?	Yes	1
	No	0

255. What parts of the interview seem questionable to you?

Family background?	Yes	1
	No	0
OMIT IF 4 Residence?	Yes	1
	No	0
OMIT IF 3 OR 4 Occupational history?	Yes	1
	No	0
OMIT IF 3 OR 4 After-care?	Yes	1
	No	0
Opinions of Farview?	Yes	1
	No	0
KAS?	Yes	1
	No	0
OMIT IF 3 OR 4 Victimization?	Yes	1
	No	0
OMIT IF 3 OR 4 Self-reported delinquency?	Yes	1
	No	0

APPENDIX 7
Respondent Interview Schedule

COMMUNITY RESPONDENT INTERVIEW

This interview is part of a research project being conducted by a group of sociologists, psychiatrists, and lawyers at the University of Pennsylvania and it concerns people who have been in state hospitals. Since _____ has been in a hospital, we would like your opinions about how he is doing now. He told us that he spends much of his time with you and he has agreed to our contacting you. But we will not tell him any of the answers you give us.

You don't have to answer our questions if you don't want to, but by helping us you could help other people who are in state hospitals.

Anything you say will be held in strictest confidence and will be treated as part of the information we are collecting on over 600 other men. No one beyond our research group will ever know your answers about _____. We are an independent research group not connected with any hospital or state agency.

Name _____

Address _____ Apartment No. _____

City _____ Telephone No. _____

4

A. What is your relationship to _____? _____		People differ in what they are able to do after they come home from the hospital. I would like you to listen to each item on this list and decide which of these things _____ is doing or has done since his return. For each item tell me whether he is not doing it, doing it some, or doing it regularly.

	1 is not doing	2 is doing some	3 is doing regularly	0 does not apply

B. How long have you known him? _____			
C. Do you live with him?	Yes	1	1. Helps with household chores. — — — —
Skip to #1	No	0	2. Visits his friends — — — —
			3. Visits his relatives — — — —
D. How many days do you see him each week, on the average? _____ days			4. Entertains friends at home — — — —
			5. Dresses and takes care of himself — — — —
E. On the days that you do see him, about how many hours do you actually spend with him? _____ hours			6. Helps with the family budgeting — — — —
			7. Remembers to do important things on time — — — —
IF THE TOTAL NUMBER OF HOURS RESPONDENT SEES SUBJECT EACH WEEK IS LESS THAN 5, DO NOT COMPLETE THE INTERVIEW			8. Gets along with family members — — — —
			9. Goes to parties and other social activities — — — —
			10. Gets along with neighbors — — — —
			11. Helps with family shopping — — — —
			12. Helps in the care and training of children — — — —
			13. Goes to church — — — —
			14. Takes up hobbies — — — —
			15. Works — — — —
			16. Supports the family — — — —

5

Families and friends differ in what they think their relatives and friends should do after they come home from the hospital. Now let's go back over the list we just finished. I would like you to think back to the time just before he came home and decide which of these things you expected him to be doing within a reasonable time following his return. Then tell me if you did not expect him to be doing it, you expected him to be doing some, or you expected him to be doing it regularly.

	1	2	3	0
	did not expect him to be doing	expected him to be doing some	expected him to be doing regularly	does not apply
17. Helps with household chores	—	—	—	—
18. Visits his friends	—	—	—	—
19. Visits his relatives	—	—	—	—
20. Entertains friends at home	—	—	—	—
21. Dresses and takes care of himself	—	—	—	—
22. Helps with the family budgeting	—	—	—	—
23. Remembers to do important things on time	—	—	—	—
24. Gets along with family members	—	—	—	—
25. Goes to parties and other social activities	—	—	—	—
26. Gets along with neighbors	—	—	—	—
27. Helps with family shopping	—	—	—	—
28. Helps in the care and training of children	—	—	—	—
29. Goes to church	—	—	—	—

	1	2	3	0
	did not expect him to be doing	expected him to be doing some	expected him to be doing regularly	does not apply
30. Takes up hobbies	—	—	—	—
31. Works	—	—	—	—
32. Supports the family	—	—	—	—

There are a number of statements on this list which describe different kinds of behavior and mood. These include symptoms that people who have been in the hospital sometimes show. Would you listen to each of these items as I read it and decide how he has looked to you during the past few weeks on this item. Then tell me if, in you opinion, he is never like this or only rarely, if he is this way sometimes, but not too frequently, if he is like this often, or if he is like this always or practically always.

	1	2	3	4
	almost never	some- times	often	almost always
33. Has trouble sleeping	—	—	—	—
34. Gets very self-critical, starts to blame himself for things	—	—	—	—
35. Cries easily	—	—	—	—
36. Feels lonely	—	—	—	—
37. Acts as if he has no interest in things	—	—	—	—
38. Is restless	—	—	—	—
39. Has periods where he can't stop moving or doing something	—	—	—	—
40. Just sits	—	—	—	—

	1 almost never	2 some-times	3 often	4 almost always
41. Acts as if he doesn't have much energy	—	—	—	—
42. Looks worn out	—	—	—	—
43. Feelings get hurt easily	—	—	—	—
44. Feels that people don't care about him	—	—	—	—
45. Does the same thing over and over again without reason	—	—	—	—
46. Passes out	—	—	—	—
47. Gets very sad, blue	—	—	—	—
48. Tries too hard	—	—	—	—
49. Needs to do things very slowly to do them right	—	—	—	—
50. Has strange fears	—	—	—	—
51. Afraid something terrible is going to happen	—	—	—	—
52. Gets nervous easily	—	—	—	—
53. Jittery	—	—	—	—
54. Worries or frets	—	—	—	—
55. Gets sudden fright for no reason	—	—	—	—
56. Has bad dreams	—	—	—	—
57. Act as if he sees things that aren't there	—	—	—	—

	1 almost never	2 some-times	3 often	4 almost always
58. Does strange things without reason	—	—	—	—
59. Attempts suicide	—	—	—	—
60. Gets angry and breaks things	—	—	—	—
61. Talks to himself	—	—	—	—
62. Acts as if he has no control over his emotions	—	—	—	—
63. Laughs or cries at strange times	—	—	—	—
64. Has mood changes without reason	—	—	—	—
65. Has temper tantrums	—	—	—	—
66. Gets very excited for no reason	—	—	—	—
67. Gets very happy for no reason	—	—	—	—
68. Acts as if he doesn't care about other people's feelings	—	—	—	—
69. Thinks only of himself	—	—	—	—
70. Shows his feelings	—	—	—	—
71. Generous	—	—	—	—
72. Thinks people are talking about him	—	—	—	—
73. Complains of headaches, stomach trouble, other physical ailments	—	—	—	—

7

	1 almost never	2 some- times	3 often	4 almost always			1 almost never	2 some- times	3 often	4 almost always
74. Bossy	_	_	_	_		92. Gets into trouble with law	_	_	_	_
75. Acts as if he's suspicious of people	_	_	_	_		93. Gets drunk	_	_	_	_
76. Argues	_	_	_	_		94. Is dependable	_	_	_	_
77. Gets into fights with people	_	_	_	_		95. Is responsible	_	_	_	_
78. Is cooperative	_	_	_	_		96. Doesn't argue (talk) back	_	_	_	_
79. Does the opposite of what he is asked	_	_	_	_		97. Obedient	_	_	_	_
80. Stubborn	_	_	_	_		98. Shows good judgement	_	_	_	_
81. Answers when talked to	_	_	_	_		99. Stays away from people	_	_	_	_
82. Curses at people	_	_	_	_		100. Takes drugs other than recommended by hospital or clinic	_	_	_	_
83. Deliberately upsets routine	_	_	_	_		101. Shy	_	_	_	_
84. Resentful	_	_	_	_		102. Quiet	_	_	_	_
85. Envious of other people	_	_	_	_		103. Prefers to be alone	_	_	_	_
86. Friendly	_	_	_	_		104. Needs a lot of attention	_	_	_	_
87. Gets annoyed easily	_	_	_	_		105. Behavior is childish	_	_	_	_
88. Critical of other people	_	_	_	_		106. Acts helpless	_	_	_	_
89. Pleasant	_	_	_	_		107. Is independent	_	_	_	_
90. Gets along well with people	_	_	_	_		108. Moves about very slowly	_	_	_	_
91. Lies	_	_	_	_		109. Moves about in a hurried way	_	_	_	_

	1 almost never	2 some-times	3 often	4 almost always		1 almost never	2 some-times	3 often	4 almost always
110. Clumsy; keeps bumping into things or dropping things	—	—	—	—	124. Acts as if he can't concentrate on one thing	—	—	—	—
111. Very quick to react to something you say or do	—	—	—	—	125. Acts as if he can't make decisions	—	—	—	—
112. Very slow to react	—	—	—	—	126. Talks without making sense	—	—	—	—
113. Gets into peculiar positions	—	—	—	—	127. Hard to understand his words	—	—	—	—
114. Makes peculiar movements	—	—	—	—	128. Speaks clearly	—	—	—	—
115. Hands tremble	—	—	—	—	129. Refuses to speak at all for periods of time	—	—	—	—
116. Will stay in one position for a long period	—	—	—	—	130. Speaks so low you cannot hear him	—	—	—	—
117. Loses track of day, month, or year	—	—	—	—	131. Speaks very loudly	—	—	—	—
118. Forgets his address or other places he knows well	—	—	—	—	132. Shouts or yells for no reason	—	—	—	—
119. Remembers the names of people he knows well	—	—	—	—	133. Speaks very fast	—	—	—	—
120. Acts as if he doesn't know where he is	—	—	—	—	134. Speaks very slowly	—	—	—	—
121. Remembers important things	—	—	—	—	135. Acts as if he wants to speak but can't	—	—	—	—
122. Acts as if he's confused about things; in a daze	—	—	—	—	136. Keeps repeating the same idea	—	—	—	—
123. Acts as if he can't get certain thoughts out of his mind	—	—	—	—	137. Keeps changing from one subject to another for no reason	—	—	—	—
					138. Talks too much	—	—	—	—
					139. Says that people are talking about him	—	—	—	—

9

	1 almost never	2 some-times	3 often	4 almost always
140. Says that people are trying to make him do or think things he doesn't want to	—	—	—	—
141. Talks as if he committed the worst sin	—	—	—	—
142. Talks about how angry he is at certain people	—	—	—	—
143. Talks about people or things he is afraid of	—	—	—	—
144. Threatens to injure certain people	—	—	—	—
145. Threatens to tell people off	—	—	—	—
146. Says he is afraid that he will injure somebody	—	—	—	—
147. Says he is afraid he will not be able to control himself	—	—	—	—
148. Talks about strange things that are going on inside his body	—	—	—	—
149. Says how bad or useless he is	—	—	—	—
150. Brags about how good he is	—	—	—	—
151. Says the same thing over and over again	—	—	—	—
152. Complains about people and things in general	—	—	—	—

	1 almost never	2 some-times	3 often	4 almost always
153. Talks about big plans he has for the future	—	—	—	—
154. Says or acts as if people are after him	—	—	—	—
155. Says that something terrible is going to happen	—	—	—	—
156. Believes in strange things	—	—	—	—
157. Talks about suicide	—	—	—	—
158. Talks about strange sexual ideas	—	—	—	—
159. Gives advice without being asked	—	—	—	—

What does he do with his free time? I would like you to listen to the items on this list and decide which of these things he is now doing. Tell me if he is doing it frequently, sometimes, or practically never.

	1 frequently	2 some-times	3 practically never	0 does not apply
160. Work in and around the house	—	—	—	—
161. Work in the garden or yard	—	—	—	—
162. Work on some hobby	—	—	—	—
163. Listen to the radio	—	—	—	—
164. Watch television	—	—	—	—

	1 frequently	2 some-times	3 practically never	0 does not apply
165. Write letters	—	—	—	—
166. Go to the movies	—	—	—	—
167. Attend lectures, theatre	—	—	—	—
168. Attend club, lodge, other meetings	—	—	—	—
169. Shop	—	—	—	—
170. Take part in community or church work	—	—	—	—
171. Bowl or other sports	—	—	—	—
172. Play cards or other table games	—	—	—	—
173. Take rides	—	—	—	—
174. Visit friends	—	—	—	—
175. Entertain friends	—	—	—	—
176. Sew, crochet or knit	—	—	—	—
177. Read	—	—	—	—
178. Go to the library	—	—	—	—
179. Just sit and think	—	—	—	—
180. Take courses at home	—	—	—	—
181. Go to school	—	—	—	—
182. Other (what?) _____	—	—	—	—

Are you satisfied with the way he spends his free time? Let's go through the list again and this time decide whether you would like him to do more or less of these things. Then tell me whether you are satisfied with what he does here, you would like to see him do more of this, or you would like to see him do less.

	1 satisfied with what he does here	2 would like to see him do more of this	3 would like to see him do less	0 does not apply
183. Work in and around the house	—	—	—	—
184. Work in the garden or yard	—	—	—	—
185. Work on some hobby	—	—	—	—
186. Listen to the radio	—	—	—	—
187. Watch television	—	—	—	—
188. Write letters	—	—	—	—
189. Go to the movies	—	—	—	—
190. Attend lectures, theatre	—	—	—	—
191. Attend club, lodge, other meetings	—	—	—	—
192. Shop	—	—	—	—
193. Take part in community or church work	—	—	—	—
194. Bowl or other games	—	—	—	—
195. Play cards or other table games	—	—	—	—
196. Take rides	—	—	—	—

II

	1 satisfied with what he does here	2 would like to see him do more of this	3 would like to see him do less	0 does not apply		
197. Visit friends	_	_	_	_		
198. Entertain friends	_	_	_	_		
199. Sew, crochet, or knit	_	_	_	_		
200. Read	_	_	_	_		
201. Go to the library	_	_	_	_		
202. Just sit and think	_	_	_	_		
203. Take courses at home	_	_	_	_		
204. Go to school	_	_	_	_		
205. Other (what?)	_	_	_	_		

206. Finally, how would you describe the time you spend with _____ ?

Enjoyable	1
Distressing	2
Neither	3
Some other way	4

HOSPITAL RESPONDENT QUESTIONNAIRE

This questionnaire is part of a research project being conducted by a group of sociologists, psychiatrists, and lawyers at the University of Pennsylvania about the adjustment of people who have been in state hospitals. This research has been approved by the Department of Public Welfare and the superintendent of this hospital.

We have selected a group of patients and are attempting to assess their present condition. We understand that you have considerable contact with one of these patients, _____. We have talked to him and he has consented to your answering some questions about his present condition.

You don't have to answer these questions, but by helping us you could help some of the people who are in state hospitals. Anything you tell us will be held in strictest confidence. We will not show your answers to the patient or to any other hospital or Department employee. Your answers will be treated as part of the information we are collecting on over 600 other men. No one beyond our research group will ever know your answers.

Since the information you provide will not be used in making any decisions regarding this particular patient, we request that you try to be as open and forthright in your answers as possible.

Your Name	_____
Hospital Name	_____
Ward Number of ward you are assigned to	_____

A. What is your relationship to the patient?

CIRCLE THE CORRECT ANSWER

| Ward nurse |
| Aide |
| Other (specify) |
| _____ |

B. How long have you known him?

_____

C. How long has he been under your direct care or supervision?

_____

IF THE PATIENT HAS BEEN UNDER YOUR DIRECT CARE OR SUPERVISION FOR LESS THAN TWO WEEKS, DO NOT COMPLETE THE QUESTIONNAIRE

D. How many days each week do you see the patient, on the average?

_____ days

E. On the days that you do see him, about how many hours do you actually spend with him or observing him?

_____ hours

IF THE TOTAL NUMBER OF HOURS YOU SPEND WITH THE PATIENT EACH WEEK IS, ON THE AVERAGE, LESS THAN 5, DO NOT COMPLETE THE QUESTIONNAIRE.

There are a number of statements on this list which describe different kinds of behavior and mood. These include symptoms that people who have been in the hospital sometimes show. Would you go through them and indicate how the patient has looked to you during the past few weeks on these things. Alongside each statement are four possible answers. If, in your opinion, he is never like this or only rarely, then place a check in the first blank (1). If he is this way sometimes, but not too frequently, place a check in blank (2). If he is like this often, check blank (3). Place a check in blank (4) if the statement would describe him or his behavior always or practically always.

Do not spend too much time on any one question, but make sure that you check every question.

	1 almost never	2 some- times	3 often	4 almost always
1. Has trouble sleeping	__	__	__	__
2. Gets very self-critical, starts to blame himself for things	__	__	__	__
3. Cries easily	__	__	__	__
4. Feels lonely	__	__	__	__
5. Acts as if he has no interest in things	__	__	__	__
6. Is restless	__	__	__	__
7. Has periods where he can't stop moving or doing something	__	__	__	__
8. Just sits	__	__	__	__
9. Acts as if he doesn't have much energy	__	__	__	__
10. Looks worn out	__	__	__	__
11. Feelings get hurt easily	__	__	__	__

3

	1 almost never	2 some-times	3 often	4 almost always	
12. Feels that people don't care about him	—	—	—	—	
13. Does the same thing over and over again without reason	—	—	—	—	
14. Passes out	—	—	—	—	
15. Gets very sad, blue	—	—	—	—	
16. Tries too hard	—	—	—	—	
17. Needs to do things very slowly to do them right	—	—	—	—	
18. Has strange fears	—	—	—	—	
19. Afraid something terrible is going to happen	—	—	—	—	
20. Gets nervous easily	—	—	—	—	
21. Jittery	—	—	—	—	
22. Worries or frets	—	—	—	—	
23. Gets sudden fright for no reason	—	—	—	—	
24. Has bad dreams	—	—	—	—	
25. Acts as if he sees people or things that aren't there	—	—	—	—	
26. Does strange things without reason	—	—	—	—	
27. Attempts suicide	—	—	—	—	
28. Gets angry and breaks things	—	—	—	—	
29. Talks to himself	—	—	—	—	
30. Acts as if he has no control over his emotions	—	—	—	—	

	1 almost never	2 some-times	3 often	4 almost always	
31. Laughs or cries at strange times	—	—	—	—	
32. Has mood changes without reason	—	—	—	—	
33. Has temper tantrums	—	—	—	—	
34. Gets very excited for no reason	—	—	—	—	
35. Gets very happy for no reason	—	—	—	—	
36. Acts as if he doesn't care about other people's feelings	—	—	—	—	
37. Thinks only of himself	—	—	—	—	
38. Shows his feelings	—	—	—	—	
39. Generous	—	—	—	—	
40. Thinks people are talking about him	—	—	—	—	
41. Complains of headaches, stomach trouble, other physical ailments	—	—	—	—	
42. Bossy	—	—	—	—	
43. Acts as if he's suspicious of people	—	—	—	—	
44. Argues	—	—	—	—	
45. Gets into fights with people	—	—	—	—	
46. Is cooperative	—	—	—	—	
47. Does the opposite of what he is asked	—	—	—	—	
48. Stubborn	—	—	—	—	

4

	1 almost never	2 some-times	3 often	4 almost always			1 almost never	2 some-times	3 often	4 almost always	
49. Answers when talked to	—	—	—	—		69. Shy	—	—	—	—	
50. Curses at people	—	—	—	—		70. Quiet	—	—	—	—	
51. Deliberately upsets routine	—	—	—	—		71. Prefers to be alone	—	—	—	—	
52. Resentful	—	—	—	—		72. Needs a lot of attention	—	—	—	—	
53. Envious of other people	—	—	—	—		73. Behavior is childish	—	—	—	—	
54. Friendly	—	—	—	—		74. Acts helpless	—	—	—	—	
55. Gets annoyed easily	—	—	—	—		75. Is independent	—	—	—	—	
56. Critical of other people	—	—	—	—		76. Moves about very slowly	—	—	—	—	
57. Pleasant	—	—	—	—		77. Moves about in a hurried way	—	—	—	—	
58. Gets along well with people	—	—	—	—		78. Clumsy; keeps bumping into things or dropping things	—	—	—	—	
59. Lies	—	—	—	—		79. Very quick to react to something you say or do	—	—	—	—	
60. Gets into trouble with law	—	—	—	—		80. Very slow to react	—	—	—	—	
61. Gets drunk	—	—	—	—		81. Gets into peculiar positions	—	—	—	—	
62. Is dependable	—	—	—	—		82. Makes peculiar movements	—	—	—	—	
63. Is responsible	—	—	—	—		83. Hands tremble	—	—	—	—	
64. Doesn't argue (talk) back	—	—	—	—		84. Will stay in one position for a long period	—	—	—	—	
65. Obedient	—	—	—	—		85. Loses track of day, month, or year	—	—	—	—	
66. Shows good judgment	—	—	—	—		86. Forgets his address or other places he knows well	—	—	—	—	
67. Stays away from people	—	—	—	—		87. Remembers the names of people he knows well	—	—	—	—	
68. Takes drugs other than recommended by hospital or clinic	—	—	—	—							

5

	1 almost never	2 some-times	3 often	4 almost always			1 almost never	2 some-times	3 often	4 almost always
88. Acts as if he doesn't know where he is	—	—	—	—		105. Keeps changing from one subject to another for no apparent reason	—	—	—	—
89. Remembers important things	—	—	—	—		106. Talks too much				
90. Acts as if he's confused about things; in a daze	—	—	—	—		107. Says that people are talking about him	—	—	—	—
91. Acts as if he can't get certain thoughts out of his mind	—	—	—	—		108. Says that people are trying to make him do or think things he doesn't want to	—	—	—	—
92. Acts as if he can't concentrate on one thing	—	—	—	—		109. Talks as if he committed the worst sin	—	—	—	—
93. Acts as if he can't make decisions	—	—	—	—		110. Talks about how angry he is at certain people	—	—	—	—
94. Talks without making sense	—	—	—	—		111. Talks about people or things he's very afraid of	—	—	—	—
95. Hard to understand his words	—	—	—	—		112. Threatens to injure certain people	—	—	—	—
96. Speaks clearly	—	—	—	—		113. Threatens to tell people off	—	—	—	—
97. Refuses to speak at all for periods of time	—	—	—	—		114. Says he is afraid that he will injure somebody	—	—	—	—
98. Speaks so low you cannot hear him	—	—	—	—		115. Says he is afraid that he will not be able to control himself	—	—	—	—
99. Speaks very loudly	—	—	—	—		116. Talks about strange things that are going on inside his body	—	—	—	—
100. Shouts or yells for no reason	—	—	—	—		117. Says how bad or useless he is	—	—	—	—
101. Speaks very fast	—	—	—	—		118. Brags about how good he is	—	—	—	—
102. Speaks very slowly	—	—	—	—		119. Says the same thing over and over again	—	—	—	—
103. Acts as if he wants to speak but can't	—	—	—	—						
104. Keeps repeating the same idea	—	—	—	—						

6

	1 almost never	2 some-times	3 often	4 almost always
120. Complains about people and things in general	—	—	—	—
121. Talks about big plans he has for the future	—	—	—	—
122. Says or acts as if people are after him	—	—	—	—
123. Says that something terrible is going to happen	—	—	—	—
124. Believes in strange things	—	—	—	—
125. Talks about suicide	—	—	—	—
126. Talks about strange sexual ideas	—	—	—	—
127. Gives advice without being asked	—	—	—	—

APPENDIX 8
Items in the Subscales of
the Katz Adjustment Scale

The items that compose the five patient scales can be readily found in the interview schedule presented in appendix 6, since the interview schedule is grouped according to the various scales. The items are related to the scales in the following manner:

No.	Scale
87–140	Symptom Discomfort
141–56	Level of performance of socially expected activities
157–72	Level of expectation of socially expected activities
173–95	Level of free-time activities
196–218	Level of satisfaction with free-time activities

The four informant scales that deal with social behavior can be found in a similar manner in the community respondent interview schedule presented in appendix 7. The items are related to the scales in the following manner:

No.	Scale
1–16	Level of performance of socially expected activities
17–32	Level of expectation of socially expected activities
160–82	Level of free-time activities
183–205	Level of satisfaction with free-time activities

The items that compose each of the thirteen informant scales relating to symptom discomforts cannot be easily found in the interview schedules since they are randomly distributed throughout that section of the interview. Hence, they are presented below.

270

(1) *Belligerence*
Got angry and broke things
Cursed at people
Got into fights with people
Threatened to tell people off

(2) *Verbal Expansiveness*
Shouted or yelled for no reason
Talked too much
Spoke very loud
Kept changing from one subject to
  to another for no reason
Bragged about how good he was

(3) *Negativism*
Was not cooperative
Acted as if he did not care about other
  people's feelings
Did the opposite of what he was asked
Stubborn
Critical of other people
Deliberately upset routine
Lied
Thought only of himself
Got into trouble with the law

(4) *Helplessness*
Acted as if he could not make decisions
Acted helpless
Acted as if he could not concentrate on
  one thing
Cried easily

(5) *Suspiciousness*
Thought people were talking about him
Acted as if he were suspicious of people
Said that people were trying to make
  him do or think things he did not
  want to

(6) *Anxiety*
Afraid something terrible was going to
  happen
Said that something terrible was going
  to happen
Had strange fears
Talked about people or things
  he was afraid of
Got suddenly frightened for no reason
Talked about suicide

(7) *Withdrawal & Retardation*
Moved about very slowly
Just sat
Very slow to react
Quiet
Needed to do things very slowly to do
  them right
Would stay in one position for long
  period of time

(8) *General Psychopathology*
Acted as if he had no interest in things
Felt that people did not care about him
Acted as if he had no control over his
  emotions
Laughed or cried at strange times
Had mood changes without reason
Had temper tantrums
Got very excited for no reason
Bossy
Argued
Resentful
Got annoyed easily
Stayed away from people
Preferred to be alone
Behavior was childish
Very quick to react to something
  said or done
Acted as if he were confused about
  things; in a daze

Acted as if he could not get certain thoughts out of his mind

Talked without making sense

Refused to speak at all for periods of time

Spoke so low you could not hear him

Talked about how angry he was at certain people

Said the same things over and over again

Talked about big plans he had for the future

Gave advice without being asked

(9) *Nervousness*

Got nervous easily

Jittery

Showed his feelings

Worried or fretted

(10) *Confusion*

Lost track of day, month, or the year

Forgot his address or other places he knows well

Acted as if he did not know where he was

(11) *Bizarreness*

Talked about strange things that were going on inside his body

Did strange things without reason

Acted as if he saw people or things that weren't there

Believed in strange things

Had bad dreams

(12) *Hyperactivity*

Had periods where he could not stop moving or doing something

Did the same thing over and over again without reason

Was restless

(13) *Emotional Stability*

Generous

Not envious of other people

Friendly

Pleasant

Gets along well with people

Is dependable

Is responsible

Shows good judgment

Is independent

The scale format for all these scales is as follows: 1, almost never; 2, sometimes; 3, often; 4, almost always.

NOTES

CHAPTER 1

1. In the United States a person sentenced to "life" actually serves, on the average, twelve years of that sentence in prison before being paroled.

2. The following description of treatment facilities at Farview refers to the situation that existed during the late 1960s and early 1970s, that is, the situation at Farview while our subjects were still confined there. A more recent description of the treatment facilities at Farview is provided in a 1976 Medicare certification examination conducted by the National Institute of Mental Health (see NIMH 1976).

CHAPTER 2

1. A more complete chronology of the Dixon case can be found in appendix 1.

2. The Barr-Walker Act was declared unconstitutional in 1964, but Dixon patients committed under the provisions of that act remained at Farview until the Dixon decision.

3. An explanation of the inclusion of a small group of civil commitments in the class is found below.

4. This aspect of the court's decision explains the presence of a small number of civilly committed patients in the Dixon class. Although the class was initially defined as time-expired criminal

273

commitments, the court's decision extended it to include all section 404 commitments at Farview at the time of the suit.

5. Although many commitments were thus invalidated, the Dixon decision did not result in wholesale discharges from civil mental hospitals. In December 1971 the Department of Public Welfare reported that the following commitment conversions had occurred among patients who had been committed to all state schools and hospitals under section 404 after it had been declared unconstitutional (Brunetti 1972, p. 676): 1.5 percent were discharged, 88 percent were converted to voluntary commitments, 8 percent were placed under thirty-day voluntary commitment, and 2.5 percent were committed or were being processed by civil court involuntary commitment. The major impact on the civil hospitals was the generation of a large volume of paperwork as new commitments were obtained.

6. See appendix 1 for this information.

7. At the time of this hearing there were approximately four hundred members of the class.

8. This objection has been raised in the past when the authors presented papers based on preliminary analyses of these data.

9. These studies have been reviewed elsewhere (see Jacoby 1976, pp. 39–47). The high rates of overprediction are not exclusively the products of inadequately staffed institutions like Farview, although conditions under which predictions of dangerousness are made are usually more like those at Farview than not. Even under the best of circumstances, when staff numbers and qualification approach an apparent optimum, overprediction still occurs, although at a reduced rate. (see Kozol et al. 1972).

10. Dates in these exchanges are fictitious, although years and time intervals between events are accurate.

11. See chapter 7 for a further discussion of this point.

CHAPTER 3

1. The material presented in the previous chapter indicating the political pressures surrounding decisions to release mentally ill offenders suggests, correctly, that similar pressures would occur around efforts to change the location at which care is delivered to this population. As the state began to implement its plan in 1973 and 1974, they encountered strong opposition. At two of the five hospitals where units were to be located, the surrounding communities were successful in having the plans canceled. In one case the citizenry sought injunctive relief, and in the other they brought informal pressure through locally elected officials.

2. The issue of the course of previous attempts to transfer

patients was included after discussion with Farview staff in which they noted difficulty in convincing other hospitals to accept transfers.

3. These offenses include the 10,214 offenses in the original cohort as well as an additional 636 offenses committed by a 10 percent sample of the cohort between the ages of eighteen and twenty-six.

4. See the section on Offense Histories in chapter 4 for more detail and an example of the application of the total seriousness score.

5. The term *Dixon offense* is used in this study in reference to the criminal offense with which a subject was charged resulting in the period of hospitalization at Farview which was terminated by the Dixon court suit.

6. Katz and Lyerly used the term *informant* in reference to these interviews. Since that term seemed unnecessarily threatening to print in the title of a questionnaire, *respondent* was selected as being more emotionally neutral.

CHAPTER 4

1. Since Pennsylvania admits only men to the hospital for the criminally insane—sending mentally ill women offenders to closed wards of civil mental hospitals—all the Dixon patients are men.

2. The Dixon commitment refers to that offense or hospitalization which began the series of institutional moves that ended in transfer from Farview under the Dixon decision.

3. When prior periods of criminal incarcerations are included, 80 percent of the Dixon patients were institutionalized before the Dixon commitment.

CHAPTER 5

1. The possibility that violence was constrained by the maximum security conditions is discussed and examined in chapter 6. Here we are asking whether empirical, logical support for the prediction of dangerousness could have been offered to support the political predictions.

2. These figures present the annual incident rate for all subjects who spent their X^{th} year of age in confinement at Farview. For example, each subject who spent his twentieth year of age at Farview was counted in the base for the twentieth year and all of his incidents that occurred during his twentieth year were included in the numerator to generate the annual incident rate for twenty-year-olds. The same process was repeated for each of the other years of age.

The identical technique was used to produce the annual

rates based on the year of confinement at Farview (fig. 5.4 to 5.6). Here all subjects who spent a first year at Farview, a second year, and so on, are grouped together to form the annual rates for year 1, year 2, and so on.

3. Although a comparison with incident rates of a representative sample of patients at civil mental hospitals would be informative here, we have not discovered any such comparable data. Moreover, should such data exist, difficulties would arise in making valid comparisons because every hospital has distinctive formal policies and informal practices regarding the type and seriousness of events which qualify as incidents.

4. If the guard injured the subject after the subject assaulted the guard, that incident would be counted in the category labeled "assault initiated by subject" and not in this category.

5. We note again that these data should be viewed as approximations of the actual pattern of violence at Farview. A number of factors, discussed in chapter 3, suggest that intentional and unintentional errors in staff reporting of violence in the hospital can lead to the underreporting of incidents.

6. In the mid-1950s, psychotropic drugs came into common use in mental hospitals, including Farview. Although it would be preferable to be able to gauge the effect of these drugs in reducing violence, we are unable to do so within the context of the experience of our subjects. The variety of drugs, different dosages, varying combinations in which they were given, and various time periods during which they were administered create a crazy-quilt pattern that defies analysis. About half of the Farview population was receiving psychotropic drugs at the time of the Dixon case, so the low levels of violence cannot be attributed exclusively to the use of such drugs.

7. See chapter 3 for a discussion of this methodology.

8. In addition, there was a series of questions asking the subject to indicate which he liked best—Farview, the transfer hospital, or the community—in relation to a number of criteria. Those data will be represented in the next chapter.

CHAPTER 6

1. A more detailed analysis of these data, including correlates of in-hospital violence, can be found in Jacoby (1976).

CHAPTER 7

1. In chapter 9, which analyzes recidivism and dangerousness, we will more fully examine the consequences of these escapes.

2. Alternative explanations for the rapid discharge of the sub-

jects—a hospital's desire to be enthusiastically compliant with the court order or a desire to be rid of a group of troublesome patients in the quickest way—are not supported by the opinions expressed by the employees of the transfer hospitals who were interviewed.

3. For the Dixon patients the period between the date of transfer from Farview and the date of our follow-up averaged 3.7 years. All of the patients classified as "not discharged" had follow-up periods greater than 2 years, the time within which 90 percent of the discharged subjects were discharged. Only 5 percent of "not discharged" subjects had follow-up periods of less than 3 years. Therefore it appears as though our follow-up permitted ample time for hospitals to discharge subjects if they were likely to do so.

4. The conventional .05 level was used to determine significance in this analysis.

5. In addition, the Baxstrom research also demonstrated the significance of two other variables—psychiatric evaluation and the presence of an interested family. These two variables were the best predictors of release from the civil hospitals, with an interested family being the most important. Since this research project was unable to collect data that would allow us to measure these variables, however, we will confine our discussion to the age-related variables.

CHAPTER 8

1. See the introduction to chapter 7 for a discussion of these procedures.

2. Of course the possibility exists that, despite the interviewers' attempts to convince the subjects in the community of the interviewers' disinterested role, some subjects may have been wary in revealing any problems in fear that such revelations could somehow lead to their rehospitalization.

3. The small cell sizes made this analysis possible only for the first two residences.

4. An alternative explanation for the higher rates of rehospitalization among subjects who lived with their families may be that family members may be less tolerant of a former patient's unadjusted behavior, perhaps having previously experienced the unpleasantness of a psychotic episode, and may therefore be more likely than boarding house or apartment managers to seek rehospitalization.

5. This figure is somewhat inflated by the negative responses of some subjects who secured jobs without "looking for work."

6. The nature of the Michaux study and the characteristics of its subjects will be discussed in a later section of this chapter.

7. A copy of the subject interview schedule appears in appendix 6 and the respondent schedule appears in appendix 7.

8. We can also point out that the other comparisons—with the normal population and with the second mental patient group—will not be affected in this way since in both cases data are available for male subjects only.

9. The difference between the larger number of 254 patients in the community and the 92 subjects who will be used in this analysis is a function of the sex variable. Most of the subjects in the study were female but we will confine our comparisons to the 92 male subjects for whom KAS data are available.

The authors would like to thank Alice Lowery of the National Institute of Mental Health for supplying these data and other material on the KAS.

10. There is only one exception to this and it concerns the large proportion of females in the Spring Grove sample. This difference cannot be overcome since the female scores cannot be separated from the male scores in this analysis.

11. The reader should bear in mind that *lower mean scores* are indicative of *better adjustment* while *lower percentage differences,* that is, greater negative percentages, are indicative of *poorer adjustment.*

12. These means were presented in table 8.24.

13. While it would have been appropriate to examine the adjustment of patients confined at Farview for shorter periods, say, less than three years, the small number of subjects prohibit such an analysis. As it is, the number of subjects in tables 8.28 and 8.29 is rather small for the less-than-six-years group.

CHAPTER 9

1. In some earlier publications relating to this topic, we reported that 432 subjects had been released to the community. Subsequent analyses and computer file modifications indicate, however, that the correct number is 414, as noted here. Although slight differences occur because of the modifications, the modifications have no effect on the substantive findings of the analyses.

2. Subjects who were at liberty only one or two days at a time on home visits or brief unauthorized absences were not included in this group, however. The issue of whether the escapees pose a special threat to the community will be addressed below.

3. The authors would like to thank their demographic col-

leagues, Drs. Peter J. Donaldson, Ronald R. Rindfuss, and Philip C. Sagi for suggesting this type of analysis.

4. Some of the subjects were released, rehospitalized, rereleased, and so forth. Periods of rehospitalization were simply subtracted from the total interval between release and termination date to produce a net time at risk. This adjustment should not distort the findings since only seventy-five, or 18 percent, of the subjects released to the community were rehospitalized. In addition, the periods of rehospitalization tended to be rather brief, with virtually all of them lasting less than three months.

5. The same age groupings were used in this analysis as elsewhere: under 35, 35 to 49, 50 to 64, over 65.

CHAPTER 10

1. An example of these consequences can be seen in a recent Pennsylvania case, *Freach and Keen* v. *Shovlin et al.* (Commonwealth Court of Pennsylvania, 1978). In this case twenty-two employees of Farview were sued for liability and punitive damages by the parents of two boys who were sexually assaulted and murdered by a patient released from Farview. While twenty of the defendants were acquitted, there was a hung jury for the superintendant and director of clinical services at Farview and they may yet face another trial. Although damages were not assessed against any of the defendants, the mere occurrence of such a trial is enough to suggest to clinicians they they should proceed very cautiously in decisions to release patients from institutions like Farview.

2. Offenders under sentence may have to be housed on security wards, but they should be given the opportunity to participate in the same types of programs as other patients. These patients cannot legally be released until their sentence has expired or until they are paroled. It is hoped that participation in effective programs would improve the inmate's chances of being paroled.

3. *U.S. ex rel Souder* v. *Watson* (413 F. Supp. 711[1976]) is the case in question.

REFERENCES

Brooks, Alexander D.
  1974 *Law, psychiatry and the mental health system.* Boston: Little, Brown and Company.
Brunetti, Frank Leo
  1972 Case Comment: Mental health—validity of commitment statute. *Duquesne Law Review* 10:674-84.
Burt, R., and Morris, N.
  1972 A proposal for the abolition of the incompetency plea. *University of Chicago Law Review* 40:66-95.
Chapin, F. Stuart
  1947 *Experimental design in sociological research.* New York: Harper & Brothers Publishers.
Cole, Jonathan R., and Cole, Stephen
  1973 *Social Stratification in Science.* Chicago: University of Chicago Press.
Collins, James J. Jr.
  1977 *Offender careers and restraint: Probabilities and policy implications.* Report submitted to the United States Department of Justice, Law Enforcement Assistance Administration, National Institute of Juvenile Justice and Delinquency Prevention.
Dixon, Donald, et at. *v.* Attorney General of the Commonwealth of Pennsylvania, *Order and Opinion*, 325 F. Supp. 966.

Giovannoni, Jeanne M., and Gurel, Lee
    1967 Socially disruptive behavior of ex-mental patients. *Archives of General Psychiatry* 17:146-53.
Gottfredson, Don M.; Neithercutt, M. G.; Nuffield, J.; and O'Leary, V.
    1973 *Four thousand lifetimes: A study of time served and parole outcomes.* Davis, Calif.: National Council on Crime and Delinquency.
Guilford, J. P.
    1956 *Fundamental statistics in psychology and education.* New York: McGraw-Hill.
Hindelang, Michael J.; Dunn, Christopher S.; Aumick, Alison L. and Sutton, L. Paul
    1975 *Sourcebook of criminal justice statistics—1974.* Washington, D.C.: U.S. Government Printing Office.
Hogarty, Gerard E., and Katz, Marvin M.
    1971 Norms of adjustment and social behavior. *Archives of General Psychiatry* 25:471-80.
Hospitalization of mentally ill criminals in Pennsylvania and New Jersey. *University of Pennsylvania Law Review* 110 (1961): 78-112.
Jacoby, Joseph E.
    1976 The dangerousness of the criminally insane. Ph.D. diss., University of Pennsylvania.
Katz, Martin M., and Lyerly, Samuel B.
    1963 Methods for measuring adjustment and social behavior in the community. *Psychological Reports* 13:503-35.
Kittrie, Nicholas
    1971 *The right to be different: Deviance and enforced therapy.* Baltimore: Johns Hopkins University Press.
Kozol, Harry L.; Boucher, Richard J.; and Garofalo, Ralph
    1972 The diagnosis and treatment of dangerousness. *Crime and Delinquency* 18:371.
Levine, David
    1970 Criminal behavior and mental institutionalization. *Journal of Clinical Psychology* 26:279-84.
Meehl, Paul
    1954 *Clinical vs. statistical prediction: A theoretical analysis and a review of the evidence.* Minneapolis: University of Minnesota Press.
Michaux, William M.; Katz, Martin M.; Kurland, Albert A.; and Gansereit, Kathleen H.
    1969 *The first year out: Mental patients after hospitalization.* Baltimore: Johns Hopkins University Press.

Monahan, John
   1975a The prediction of violence. In *Violence and criminal justice*, edited by Duncan Chappell and John Monahan, pp. 15-23. Lexington: Lexington Books.
   1975b *Community mental health and the criminal justice system.* New York: Pergamon Press.
Moran, Richard
   1975 The future of crime and crime control. Paper presented at the National Institute on Crime and Delinquency, Minneapolis.
Morris, Norval
   1966 Impediments to penal reform. *University of Chicago Law Review* 33:627-56.
National Institute of Mental Health
   1964 Phenothiazine treatment in acute schizophrenia. *Archives of General Psychiatry* 10:246-60.
   1975 *Statistical note 117.* Washington D.C.: Department of Health, Education, and Welfare, Division of Biometry.
   1976 Medicare certification report [for Farview State Hospital]. Mimeographed.
Pasamanick, Benjamin; Scarpitti, Frank R.; and Dinitz, Simon
   1967 *Schizophrenics in the community.* New York: Appleton-Century-Crofts.
Peto, R.; Pike, M. C.; Armitage, P.; Breslow, N. E.; Cox, D. R.; Howard, S. N.; Mantel, N.; McPherson, K.; Peto, J.; and Smith, P. G.
   1976 Design and analysis of randomized clinical trials requiring prolonged observation of each patient. *British Journal of Cancer* 34:585-612.
Potter, Robert G.
   1966 Application of life table techniques to measurement of contraceptive failure. *Demography* 3:297-304.
Prettyman, E. Barrett
   1972 The indeterminate sentence and the right to treatment. *American Criminal Law Review* 11:7-37.
Rindfuss, Ronald, and Bumpass, Larry L.
   1977 Fertility during marital disruption. *Journal of Marriage and the Family* 39:517-28.
Sawyer, Jack
   1966 Measurement and prediction, clinical and statistical. *Psychological Bulletin* 66:178-200.
Schooler, Nina R.; Goldberg, Solomon C.; Boothe, Helvi; and Cole, Jonathan O.
   1967 One-year after discharge: Community adjustment of

schizophrenic patients. *American Journal of Psychiatry*
123:986-95.

Sellin, Thorsten, and Wolfgang, Marvin E.
1964 *The measurement of delinquency*. New York: John Wiley.

Steadman, Henry J.
1972 The psychiatrist as a conservative agent of social control.
Social Problems 20:263-73.

n. d. Legal dangerousness scale. Albany: Mental Health Research Unit, New York State Department of Mental
Hygiene. Unpublished paper.

Steadman, Henry J., and Braff, Jeraldine
1974 Incompetency to stand trial: The easy way in? In *Crime
and delinquency: Dimensions of deviance,* edited by Marc
Riedel and Terence P. Thornberry, pp. 178-91. New
York: Praeger Press.

Steadman, Henry J., and Cocozza, Joseph J.
1974 *Careers of the criminally insane.* Lexington, Mass.: D. C.
Heath and Company.

1975 We can't predict who is dangerous. *Psychology Today*
January 1975, pp. 32-35.

Steadman, Henry J.; Cocozza, Joseph J.; and Melick, Mary Evans
n. d. Explaining the increased crime rate of mental patients:
The changing clientele of state hospitals. *American Journal of Psychiatry,* in press.

Steadman, Henry J., and Keveles, Gary
1972 The community adjustment and criminal activity of the
Baxstrom patients: 1966-1970. *American Journal of
Psychiatry* 129:304-19.

Stone, Alan A.
1975 *Mental health and law: A system in transition.* Rockville,
Md.: National Institute of Mental Health.

Thornberry, Terence P.
1974 Community follow-up and dangerous mental patients.
Paper presented at the National Institute of Mental
Health, Symposium on Dangerousness and Mentally
Disturbed Persons, May 1974. Rockville, Md.

Treffert, Darold A.
1974 Dying with your rights on. Paper presented at the Annual
Meeting of the American Psychiatric Association, May
1974. Detroit, Mich.

Wexler, David B.
1976 *Criminal commitments and dangerous patients: Legal
issues of confinement, treatment and release.* Rockville,
Md.: National Institute of Mental Health.

Wolfgang, Marvin E.; Figlio, Robert M.; and Sellin, Thorsten
1972 *Delinquency in a birth cohort.* Chicago: University of Chicago Press.
Zitrin, Arthur; Hardesty, Anne S.; Burdock, Eugene I.; and Drossman, Ann K.
1975 Crime and violence among mental patients. Paper presented at the annual meeting of the American Psychiatric Association, Anaheim, Calif., May 1975.

INDEX